Theological Education and Moral Formation

Essays by

Dennis Campbell
Rowan A. Greer
E. Brooks Holifield
John W. O'Malley, S.J.
Merle D. Strege

and
The Story of an Encounter by
Paul T. Stallsworth

Edited and with a Foreword by
Richard John Neuhaus

WILLIAM B. EERDMANS PUBLISHING COMPANY
GRAND RAPIDS, MICHIGAN

Published by Wm. B. Eerdmans Publishing Co.
in cooperation with
The Rockford Institute Center on Religion and Society

Library of Congress Cataloging-in-Publication Data

Theological education and moral formation / essays by Dennis Camp-
    bell . . . [et al.]; edited and with a foreword by Richard John Neuhaus.
        p.   cm.   — (Encounter series; 15)
    Papers presented at a conference.
    Includes bibliographical references.
    ISBN 0-8028-0215-X
    1. Theology — Study and teaching — Congresses. 2. Moral educa-
tion — Congresses. I. Campbell, Dennis M., 1945-   . II. Neuhaus,
Richard John. III. Series: Encounter series (Grand Rapids, Mich.); 15.
BV4020.T47 1991
207'.1 — dc20   91-37167
                                                              CIP

ENCOUNTER SERIES

Contents

Foreword

Both references in the somewhat cumbersome title of this book
— "theological education" and "moral formation" — are anything but self-evidently clear today. We might be inclined to
think that moral formation is the relatively new subject,
whereas we assume that we know what is meant by theological education. But that would be a mistake. The papers and
discussion in this volume make it evident that there are different, and sometimes conflicting, notions of theological education in contention today. According to some construals of theological education, the question of moral formation must be
resisted as an unwelcome intrusion. Theological education, like
other graduate studies, is a matter of the mind, it is suggested.
Theological education is learning and doing theology, and what
that does or does not do for the moral character of the participants is a matter of indifference. At least it is not the proper
business of the academic institution where theological education is pursued.

Not all seminaries or divinity schools take that view. Some
are academic institutions devoted to the "critical" study of
religious traditions; others understand themselves to be training schools; yet others intend to be schools of formation for
spiritual leadership. From university-connected graduate
school to Bible college, however, the worlds of theological education are entangled with one another in complicated ways.
The ministerial training school boasts of its faculty member
with a "respectable" doctorate from Yale — and simul-

taneously worries that Dr. Ivyleague thinks that the school should be more like Yale.

The participants in the conference that produced this book reflect great diversity in their engagement with theological education. They are evangelical, mainline/old-line, and Roman Catholic. Most are teachers or administrators in seminaries or divinity schools. They bring to this conference the questions being debated among colleagues and students in their several institutions. All recognize that they are, however diversely, involved in the common enterprise called theological education.

The second referent in our title, "moral formation," is not a settled part of the vocabulary of many involved in theological education. For some Protestants, the language of moral formation has a suspiciously Catholic flavor. And it is true that Roman Catholics have for a long time spoken of "priestly formation" as an important, perhaps dominant, purpose of theological education. In fact, some Catholic seminaries are as uneasy with the language of "theological education" as some Protestant schools are uneasy with talk about "moral formation." It is not that Catholics have usually been concerned about spiritual and moral development while Protestants have been preoccupied with the mind and professional skills. Far from it. As Brooks Holifield suggests in his paper, an enculturated Protestantism of the past confidently assumed that it knew what was meant by moral formation, even if it did not use the term.

As recently as forty years ago there was very little disagreement among Christians — indeed, among Americans in general — about what kind of people we ought to be and how we ought to live our lives. The witness of the churches was virtually unanimous on numerous questions that are today hotly controverted. Marriage, adultery, divorce, gender roles, homosexuality, abortion — none of these were deemed "controversial" issues forty years ago. Forty years is not a long time in the history of societies, nor in the history of the Christian church. The rapidity of social and moral change in our time is often exaggerated. Sometimes it seems that a new "revolution" in attitudes and behavior is proclaimed every month or so. Nonetheless, there is no denying the fact that much that was,

until fairly recently, taken for granted must now be argued for.
People do not usually hold conferences on the self-evident. A
conference and a book on moral formation are evidence that
many people are not very sure about what is meant by moral
formation.

Questions of character, virtue, and morality may not be
the most important concerns in the Christian life. Our several
traditions differ in the weight they give to the moral, as distinct
from questions of doctrine, faith, experience, and liturgy. But
all agree that an important part of the newness of the new man
and new woman in Christ is the new kind of people we are
called to be. In recent decades the argument has been made that
Christian morality that is genuinely Christian gives priority to
social and political transformations. Sometimes the questions
of "personal morality" are denigrated as bourgeois and individualistic vestiges of a politically benighted past. Most
Christians, however, likely agree that the testing of our new life
in Christ has at least as much to do with, for example, how we
treat our children, how we cope with sexual temptation, and
how we handle our finances as it has to do with our holding
the correct views on, say, current political struggles in Latin
America. For a long time now it has been common to make a
distinction between social ethics and personal ethics. In fact, all
ethics is by definition social, having to do with how we treat
others. The distinction is between whether the others are near
to or remote from the circumstances of our lives.

Most people in theological education understand that
their work is related to specific religious communities. Most
students in seminaries or divinity schools are preparing to be
or to train the clergy of churches. From the New Testament era
to the present, the church has always expected its leadership to
be morally exemplary, or, as some ordinals put it, "to adorn the
gospel with a holy life." While complaints about a "double
standard" for clergy and laity are perennial in church history,
the fact that there will be higher expectations of clergy is probably sociologically inevitable. If there are to be those whom we
call leaders, there must be those whom we call followers, and
people are not likely to follow those whom they do not respect
— in moral as well as in other ways.

Today's disputes about the moral expectations attached to church leadership are not about what is *permissible* but about what is *exemplary*. That is as true for the priest or minister who aspires to exemplify a liberated life of "authentic selfhood" as it is for those who would exemplify "traditional values." A persistent theme in the following pages is the necessarily communal nature of any useful discussion of moral formation. Different Christian communities have different doctrines of the ministry. A very few claim to have no doctrine of the ministry because they have no ministry, but of course they do have both to the extent that they have sustaining roles of communal leadership. It will perhaps strike some readers, as it strikes me, that this book is not simply about community; it is about ecclesiology, our understanding of what the church is or is supposed to be. One question addressed is whether moral formation is a necessary or appropriate part of theological education. Another question involves the continuing contest over the content of moral formation. But at the beginning, at the end, and all along the way, the question that keeps pressing for an answer is this: What is the church?

In response to that question, a personal word might be in order. Since the discussion that gave birth to this book, I have been received into full communion and ordained to the priesthood in the Roman Catholic Church. However, nothing that is said later in these pages about the Lutheran tradition is substantively altered by this admittedly momentous transition.

As with so many conferences, publications, and other projects, I am again most particularly indebted to Davida Goldman and Paul Stallsworth, without whom . . .

NEW YORK CITY   RICHARD JOHN NEUHAUS

Theological Education and Moral Formation: What's Going On in Seminaries Today?

Dennis M. Campbell

INTRODUCTION

Several years ago a judicatory visitation team came to the divinity school. Beginning their visit with an interview in the dean's office, they asked me, "Is Duke Divinity School doing a good job?" "Yes," I answered immediately. Then I proceeded to enumerate the predictable criteria that academic institutions use to measure their quality: faculty, students, curriculum, library, financial resources, graduate placement. After the team was gone, I reflected further on the question. How can we really measure success in theological education?

Later that same day I attended a luncheon at the university's business school to celebrate the inauguration of a new program. After lunch an associate dean fielded questions. The first one came from a guest from outside the university. "Is the business school doing a good job?" "Yes," was the answer. And he proceeded to cite concrete evidence: "Our graduates from last year entered jobs with an average compensation of $32,500, and if personnel and public relations jobs are factored out, the average was $34,000." I was impressed by the certainty in his voice, which came from his confidence that the average salary of graduates was a satisfactory and accurate indicator of the school's success. I would guess that the money itself was not as important as what it symbolized. It served as a specific measure by which judgment could be made.

As I walked back to the divinity school, I pondered further the question of success and achievement in theological education. Success in theological education, in ministry — indeed, in the total life of the church — is not easily, accurately, or faithfully measured. Ministry often imports models of success from other arenas of life. One thinks, for instance, of the "market model," the "entertainment model," the "management model," or the "celebrity model." But when such models are applied to ministry, we know there is something wrong. Inherent in Christian ministry is a moral dimension that is not easily articulated in its fullness but that must be present in authentic ministry.

If theological education is to be evaluated, a major factor presumably should be the capacity of a school to help students come to terms with the complex and multiple factors that make up the moral fabric of Christian ministry.

This essay explores the issues involved in theological education and moral formation by taking a look at what actually is going on today in theological schools. Before addressing the setting and culture of theological education, however, it is necessary to explore briefly my understanding of ordained ministry, because subsequent judgments derive from these presuppositions.

THE NATURE OF ORDAINED CHRISTIAN MINISTRY

All Christians are called to ministry, and this is understood as the ministry of the whole people of God. Some Christians are called to ordained ministry and are set apart to serve in the particular ministries of Word, sacrament, and order. Christian ministry, both lay and ordained, involves particularity and distinctiveness. Particularity results from Christian identity. The uniqueness of Jesus Christ characterizes ministry and distinguishes Christian community. The life of the Christian believer is shaped in community and is identifiable as such. Christian faith evidences itself in the way one lives.

A consistent theme in the New Testament and in Christian tradition is the distinctiveness of life in Christ. Jesus said "For I am come to set . . . at variance . . . (Matt. 10:35, KJV). "To set at variance" suggests that Christians and Christian communities are to develop lifestyles that are different from those of others and of the general society. Theological education for ordained ministry therefore requires consideration of the particularity of Christian commitment and identity. There are five aspects of this which need to be noted.

1. *Vocation.* Education for ministry is tied to exploration of vocation to ordination. This immediately distinguishes theological education from other professional education, since vocation to ordained ministry involves a call from God to the inner self as well as a call from the church. Both must be present for authentic vocation. The complexity of vocation is that these calls come in a variety of ways and at different times for different people.

Sometimes God's call to the inner self precedes the call from the church; but the call from the church may also precede the experience of God's specific call. The nature of the calls cannot be easily categorized.

The decision to pursue ordained ministry is not merely an individual decision about what one wants to do with one's life. The role of the church is crucial because it is finally the church that must establish criteria and judge specific candidates' suitability for ordination. This must include the conviction on the part of the church that a candidate has indeed been called by God.

Different churches carry out the task of assessing candidates in a variety of ways, but one of the jobs of the church is to order its life to fulfill the task of determining appropriateness for ordination. The fact that vocation is a dynamic reality involving God, individual, and community clearly indicates the reality that vocation for ordination is not an individual matter. No one has a right to be ordained. The church sets criteria and standards and makes judgments. This has always been the case.

2. *The Meaning of Ordination.* Ordination is God's act in the church. Through the laying on of hands, with prayer for the gift of the Holy Spirit, the church receives the gift of ministry from God through Jesus Christ. Ordination is not credentialing

for ministry; that is done in other ways and at other times. Ordination sets people apart for particular leadership, especially sacramental leadership. This essay cannot explore the important and complex history and theology of ordination and particularly the relationship between ordination, sacramental leadership, and teaching authority.[1] It is essential, however, to make the point that ordination carries with it the *obligation* to set aside the self for the church. Elsewhere, borrowing from Wesley, I have called this the yoke of obedience.

Just as no one has a right to be ordained, so no one is forced to shoulder the yoke of obedience. But if one consents to take the vows of ordination, then one is bound to the church. The sacramental ministries exemplify the major aspects of this binding because they bring together the fullness of the gospel, including teaching and living the faith. Teaching and living cannot be separated. By "teaching" I am referring especially to the systematic doctrinal matters that have concerned the church from its beginning. In Scripture and Christian tradition, God has given guidance to contemporary Christians concerning the faith. To rightly know and understand is to bear witness in the way life is lived.

Ordination requires that the ordinand explicitly and publicly affirm that he or she is willing to have the church play a large role in the shaping of the self. An ordained person's identity is inevitably linked to and determined by the church.

3. *The Ordained Minister as a Representative.* The idea of the ordained minister as a representative has always been one element of the theology of Christian ministry. As representatives of Christ, ordained people are called to exemplify and to fulfill several roles that are aspects of Christ's ministry. The roles of prophet, priest, and ruler are incorporated through ministries of Word, sacrament, and order. The representative character of ordained ministry is twofold: the ordained represent Christ to the church and represent the church to the world. Later in the essay I will discuss some specific implications of this representative character.

---

1. See my book entitled *The Yoke of Obedience: The Meaning of Ordination in Methodism* (Nashville: Abingdon, 1988).

The discussion of particular issues of the moral life of clergy has its theological foundation in the ecclesiological reality that the clergy are representatives by the nature of the office they hold. "Office" is a theological concept that has important ramifications. By accepting the call of God and the church to ordained ministry, one takes upon oneself an "official" role that transcends the self. It is not that the self is unimportant, but that the representative character of the office is such that one's selfhood is secondary to the primary fact that one represents the wholeness of Christ and the Christian community.

Accordingly, there is no way for an ordained minister to escape the "office" for a while. One cannot segment aspects of one's life to escape the representative reality. Although I have not been able to explore in detail the theology of ordination, it is important to note that the wholeness, permanence, and character of ordination point to why the Catholic tradition calls ordination a sacrament, and why many Protestants want to understand ordination as "sacramental."

When asked what he did as the rector of Justin, Frank Prescott replied, "It is not what I *do* but what I *am* that matters."[2] Obviously, ordained ministry involves specific and essential tasks. What one "does" matters. But in a larger sense, the representative character of ordained ministry means that what one "is" finally is more important. The implications of this insight for moral formation and theological education are enormous.

4. *The Ordained Minister as a Servant Leader.* The servant character of ordained ministry derives directly from Jesus Christ, and because of this the nature of leadership is defined with reference to service. The Gospels show Jesus as an intentional leader who gathered around himself a group of individuals who were also commissioned as leaders. The nature of this leadership was difficult for his followers to grasp because Jesus presented a new vision of a community of service led by people who were themselves servants of the servant

---

2. Prescott, cited by Louis Auchincloss in *The Rector of Justin* (Boston: Houghton Mifflin, 1964).

community. This model was exemplified by Jesus himself, who, "though he was in the form of God, did not count equality with God a thing to be grasped, but emptied himself, taking the form of a *servant*, being born in the likeness of men. And being found in human form he *humbled* himself and became *obedient* unto death, even death on a cross" (Phil. 2:6-8, RSV, emphasis mine).

Clergy sometimes fail to achieve an authentic and effective style of ministry because they are unable to come to terms with the reality that the church must have strong leadership which does not become corrupted with self-service. The result is that some clergy shrink from leadership and others use the church for their own ends. I have been helped in my thinking about servant leadership by Robert Greenleaf. Drawn from his wide experience with profit and non-profit organizations, the concept of servant leadership is applicable to the church because it advances the idea of the leader as one who allows the mission of the community to be determinative.[3] The servant leader is advancing the goals and objectives of the community, not personal goals and objectives. In the case of the church, the commands of the gospel of Jesus Christ shape the community and come to focus with the help of "official" representatives: ordained ministers.

Warren Bennis once observed that American organizations are "overmanaged and underled."[4] This seems to me an apt description of the church today. Leadership is essential, and ordination carries with it a mandate for leadership. But the style of leadership must be such that it feeds not on personal aggrandizement but on service shaped by Christ. This means that strong leadership in the church serves the church's ends when it helps the community to order its life for ministry. The focus and end of authentic Christian leadership, therefore, is not determined by the self-interest of the leader, but by the

---

3. Greenleaf, *Servant Leadership: A Journey into the Nature of Legitimate Power and Greatness* (New York: Paulist Press, 1977). See especially pp. 7-48 and his chapter entitled "Servant Leadership in Churches," pp. 218-48.

4. Bennis, cited by Tom Peters and Nancy Austin in *A Passion for Excellence: The Leadership Difference* (New York: Random House, 1985), p. xix.

self-giving nature of leadership characterized by humility and obedience.

5. *The Moral Character of Ordained Ministry.* In my consideration of the nature of ordained ministry, I have stressed those aspects of the theology of ministry that are suggestive of the moral character of ordination. The purpose has been to suggest a framework within which current realities concerning theological education can be assessed. In using the phrase "moral character of ordination," I suggest that the reality of ordination, when rightly understood, has to do with the wholeness of the life of the ordained and not simply specific decisions, acts, or discrete functions.

Perhaps the moral character of ordination is best described with reference to obedience. Franz Hildebrandt argues that no one could read the New Testament and fail to understand that a minister of the gospel is not so much one "in orders" as one "under orders."[5] The image of being "under orders" suggests obedience and accountability. Calvin asserted that an ordained person must understand that "he is no longer a law unto himself, but bound in servitude to God and the church."[6] The language of service, orders, and obedience is not easily compatible with secular, liberal, twentieth-century America. We do not like to admit to any limitations on individual freedom. But if ordained Christian ministers are to be like Christ, in terms of the servant leadership he exemplified, then we are called to representative self-emptying lives of obedience and service.

The question now is in what way and to what extent is contemporary theological education able to help with the formation of men and women for the kind of servant leadership ministry that is the true nature of ordination.

---

5. Hildebrandt, "The Meaning of Ordination in Methodism," in *The Ministry in the Methodist Heritage,* ed. Gerald O. McCulloh (Nashville: Board of Education of the Methodist Church, 1960), p. 74.
6. *Institutes of the Christian Religion,* ed. John T. McNeill (Philadelphia: Westminster Press, 1960), 4.3.16.

THE SETTING AND CULTURE OF
THEOLOGICAL EDUCATION

1. *The Context of Theological Education in Late-Twentieth-Century America.* It is almost preposterous to attempt a brief description of theological education in contemporary America. Perhaps the only generalization which holds true is that the picture is complex and variegated. The Association of Theological Schools, the accrediting agency for graduate-professional schools of theology in the United States and Canada, includes a vast array of Protestant, Orthodox, and Roman Catholic institutions. These vary in size from tiny seminaries of under a hundred students to large schools enrolling thousands of degree candidates. They include both schools related to most denominations and schools that are non-denominational. Some are freestanding institutions with their own trustee boards, and some are integral parts of larger institutions, colleges, or universities.

Despite the tremendous diversity, however, there is at least one characteristic that, in my experience, virtually all contemporary American theological schools share. This is the predominance of the academic culture. In a sense this is obvious, since they are all schools by definition, but the meaning of academic culture and its relevance to moral formation need exploration. That the academic culture is a prevailing reality and common denominator is evidenced by examination of standards for accreditation. The criteria by which seminaries are judged for accreditation are primarily academic. Judgments concerning the quality of students, faculty, library, resources, and governance, for instance, are rendered in terms not unlike those applied to any academic institution. One result of this is constant confusion about the proper relationship between the church and the church's schools.

All professional schools experience tensions between the academy and the profession. Physicians and their associations are always complaining that medical schools do not do a good enough job of preparing men and women for the actual practice of medicine, and lawyers say the same thing about the theoretical character of legal education. So we are not surprised at the perpetual gripes from the clergy about the lack of immediate applicability of much of what is studied in seminary.

My concern here, however, is not this age-old and largely unrewarding discussion of the relative importance of the theoretical and the practical and how they are held together. I am pointing at the more subtle and difficult tension that inevitably exists between academic culture and church culture. It is not simply a matter of the academic or theoretical and the churchly or practical. It is rather a tension between communities shaped by different goals and priorities. Seminary faculties, for the most part, have adopted the values and norms of academic culture. For many faculty members the primary community of identification is the academy rather than the church. The predominance of the academic culture is evidenced in numerous ways that have implications for our consideration of moral formation.

The almost universal affirmation of "academic freedom" as an absolute value within the theological-education establishment is one example of the ascendance of academic culture. I do not want to be misunderstood on this point. Academic freedom has had a distinguished role in American higher education and continues to be an essential component in higher education. The protection of a faculty member from fear of expressing a bold and unpopular opinion needs no defense. Nevertheless, the uncritical affirmation of academic freedom in the context of theological education frames the issue in terms of academic culture rather than in terms of obedience and service to the church.

It is interesting to me that at the last biennial meeting of the Association of Theological Schools a good bit of time was spent affirming academic freedom and the "right" of a faculty member to his or her opinion about anything. What was absent was serious reflection on the obligation of theological educators to consider their role as an example to students of how faithful and responsible critique goes on in the context of the church community. I understand why. There remain too many church leaders who want to exert inappropriate control on their schools. But I am suggesting that an uncritical asserting of "the principle of academic freedom" is too simpleminded and invites students to think that they should have the same "freedom" to express any idea they may have as pastors. It is problematic also because it fails to grapple with the complex interaction of the obligation of Christians with the community of faith.

Ironically, uncritical thinking about academic freedom may lead seminaries to make bad judgments about faculty appointments and promotions. Such thinking hampers an institution's ability to develop a clear understanding of its own distinctive character and then to make judgments about the appropriate academic excellence required for faculty appointments and promotions. The phrase "academic excellence" is in fact as imprecise as "academic freedom." But theological educators must be able to articulate exactly what "academic excellence" means in the context of preparation for the church's ministry.

The way a theological faculty deals with these issues is for students a model for the role of critical theological thought in the Christian community. One of the perennial challenges faced by theological education is how to provide students with a rigorous theological education that does not fundamentally alienate them from the people they are called to serve. The process of education and preparation for ordination almost inevitably removes candidates from the settings in which the initial calls to ministry took place and introduces them to a life-style of study and reflection. It can be difficult to go back.

This reality is present in all education because, by definition, education is designed to expose one to new ideas and thus engender a certain alienation from previous experience. The problem is especially acute for theological education since its purpose is to send graduates back to their communities of origin as servant leaders. The tension is exacerbated if students perceive that the seminary gives uncritical priority to concepts such as "academic freedom" or "academic excellence" without substantial and explicit interpretation of what these might mean in the context of the priority of the church.

I have suggested that the context of theological education in late-twentieth-century America is the academic culture of higher education. I am aware of the history of theological education, which demonstrates that theological education was sometimes slow to adopt and champion the academic model. But I am suggesting that the time has now come for us at least to consider the proposition that our situation in the latter part of the twentieth century is different from that of earlier days. It may be that unwittingly we in theological education have given over too much to the principles and visions of the secular Enlightenment, which are now ascendant.

2. *The Current State of American Higher Education.* Higher education in America reflects American culture even as it endeavors to shape it. In recent years higher education can be characterized as dominantly relativistic, secular, and materialist. I think there is increasing evidence that the unquestioned pre-eminence of secular Enlightenment thinking may be waning, but change in higher education will be slow. While there is much that is wrong with Allan Bloom's *The Closing of the American Mind,* his claim that relativism pervades elite culture is persuasive.[7] College and university faculties seldom share the conviction that there is truth, and that it can be known and shared. President James T. Laney of Emory University recently asserted his view that the relativism of higher education is inseparable from its secular commitments. Most students and faculty of the modern university deem the reality of God to be irrelevant to the daily research, teaching, and learning activities of their institution. It is not necessarily that they deny God, but they deny that the matter makes any difference to the work of higher education.

The pervasive materialism of higher education stems both from the American conviction that the value of education is that it improves one's chance for financial gain and from the inability of institutions to make value judgments on any basis other than the market model. Faculty therefore tend to adopt the same entrepreneurial values that characterize business. Former Harvard president Derek Bok, in his address marking the 350th anniversary of Harvard, cautioned that professors are becoming increasingly caught up in the pursuit of affluence by extensive lecturing, consulting, development of businesses, and

---

7. Bloom, *The Closing of the American Mind* (New York: Charles Scribner's Sons, 1987), p. 25.

government service. "In a world that honors success and opulent lifestyles," he said, "we could easily find ourselves harboring more and more professors who try to combine the freedom and security of a tenured academic post with the income and visibility traditionally reserved for people who take much greater risks and work at much less elevating tasks."[8]

The impact of relativism, secularism, and materialism has altered the traditional idea that a college education was designed to shape students' moral values in an explicit way. This was noted by Ernst L. Boyer, the president of the Carnegie Corporation, in his book titled *College: The Undergraduate Experience in America:* "We have moved from the ideal of shaping students to a certain sense of values to that of offering a smorgasbord of options and letting them pick their way to a degree."[9]

Running through most recent commentaries on higher education is the theme that what is lacking is *unity* and *purpose*. John Henry Newman, of course, articulated the lack of unity and purpose in *The Idea of a University* over a century ago, so the problem is neither new nor unique to American higher education. Nevertheless, historically the Christian vision was thought to provide both unity and purpose for at least some institutions. These institutions were explicit in asserting the importance of moral formation, and faculty members were selected with this view in mind. Helen Lefkowitz Horowitz makes this point in *Alma Mater,* using Wellesley as an example: "The original status of the college announced that 'the College was founded for the glory of God and the service of the Lord Jesus Christ. . . .' A necessary corollary followed: 'It is required that every Trustee, Teacher, and Officer, shall be a member of an Evangelical Church, and that the study of the Holy Scriptures shall be pursued by every student throughout the entire college course under the direction of the Faculty.' "[10]

---

8. Bok, cited in the *New York Times,* 7 Sept. 1986.

9. Boyer, *College: The Undergraduate Experience in America* (New York: Carnegie Corporation, 1986).

10. Horowitz, *Alma Mater: Design and Experience in the Women's Colleges from Their Nineteenth-Century Beginnings to the 1930s* (Boston: Beacon Press, 1984), p. 54.

The same kind of affirmations were made by virtually all the early private colleges in this country. One thinks immediately of Harvard, Yale, Princeton, and Brown, but many others could be named. This assumption that Christian conviction provided unity and purpose continued through the nineteenth century and early twentieth century as the early colleges expanded into universities and as new universities with church affiliations were founded. The presence of divinity schools at Harvard, Yale, Boston, Chicago, Duke, and Vanderbilt is the result of the historical assumption that universities both could and should be preparing men for ordained Christian ministry. The position of divinity schools in modern secular universities characterized by relativism and materialism is ambiguous. A full analysis of the philosophical issues involved cannot be undertaken here, but in the next section of the essay I will take up the complexity this ambiguous position presents for serious attention to moral formation for ordained Christian ministry.

The current state of American higher education presents complex issues for education for ordained ministry. Until we understand this and think these issues through, we will be unable to deal with moral formation more creatively. If what I have suggested about the nature of ordained Christian ministry is true, theological education cannot uncritically accept and adopt the values and assumptions of the modern university. By making such comments I am not suggesting that the picture is all negative. In fact, serious attention to the reality of these issues can be salutary for the integrity of theological education.

3. *The Current State of the Church with Regard to Moral Formation.* Theological schools exist not only in the context of the academic culture but also in the context of the churches. Problems with regard to moral formation derive not only from the intellectual confusion about what is good and right in higher education but also from similar confusion in the churches. To put the matter directly, the crisis in the seminaries regarding the moral lives of students and faculty reflects the crisis in the churches on these issues.

The problem has to do with teaching authority. Fundamental is the way the Christian community understands the sources given to it through which judgments are made concerning the shape of the Christian life. The place and authority of Scripture and church tradition and their relationship to the experience of the church and of individual believers need careful examination. Contemporary disciplines outside the traditional theological curriculum now make claims on the modern Christian mind. In fact, some contemporary Christian thinkers elevate either personal experience or what they argue to be the shared experience of a group (feminist experience, for instance) to hermeneutical priority.

All Christian churches have problems with teaching authority, and the history of Christianity shows that this has always been the case. The problem is more acute now, however, because of the dominance of Western Enlightenment thought within the churches' intellectual elite. The unmitigated individualism of so much of modern Christian theology and ethics stands in sharp contrast to the view of ordained Christian ministry I set forth earlier in this essay.

Liberal Protestant churches have the greatest problems dealing with teaching authority. My own denomination, United Methodism, is a case in point. The gradual democratization of governance from the eighteenth century to now has resulted in a situation where major questions of doctrine and theological ethics are dealt with as simply political issues. Delegates to the General Conference, one half of whom are laypersons, are asked to render judgments on issues about which they quite literally know nothing. Thus in the case of the theology of ministry, for instance, debate usually concerns not biblical or doctrinal considerations but questions of perceived "fairness" or "rights and justice" in terms of twentieth-century American political opinion. The question of ordination then is treated like another social-justice issue rather than as a matter requiring complex reflection based on biblical, historical, and theological considerations.

A similar observation could be made about the doctrine of the Trinity. In 1988 the Trinity "won" at the St. Louis General Conference; but what does it mean when a church might "vote out," quite literally, "Father, Son, and Holy Spirit" because the matter has been turned into an issue of social justice? Delegates have not studied and do not understand theology, but most of them are "good Americans," and "good Americans" are for fairness. If "Father language" offends, toss it out. The same process is used for matters of theological ethics in regard to the social teachings of the church.

Let me be clear that I am not objecting to the concept of "conference"; that is as old as the church itself. The question is who makes up the "conference" when matters of teaching authority are at stake? If my theology of ordination is right, then doctrinal definition with regard to teaching authority must be dealt with by people who have been authorized by the community to deal with the mysteries of the faith. The failure of liberal Protestants to discriminate between doctrine and theology or between doctrine and the machinery of institutional order has resulted in a crisis.

This crisis in teaching authority relates directly to our topic of moral formation because it renders the seminary vulnerable if it seeks to exert leadership with regard to the way faculty and students should live. The fact that the churches themselves find it difficult or impossible to be clear about moral teaching means that the seminaries — which precisely mirror the churches on this point because that is who their faculties, students, board members, and supporters are — also find it difficult or impossible to be clear about moral teaching.

American churches and seminaries are clear only about one moral issue: that they must be in line with the dominant thinking in modern American culture, particularly concerning the value of "justice, fairness, and openness." Here the church is borrowing contemporary popular political language and baptizing it as Christian. Ironically, liberal churches continue to be engines of Western cultural dominance, but now in the vague language of "peace, justice, and globalization." Perhaps our greatest hope regarding doctrine (what to teach) and moral discernment (how to live) lies with Third World Christianity, for which the particularity of Jesus Christ is not an embarrassment but an essential. Reinhold Niebuhr once observed that "Western civilization is not Christian. It has embraced Christianity and used it to sanctify its acts. . . . Some day the Christianity we have forgotten will come back to us from the peoples who got it from our missionaries."[11]

SEMINARIES AND EDUCATION FOR THE MORAL LIFE

I began this essay with a brief consideration of the nature of ordained ministry, and I stressed that ordained ministers are representative figures who willingly take upon themselves the obligation to live lives which adorn the gospel. The schools in which people are prepared for ordination thus have, by implication, a role in moral formation *for ordained ministry*. In fact, the moral fabric of ordained ministry is different from that of the laity because of the full theological meaning of the representative character of ordained ministry. I have also suggested that education for ordained ministry occurs in academic culture and in church context. The contemporary values of academic culture are problematic for theological schools because particular moral formation is seen to be philosophically questionable. The contemporary crisis of teaching authority in the churches further complicates any consideration of the shaping of students for the fullness of ordained ministry. In this section I will explore the question of the school's role, examine the moral fabric of ordained ministry, and offer some suggestions for consideration and discussion.

1. *The Job of the School.* Many people would argue that an academic institution *qua* academic institution must resist any evaluation of students apart from strict academic evaluation. The implication of this is that a school has no real interest in a student outside his or her academic work. In the setting of theological education, this argument calls for a strict separation between the role of the school as academic educator and the role of the church as judge of adequacy for ordination. I think such arguments are too neat and fail to see the full dimensions of education, particularly education for ordained ministry.

---

11. Niebuhr, cited by Richard Wightman Fox in *Reinhold Niebuhr: A Biography* (New York: Pantheon Books, 1985), pp. 105-6.

Is it the job of the school to be involved in moral formation for ordained ministry? If the school considers itself a place where people are prepared for the ordained ministry of the church, I think the answer is clearly "yes." This is so because the nature of ordained ministry is such that to ignore this aspect of the whole is to do only a partial job of education.

A second question concerns the ability of the school to teach morality. Can we teach morality in seminary? The question of whether and to what extent morality can be taught is an old and long philosophical debate. It seems to me that the fact is we *do* teach morality in seminary, even if we do not intentionally do so. We teach by the way we engage in our total work. The faculty and staff of every seminary are involved, consciously or unconsciously, in moral formation. This is why it matters greatly who serves in these roles and why the "neutrality" or "objectivity" with regard to the moral lives of faculty and students, which is often defended by academic culture, is unsatisfactory for theological education. (I think it is an unexamined lie for all education, but that is another story.)

Some seminaries have specific mandates from church judicatories to work with students on both spiritual and moral formation. Others, especially ecumenical or university schools, may imagine that their lack of specific ecclesiastical identity renders such considerations either impossible or inappropriate or both. In all cases, schools preparing people for ordained ministry need to create a context in which every student is confronted with the fundamental moral character of ordination. Evaluation of students needs to include specific consideration of each student's ability to reflect theologically on the total work of ministry and see his or her whole life in relation to vocation. This means that faculty must be concerned about theological education in its wholeness and must reflect on the relationship between what actually happens on a day-to-day basis in the school and the mandates of the yoke of obedience for which students are being prepared.

2. *The Moral Fabric of Ordained Ministry.* In considering the nature of ordination, I discussed the fact that the Christian community has a message of compelling urgency which defines believers because it sets them "at variance" with the

prevailing norms of secular society. Christian faith is not just a set of ideas; when rightly understood, Christianity has consequences that lead people to lifestyles of holiness. The key point is that the Christian seeks to relinquish to the will of God the overwhelming self-interest which characterizes human beings. This is true for all Christians, and the same conception of obedience and yielding of individual will and individual interests to that of the greater good of God and God's people applies to the representative ministry. The church has always cared about the moral character of the clergy because it is necessary that its leaders reflect in the wholeness of their living the gospel they proclaim. The authenticity of the ministry is in part related to its manifestation in the lives of the clergy. Calvin says it succinctly in discussing qualifications for ordination: "To sum up, only those are to be chosen who are of sound doctrine and of holy life, not notorious in any fault which might both deprive them of authority and disgrace the ministry."[12]

The moral fabric of ordained ministry refers to the fact that we are talking not about a "job" but about a total way of life of authenticity and accountability as a representative figure. *Authenticity* involves such considerations as growth in spiritual life, the meaning of full-time ministry for pay, and personal morality.

Growth in spiritual life is essential for ordained people. This may sound obvious, but this has not always been given attention by seminaries. Indeed, at many seminaries no attention is given to this aspect of a student's development; it is left to the individual. Clearly the church wants its ordained leaders to be people of growing spiritual depth and assumes that emphasis on this facet will be a part of seminary education. Spiritual formation is a matter to be considered in the context of moral formation not only because the two cannot be separated but also because failure on the part of the theological school or the student to attend to the spiritual life undermines the authenticity of ministry.

Specific reflection on the meaning of full-time ministry for

---

12. *Institutes of the Christian Religion*, 4.3.12.

pay should also be part of every theological student's education. The "careerism" that informs the lives of many clergy results in *calculated* ministries in which everything is done with an eye to advancement. Seminarians need to ponder the ways in which clergy can use the church for their own ends. This problem is often fueled by the tendency of pastors to talk and think in terms of "my ministry." Such a perspective goes against the nature of ordained ministry, which is given by Christ and belongs to the church. "My ministry" represents the model of an individual entrepreneur. In that vein it is not uncommon to find pastors discussing the "perks" that go with certain assignments. Theological schools need to structure the curriculum so that these issues of vocation can be dealt with. Furthermore, the way the faculty handles these issues is directly relevant. If faculty members adopt the prevailing norms of the academic culture, then they are modeling the materialism of contemporary higher education rather than the values and norms of the church for its clergy. The modeling provided by the faculty is thus itself a moral issue in theological education.

A cluster of issues pertain to personal morality, matters such as how clergy handle human sexuality (including fidelity in marriage), family relationships, alcohol and drug abuse, and basic professional ethics. Certain emphases need to be made here. One is that even to use the phrase "personal morality" is inadequate in the context of the moral fabric of ordained ministry. The phrase suggests that such matters are irrelevant to one's role as an ordained minister. But I have suggested that these matters are essential because the meaning of ordination is that one's life cannot be segmented into private and public spheres. One's total life is involved in the representative ministry. It goes with the territory.

What is at stake is not a catalog of rules but a clear understanding that authentic ministry is dependent on a consistency in all aspects of life, governed by the overwhelming commitment to exemplify what the Christian community wants its leadership to be. In the case of the theological school, this means that the way the institution is structured and governed matters greatly because it teaches students by example. It also means that the faculty and leadership of seminaries cannot avoid consideration of the way in which their lives exemplify the vocation for which they are preparing students. It will not do for faculty to think of themselves simply as academics. To argue that faculty are academics and therefore exempt from the demands of Christian ministry, whether lay or ordained, is to let the academic culture have priority over the demands of the gospel. Authenticity in theological education is related to the school's commitment to be an institution accountable to Christian faith.

If authenticity is one major component of the moral fabric of ordained ministry, another is *accountability*. The ethics of professional ministry should be seen less as what one does in specific situations or cases (though this obviously is not unimportant) and more as how one is accountable to the theological meaning of obedience. In this sense professional ethics is set in the context of the primary *sacramental* life of the clergy. Thus the heart of professional ethics is how one leads in worship, deals with the Scriptures, celebrates the sacraments, preaches the gospel, and cares for the parish. Accountability means that indifference to or neglect of those roles which *define* ordained ministry is the real issue of the total moral life of clergy. Authenticity and accountability go together, and they provide the framework in which all particulars are considered.[13]

3. *What Now Needs to Be Done?* I began this essay by asking the question about what it means to do a good job in theological education and how we would measure success. In particular I have explored the matter of moral formation in theological education. I have argued that the key to the endeavor is the starting point. The leadership and faculty of theological schools need to work on the question of what is primary. I began with

---

13. I want to acknowledge my indebtedness to Stanley Hauerwas for long conversations in which we have talked about these matters. I have been helped by his thinking, though I do not by any means intend to saddle him with my tentative conclusions. See especially his article entitled "Clerical Character: Reflecting on Ministerial Morality" in *Word and World*, vol. VI, no. 2, pp. 181-93. "It is not enough to train people in Scripture, church history, theology and ethics," Hauerwas points out; "that training must serve to make their lives, and their professors' lives, available to God's shaping as officials of the church" (p. 193).

a theological exploration of ordination because I think that is essential for any theological school. The state of American higher education today is such that unless theological educators get their starting point right, they end up uncritically adopting a debatable model that itself has problems, especially in regard to moral formation.

Where do we start? We start with ordained ministry itself and thus affirm the primacy of the church. If we do this, we then begin with careful analysis of the theological meaning of ordination, not simply the question of the task of the ordained. In this way there is room for varying interpretations and critique, but the theological work begins concretely. The images and models we use derive not from the general culture or the academic culture but from the Christian community as mediated in Scripture, tradition, and the life of the church. Even though the church itself is always struggling with these issues, it does so in a context of faith and thus recognizes its limitations in the light of God's grace.

What then is to be done? We need to raise anew the question of the mission and purpose of theological schools; then we can explore the way in which every facet of a school's life and work contributes to the whole. Unity and purpose derive from clarity about the rootedness of the school in the intellectual and practical life of the church.

Who Seeks for a Spring in the Mud? Reflections on the Ordained Ministry in the Fourth Century

Rowan A. Greer

W. H. Auden once observed, "The historical discontinuity between Greek culture and our own, the disappearance for so many centuries of any direct influence, made it all the easier, when it was rediscovered, for each nation to fashion a classical Greece in its own image."[1] In some such way it is inevitable that modern reconstructions of the early church reflect our own preoccupations. I am frank to confess that it is so for me, and should argue that an Enlightenment "objectivity" is a delusion. We can test the interpretations of evidence far more securely when writers are straightforward about their own prejudices and preoccupations. My own revolve around a sense that in our time traditional Christian churches are insecure about their stance toward the surrounding culture and have too often transferred that insecurity to the gospel they profess to proclaim. For this reason, the period in the early church that interests me most is the fourth century, a time when the church's relation to society was highly problematic for the simple reason

---

1. Auden, cited by Frank M. Turner in *The Greek Heritage in Victorian Britain* (New Haven and London: Yale University Press, 1981), p. 451. Auden's comment is from his introduction to *The Portable Greek Reader* published by Viking Press.

that after A.D. 312 Christians were no longer outsiders in the Roman Empire. As a result, the leadership of the church was obliged to think through not only what ordination meant in the church but also what it meant in the public life of the Empire.

It is against this background that we must read the evidence that has survived, a body of material fairly extensive for the historian of ancient Christianity who must construe the historiographical task as one limited by the absence of statistical evidence and, indeed, of much he would like to know. We possess a good deal of canonical evidence from the fourth century, and the letters of figures like Basil, Ambrose, Augustine, and Jerome help to put flesh on these bones. Moreover, there survive three treatises from the late fourth century that seek to define an ideal for the ordained ministry. The Second Oration of Gregory of Nazianzus, probably preached in part in A.D. 362 and then later revised, is an apology for his flight from Nazianzus and the presbyterate and for his subsequent return; but an ideal sketch of what ordination means is the foil for his apology. Probably a quarter of a century later, John Chrysostom, during his diaconate (A.D. 381-386), wrote six books that make up the treatise *On the Priesthood*. About the same time, Ambrose of Milan, following in the steps of Cicero, reworked some of his homilies in his *De officiis ministrorum*. This evidence enables us to see both the actual and the ideal, and my thesis is that the ideal revolves not around training or function but around the moral and spiritual character of the ordained person. This thesis explains my title, which borrows the phrase from Ambrose.[2] Only purity of character enables the priest to be the fountain providing the church with the springs of good counsel and, to elaborate Ambrose's metaphor, with the waters of salvation. Let me begin with the historical setting and then turn to the three figures who articulate the ideal of the ordained ministry.

---

2. *De officiis* 2.12; Nicene and Post-Nicene Fathers 2.10, p. 52. Hereafter this volume will be referred to as NPNF.

THE HISTORICAL SETTING

The Constantinian Revolution, which began with Constantine's patronage of the church and ended in the late fourth century with the official recognition of a Christian empire, was, like most revolutions, in some measure of continuity with the past. Not all Christians shared Tertullian's hostile attitude toward the state and the surrounding culture, and as early as the time of Melito of Sardis (c. A.D. 180) there were those who saw the church's destiny linked with that of the Empire. Moreover, if Eusebius is to be believed, on the eve of the Diocletian persecution (A.D. 303) the church occupied a visible and important place in the Empire. It is certainly the case that before A.D. 312 the church had become an ecumenical religious society with reasonably clear norms of belief and practice. Nor was the church any longer the suspicious stranger it had been in the Roman world two centuries before.

Nevertheless, the revolution was a real one, not less for the church than for the Empire. Two changes seem to me decisive. First, the unity of the church before Constantine had been that of a purely voluntary association. To be sure, local churches were able to decide whom to expel from membership and what other churches they would regard as in communion with themselves. But there were no jurisdictional rules by which the Great Church could be clearly and easily defined. Once Constantine became the patron of the church, it became necessary to define what the church was and to eliminate heretics and schismatics. The new alliance between church and state forced the church to a new understanding of its unity that was more jurisdictional than consensual.[3] Second, for the first time the church was in

---

3. Cf. Hamilton Hess, *The Canons of the Council of Sardica A.D. 343: A Landmark in the Early Development of Canon Law* (Oxford: Clarendon Press, 1958), p. 2: "From a persecuted cultus Christianity became a legal religion, and from a society without rights in the world about her the Christian Church became the protege of the emperor, having not only rights but also responsibilities. From an organization hitherto somewhat cell-like in structure, she became immediately and awkwardly conscious of her corporate nature in a manner not before experienced." Hess goes on to point out that the new situation ended by "rapidly creating loyalties which gravely

a position to have an impact on the society in which it existed. Of course, we must not exaggerate. Christians had often been concerned with those outside the church; and, to take but one example, the church's charity was not confined to its own membership. Nevertheless, only after Constantine was the church able to have a corporate and public effect upon society.[4] In some respects the church borrowed from the Empire or had imposed upon it by the Empire solutions to these public problems. But that is not the whole story, and the church never consented to become a department of state. Post-Constantinian Christianity really begins in the fourth century, and we should not make the mistake of supposing that Eusebius and Lactantius alone define the character of the imperial church.

The issue was joined almost immediately after Constantine's victory over Maxentius in A.D. 312. The next year, certain Donatist bishops through the proconsul of Africa petitioned the emperor to appoint judges to settle their disputes with the Catholic bishops of Africa; and they asked that the judges be from Gaul, since they knew that Pope Miltiades of Rome was hostile to them. Constantine responded by appointing three Gallic bishops, but also by naming Miltiades president of the court. It looks very much as though Constantine was treating the issue as a normal civil suit on appeal to the emperor, but that Miltiades understood the court to be an ecclesiastical synod. The same ambiguity attaches to the so-called Synod of Arles in A.D. 314.[5] Increasingly the fourth-century church insisted that its synods were not to be confused with the conventions of Roman law. Despite the fact that the emperor could convene a synod, could influence its members, and alone could put real teeth into its decisions, the church continued to maintain its liberty. It is easy to find cases in which the emperor enforced the decrees of a synod but difficult to find clear evi-

---

threatened the essential unity which had its being in the one Apostolic tradition."

4. Cf. Dom Gregory Dix, *Jurisdiction in the Early Church: Episcopal and Papal* (London: Church Literature Association, 1975), p. 52: "The Church by its alliance with the Empire was suddenly called upon for *a corporate action upon society outside itself* of a kind never hitherto contemplated."

5. See the discussion in Dix, *Jurisdiction in the Early Church*, pp. 76ff.

dence that the emperor was ever able successfully to determine a synod's decisions.

We are, of course, in the presence of the beginnings of canon law. It is clear enough that the emergence of canons and of collections of canons is the product of the changed conditions of the fourth century. But it is also the case that the early canons were designed to preserve the church's custom.[6] One point that makes this reasonably clear is that a number of canons are designed to preserve the independence of the local church under its own bishop. For example, Canon 15 of Nicaea reads as follows:

> On account of the numerous troubles and divisions which have taken place, it has been thought good that the custom which has been established in some countries in opposition to the canon should be abolished; namely, that no bishop, priest, or deacon should remove from one city to another. If any one should venture, even after this ordinance of the holy and great Synod, to act contrary to this present rule, and should follow the old custom, the translation shall be null, and he shall return to the church to which he had been ordained bishop or priest.[7]

Similar canons were drafted at other synods in the fourth century.[8] One of the motives for such legislation was the strong sense that bishops (and perhaps the other clergy) were wedded to their sees. Other motives revolved around putting a stop to translations made out of ambition for wealth and power, and often reflected resistance to Arian attempts to gain authority over the church by controlling the election of bishops. But behind both motives lay the pre-Constantinian notion of the ecumenical church as a federation of more or less independent city churches.

------

6. See A. H. M. Jones, *The Later Roman Empire, 284-602* (Norman: University of Oklahoma Press, 1964), pp. 873-74: "Fundamentally the constitution of the church rested on custom, for in enacting canons councils did not claim so much to legislate as to give their sanction to established custom."

7. Charles Joseph Hefele, *A History of the Christian Councils, from the Original Documents,* 2 vols. (Edinburgh: T. & T. Clark, 1894), vol. 1, p. 422.

8. See the full discussion in Hess, *The Canons of the Council of Sardica,* pp. 71-89.

We can also see something of how a local church was organized. For example, Canon 10 of Sardica (A.D. 343) required that "should a rich man or a lawyer be proposed as bishop, he shall not be appointed until he has first discharged the office of reader, deacon, and priest, so that if he shows himself worthy, he may ascend by successive steps to the dignity of the episcopate."[9] At first we seem to be in the presence of a kind of ecclesiastical counterpart to the civil *cursus honorum*. But this is only partially true. The minor orders existed in the church long before Constantine, and their arrangement shifted according to local custom and over time.[10] The most interesting aspect of the Sardican canon is that the "successive steps" are regarded as probationary rather than as any rigid *cursus honorum*.[11] They can be regarded as one of the mechanisms by which clergy were raised up and trained for the local city church.

One of the problems reflected both in the canons and in the other literature of the period is the establishment of the bishop's control over the ecclesiastical hierarchy. Deacons, for example, are not to celebrate the Liturgy and are not to take precedence over priests.[12] Another problem revolved around

---

9. Hefele, *A History of the Christian Councils*, vol. 2, p. 143.

10. See Hess, *The Canons of the Council of Sardica*, pp. 107-8. See also Roger Gryson, *Le Prêtre selon Saint Ambrose* (Louvain: Edition Orientaliste, 1968), pp. 102ff. and pp. 133ff.

11. We should, therefore, compare the Sardican canon with Canon 2 of Nicaea: "Seeing that many things, either from necessity or on account of the pressure of certain persons, have happened contrary to the ecclesiastical canon, so that men who have but just turned from a heathen life to the faith, and who have only been instructed during a very short time, have been brought to the spiritual laver, to baptism, and have even been raised to the office of priest or bishop, it is right that in future this should not take place, for time is required for sound instruction in doctrine, and for further trial after baptism. For the apostolic word is clear, which says: 'Not a novice, lest through pride he fall into condemnation, and into the snare of the devil.' (1 Tim 3:6) If hereafter a cleric is guilty of a grave offence, proved by two or three witnesses, he must resign his spiritual office. Any one who acts against this ordinance and ventures to be disobedient to this great Synod, is in danger of being expelled from the clergy" (Hefele, *A History of the Christian Councils*, vol. 1, pp. 377-78). Needless to say, exceptions were made; Ambrose and Nectarius are the most obvious examples.

12. Deacons were not to administer the Eucharist to priests or receive

the *chorepiskopoi,* rural bishops who presided in their localities but were subject to the authority of the city bishop. They were forbidden to ordain priests and deacons, and Canon 57 of Laodicea appears to abolish them.[13] Basil the Great was obliged to deal with the problem, and he rebuked some of his rural bishops for taking money in return for ordaining men to minor orders. He also complained to them about their ordination of unworthy men to the subdiaconate, men who sought ordination to avoid military conscription.[14] While we discover a concern to establish good order in the local church, I think we should not oppose this sense of hierarchy to an understanding of the ministry as part of the body of the church. Ambrose, for example, treats the clergy as functioning within the body of Christ and appeals to 1 Corinthians 12 as a warrant for hierarchical offices in the church.[15]

When we turn to the fourth-century canons that sought to regulate the election of bishops, we move in some degree away from the independent local church to the ecumenical dimension of the church. It had long been the custom for neighboring bishops to participate in the consecration and even in the election of a city bishop, and this practice ensured that local independence would be balanced by a consenting relationship with the wider church.[16] As time passed, however, effective

communion before the bishops; they were not to sit among the priests (see Canon 18 of Nicaea in Hefele, *A History of the Christian Councils,* vol. 1, pp. 426ff.; cf. Canon 18 of Arles in Hefele, *A History of the Christian Councils,* vol. 1, pp. 194-95; see also Canon 15 of Arles in Hefele, *A History of the Christian Councils,* vol. 1, p. 193).

13. See Canon 13 of Ancyra, Canon 57 of Laodicea, Canon 10 of Antioch, Canon 6 of Sardica, and Canon 14 of Neocaesarea. Canon 13 of Neocaesarea put restrictions also on country priests.

14. See Basil, Epistles 53 and 54.

15. *De officiis* 3.3; NPNF 2.10, pp. 69ff. See also Jerome, Letter 52.9 (NPNF 2.6, p. 94): "In the church one is the eye, another is the tongue, another the hand, another the foot, others ears, belly, and so on. Read Paul's epistle to the Corinthians and learn how the one body is made up of different members." My point is simply that a hierarchical view of the church need not treat the ordained ministry as though it were separate from the church.

16. See Jones, *The Later Roman Empire,* pp. 874-75, especially p. 875: "The appointment of a bishop was thus dependent upon agreement be-

control of episcopal elections tended to pass into the hands of the provincial bishops, particularly in the East.[17] Nevertheless, the role of the people in the election of their bishop did not entirely disappear. The best-known story is that of Ambrose's election as bishop of Milan in A.D. 373:

> After the death of Auxentius, a bishop of the Arian heresy . . . , when the people were about to revolt in seeking a bishop, Ambrose [as *consularis*] had the task of putting down the revolt. So he went to the church. And when he was addressing the people, the voice of a child among the people is said to have called out suddenly: "Ambrose bishop." At the sound of this voice, the mouths of all the people joined in the cry: "Ambrose bishop."[18]

Not only did the people prevail, but Ambrose's election violated the custom of refusing to make a neophyte a bishop. As

---

tween the local community and the bishops of the district." Early in the third century, Hippolytus tells us that a bishop should be chosen "by all the people" and approved by the assembly of bishops and presbyters (*Apostolic Tradition* 2.1-2). In the middle of the third century, Cyprian is still more explicit: "So that ordinations may be rightly held, let the neighboring bishops of the same province assemble with the people for whom a bishop has been proposed, and let the bishop be chosen with the people present" (Ep. 67.5).

17. Hess provides a succinct account of this development (*The Canons of the Council of Sardica*, p. 93): "The rapid development of provincial organization in the East and the acquisition of jurisdictional rights by the provincial synod and the metropolitan bishop resulted in the early attribution, at least in theory, of effective suffrage to the body of provincial bishops. This development is clearly reflected in the legislation of several Eastern synods, including Nicaea. Canon 18 of Ancyra is concerned with the case of a bishop who has been refused by the church to which he has been appointed: this implies that the wishes of the community in question were not considered when the appointment was made. Canon 4 of Nicaea grants suffrage only to the provincial bishops, giving the metropolitan the decisive vote, and canons 19 and 23 of Antioch carry this development a step farther by introducing the provincial synod as the effective appointing body. Canon 13 of Laodicea states: 'The election of those who are to be appointed to the priesthood [episcopate] is not to be committed to the multitude.' In the West, on the other hand, the limitation of popular suffrage, even in theory, did not take place until a much later period." It is, of course, Canon 4 of Nicaea that requires at least three bishops to consecrate a new one.

18. Paulinus, *Life of Ambrose* 3.6; The Fathers of the Church, vol. 15, p. 36.

no more than a catechumen, Ambrose was not even a neophyte. Nevertheless, stories like Ambrose's are the exceptions that prove the rule that episcopal elections gradually drifted out of the hands of the people.[19]

This shift of authority must be explained by the transition in the fourth century from a voluntary to a jurisdictional understanding of the unity of the church, a transition required by the state and forced upon the church by the failure of the old consensual arrangements to resolve disputes.[20] At the heart of this development was the emergence of procedures for ecclesiastical trials and appeal procedures. Canon 5 of Nicaea established the principle that in the case of the excommunicated, "the sentence passed by the bishops of each province shall have the force of law."[21] What happened in effect was that the customary voluntary action of neighboring bishops in a province became an ecclesiastical court. The next question, of course, was whether there could be an appeal

---

19. See Jones' discussion in *The Later Roman Empire*, pp. 915ff. The riots that attended the election of Damasus as bishop of Rome in A.D. 366 provoked the scorn of Ammianus Marcellinus (27.3.12-13). In A.D. 411 Augustine had all he could do to prevent the people of Hippo from forcing him to ordain an unwilling but wealthy Christian senator called Pinianus (Letter 126). And in the early fifth century in the East, Synesius, the bishop of Ptolemais in Cyrene, was obliged to reckon with the popular will (Letters 67, 72, 76).

20. See Hess, *The Canons of the Council of Sardica*, p. 110: "The Church was at the same time attempting to re-establish peace within herself by older regulatory methods now rendered ineffective by forces too powerful to be controlled, and by new methods adapted to her present needs but which in reality she had not yet accepted. The older methods operated through the medium of mutual agreement among bishops towards a commonly desired end, cognizant of binding ecclesiastical law only as expressed in terms of universal tradition. The new methods of administration, on the other hand, operated through the medium of synodical legislation and the establishment of a rule by law, the process being borrowed from civil government and to a degree being forced upon the Church from without." I should prefer not to understand Hess to mean that the church was being forced into a position of dependence on the state, at least in all respects, and I should wish to understand the "forces too powerful to be controlled" to include not only the controversies provoked by the church's new position but also the pressure of that situation to resolve disputes.

21. Hefele, *A History of the Christian Councils*, vol. 1, p. 386.

from the provincial synod. In the East a larger synod was assembled to hear an appeal, but in the West the pope began to play a decisive role in appeals.[22]

It seems to me that there are two ways of understanding the picture as a whole. From one point of view, the church sought to preserve both the independence of the city churches and the ecumenical ties that held them together in the Great Church. From another point of view, what we see is the emergence of centralized control of the church. This second vantage point correlates with the emergence of the patriarchates in the fourth century.[23] Yet these two perspectives are coherent with one another and simply mark the third century as a period of transition. No one could have foreseen what is usually called "Caesaropapism," still less the medieval papacy. Nevertheless, the seeds of those developments were planted in the fourth century. The degree to which the older view still captured people's imagination may be judged by what Macrina said to her brother, Gregory of Nyssa, when he complained about the lot of a bishop. She told him he ought to be grateful that his was "a name to be reckoned with" all over the world, whereas their father had not been known outside his own province.[24] Perhaps what she meant is that Gregory had the best of both worlds — his own beloved country and the wider stage of the imperial church. To think of the clergy, or at least of the bishops, of the fourth century is to think of people who were called to affirm and maintain this double loyalty.

Granted that the picture I have drawn of the fourth-century church is not misleading, the next question to ask is who were the clergy that served that church.[25] If we take into account the minor orders such as subdeacon and lector as well as the threefold ministry of bishops, priests, and deacons, it is clear that the clergy were recruited from all classes of society. Slaves,

---

22. See Hess's discussion on pp. 109-27 in *The Canons of the Council of Sardica*.

23. See Jones' discussion on pp. 883-94 in *The Later Roman Empire*.

24. *Life of Macrina* 21; SC 178, pp. 210-11.

25. Something could and probably should be said about the finances of the church. On this matter I invite the reader to consult Jones, *The Later Roman Empire*, pp. 894-909, 934.

however, were supposed to be freed before entering holy orders, and the frequency of the insistence upon this leads one to suppose that the minor orders, particularly in the country districts, may well have depended upon former slaves and the *coloni*. We do not, however, hear of bishops or higher clergy who had been slaves. At the other extreme, it seems to have been rare for the senatorial class to have sought ordination. There appear to have been few aristocratic clergy, and Ambrose is the exception rather than the rule.[26]

Canon 10 of Sardica suggests that many "rich men and lawyers" became bishops and, probably, priests. This evidence dovetails with imperial legislation that began under Constantine by exempting the decurions from their liturgies and ended with attempts to restrict the flow of money out of the cities by the dispensation. It is clear enough that ordination was attractive to many who belonged to the city councils and were unable to bear the financial burdens required of them. Twice Ambrose attacked the imperial government for its attempts to ensure that decurions would discharge their financial obligations. In A.D. 384 the pagan urban prefect of Rome, Symmachus, petitioned Valentinian II to restore the Altar of Victory to the Senate House. Ambrose in turn wrote the emperor and successfully blocked the pagan petition. In the course of his argument, Ambrose said this:

> They complain, also, that public support is not considered due to their priests and ministers. What a storm of words has resounded on this point! But on the other hand even the inheritance of private property is denied us by recent laws, and no one complains; for we do not consider it an injury, because we grieve not at the loss. If a priest seeks the privilege of declining the municipal burdens, he has to give up his ancestral and all other property.[27]

Some four years later, Ambrose complained to Theodosius about his decision to punish the Christians of Callinicum for

---

26. I am dependent here upon Jones' discussion on pp. 920ff. in *The Later Roman Empire*.

27. Ambrose, Letter 18.13; NPNF 2.10, p. 419.

their role in destroying the Jewish synagogue in their town. How could he explain that a Christian emperor would punish Christians, he asked: "How shall I excuse it to those bishops, who now mourn bitterly because some who have discharged the office of the priesthood for thirty and many more years, or other ministers of the Church, are withdrawn from their sacred office, and set to discharge municipal duties?"[28]

The evidence from Ambrose's letters together with that of the relevant imperial legislation not only suggests that the curial class was the most important area for the recruitment of the higher clergy in the fourth century but also enables us to make two further inferences. First, we can explain why there seems to have been a fairly high level of literacy and even of education among the bishops and priests of the early imperial church. Second, we can see that financial motives were operative in creating the Christian clergy. The canonical legislation of the fourth century similarly suggests that it was difficult to eliminate the taint of lucre from the ordained ministry. Usury was repeatedly forbidden.[29] Moreover, the Synod of Antioch in A.D. 341 accepted two canons (24 and 25) designed to establish rules for preserving and managing church property and money. The canons show that it was extremely difficult to distinguish between a bishop's private property and that of the church. Bishops could use church moneys to care for the poor and strangers but were forbidden to use church property for private gain:

> But if the bishop be not satisfied with this, but uses the Church property for his private purposes, not dealing with her revenues or the fruits of her lands according to the wishes of the priests or deacons, but gives over the control of them to his household, brothers, sons, or other relations, and thus secretly injures the revenue of the Church, he shall be called to account by the synod of the eparchy.[30]

---

28. Ambrose, Letter 40.29; NPNF 2.10, p. 445.
29. See Canon 20 of Elvira, Canon 12 of Arles, Canon 17 of Nicaea, and Canon 4 of Laodicea.
30. See Canon 25 in Hefele, *A History of the Christian Councils*, vol. 2, p. 74.

That bishops using their office to accrue personal wealth was a problem is also testified to by frequent attacks on such people in the literature of the period.[31]

It need scarcely be said that the canons regard sex as well as money as a problem. Canon 18 of Elvira requires the excommunication of clergy convicted of fornication, while Canon 30 treats sexual offenses after baptism as a bar to the subdiaconate. Canon 9 of Neocaesarea requires a priest who confesses he has committed a carnal sin before ordination to abstain from offering the holy sacrifice, but allows him to "continue his other functions if he is zealous, for many think that other sins (except that of incontinence) were blotted out by his ordination as priest."[32] These canons only slightly mitigate the view of Cyprian in the middle of the third century that mortal sin, though forgiven through penance, disqualifies people from the ordained ministry. Another issue was the custom of clergy maintaining *subintroductae* in their households. However much the custom was supposed to establish spiritual and virginal brothers and sisters, its abuse and the scandal it caused even when not abused led the Council of Nicaea to forbid it (in Canon 3).[33]

While the canons show that the church sought to exclude sexual offenders from ordination, their evidence is somewhat more complicated with respect to clerical celibacy. On the one hand, there can be no doubt that by the end of the fourth century, celibacy was widely regarded in both East and West as desirable for bishops and priests. Early in the fifth century, Synesius of Cyrene was obliged to stipulate that he would not sacrifice his wife or his peculiar view of the resurrection, and would only reluctantly sacrifice his hunting dogs in order to be made bishop.[34] On the other hand, we know that the Council

---

31. See the subsequent discussion, pp. 49-50.

32. Hefele, *A History of the Christian Councils,* vol. 1, p. 228.

33. Canon 27 of Elvira is even stricter, since it permits clergy to include in their households only women who are their sisters or daughters upon condition that they have taken a vow of virginity.

34. See Synesius, Letter 105: "God himself, the law of the land, and the blessed hand of Theophilus himself have given me a wife. I, therefore, proclaim to all and call them to witness once for all that I will not be separated from her, nor shall I associate with her surreptitiously like an

of Nicaea deliberately refused to pass a canon requiring clerical celibacy, thanks to the intervention of Paphnutius, himself a celibate bishop and a confessor.[35] Somewhat later in the century, the Synod of Gangra in Asia Minor drafted a series of canons aimed at eliminating the extreme asceticism of the followers of Eustathius of Sebaste. Its canons condemn those who despise marriage (1), those who argue that no one should participate in the Liturgy when it is offered by a married priest (4), and those who embrace the celibate life out of contempt for marriage or from pride (9, 10).

It was in the West that clerical celibacy rapidly became a requirement. As early as Canon 33 of Elvira the attempt was made to impose celibacy on bishops, priests, deacons, and any who ministered at the altar. Later in the century, Ambrose explained that, while it might seem strange that a second marriage before baptism should exclude a man from ordination, the law was necessary so that the clergy might "exhort to widowhood." Moreover, Ambrose said, "ye know that the ministerial office must be kept pure and unspotted, and must not be defiled by conjugal intercourse."[36] Ambrose was horrified by reports of married priests who begot children after their ordination. His discussion made his reason for the reaction clear. Appealing to Exodus 19:10, he argued that Christian clergy must be ritually pure in order to offer the sacraments. The reason for clerical celibacy, then, was not so much the ascetical ideal of virginity as the notion that sexual activity would interfere with ritual purity.[37]

---

adulterer; for of these two acts, the one is impious, and the other is unlawful. I shall desire and pray to have many virtuous children" (A. FitzGerald, *The Letters of Synesius of Cyrene* [London: Oxford University Press, 1926], p. 199). See also this passage later in the letter: "No, if I am called to the priesthood [sc. episcopate], I declare before God and man that I refuse to preach dogmas in which I do not believe. . . . Even as a child, I was charged with a mania for arms and horses. I shall be grieved, indeed greatly shall I suffer at seeing my beloved dogs deprived of their hunting, and my bow eaten up by worms. Nevertheless I shall resign myself to this, if it is the will of God" (FitzGerald, p. 201).

35. See Hefele, *A History of the Christian Councils*, vol. 1, pp. 435ff.
36. Ambrose, *De officiis* 1.50; NPNF 2.10, p. 41.
37. See Gryson, *Le Prêtre selon Saint Ambrose*, and Jean-Paul Audet,

The development of clerical celibacy is, of course, a complicated matter; but the general picture may be easily summarized, and two implications of clerical celibacy may be noted. In the West, Pope Siricius held a synod in A.D. 386 that "advised" *(suademus)* that the "priests and Levites should not live with their wives."[38] And in A.D. 402, Pope Innocent I decreed in a synod that "bishops, priests, and deacons must remain unmarried."[39] In the East the custom became that bishops should be celibate, but that priests and deacons could be married provided their marriage took place before ordination. One implication of clerical celibacy was that married clergy who no longer cohabited with their wives appeared to have asked for trouble.[40] A second and more important one is that it seems likely that celibacy prevented the development of the clergy as a hereditary caste.[41]

There were, of course, other moral requirements for those seeking to be clergy. They could not be heretics or schismatics. They were not allowed to frequent taverns, practice magic or astrology, or make amulets. They were to be punished for indulging in buffoonery, using indecent language, singing during meals, or swearing by creatures.[42]

From such requirements we begin to get some sense of the standards that were set for clergy in the fourth century, but we also can see where the clergy often fell short of the ideal. Surely legislation always reflects abuses thought to be preva-

---

Structures of Christian Priesthood: Home, Marriage, and Celibacy in the Pastoral Service of the Church: The Origin of a Tradition and Its Meaning for Today (London and Melbourne: Sheed & Ward, 1967), pp. 144ff.

38. Hefele, *A History of the Christian Councils,* vol. 2, p. 387.

39. Hefele, *A History of the Christian Councils,* vol. 2, p. 429.

40. Canon 7 of the Synod of Toledo in A.D. 400 reads, "If the wife of a cleric sins, her husband shall keep her in confinement, and impose fasts and the like upon her" (Hefele, *A History of the Christian Councils,* vol. 2, p. 420).

41. There were, of course, clerical families. On the whole, however, this was not the rule. See Jones, *The Later Roman Empire,* p. 927, and Ambrose, *De officiis* 1.44 (NPNF 2.10, p. 36). Ambrose, however, ascribes the rarity of finding "a man to follow in his father's footsteps" to the "difficulties of the work," the rarity of sexual continence, and the fact that "the life seems to be too quiet for the activity of youth."

42. Hefele, *A History of the Christian Councils,* vol. 2, pp. 314, 318, 415.

lent and dangerous. In sum, the clergy of the fourth century were expected to be careful and honest in their financial dealings, chaste if not celibate in their sexual behavior, and loyal to the jurisdictional structures that redefined the unity of the church in the Roman Empire. They were, for the most part, from the middle class. And while they had received no formal training, they were expected to have received at least the grammatical education of an ordinary Roman, to have passed through the catechetical instruction of the church, and to have proved themselves by a probationary period in minor orders. We hear also that men were trained for the ministry by older bishops, and we begin to find the monasteries acting as a training ground for clergy.[43]

This is not the place to speak at length of the relation of the church and its clergy to the surrounding world, and to do so would take me far beyond my purpose. Nevertheless, a few general remarks are in order before turning to the ideal proposed for the clergy by Gregory of Nazianzus, John Chrysostom, and Ambrose. In broad terms, the post-Constantinian church saw its task as the sacralization of the Roman order. The Empire's espousal of Christianity had, as it were, enabled heaven to come down to earth. Most Christian leaders saw the Empire as having taken on a sacred character. Sacralizing imperial society took many forms. A Chrysostom preached the moral transformation now required. A Eusebius or a Lactantius sought for a political theory that would explain and justify the new situation. The development of the cult of the saints and the emergence of holy men and women in the new ascetical movement made the power of heaven available to people on

---

43. In Letter 21 Augustine speaks of a bishop who trained a man for the clergy, and his biographer speaks of clergy ordained from Augustine's monastery at Hippo (Possidius, *Life of Augustine* 11; The Fathers of the Church, vol. 15, p. 85). One thinks also of Diodore of Tarsus' *asketerion* in Antioch in the late fourth century. Formalizing the training of the clergy, however, lay much in the future. In the fifth century there were the schools of Edessa and Nisibis, and in the sixth there was Cassiodorus' proposal to establish such a school in the West. It is by no means clear, however, that either the monasteries or these schools were primarily designed to train clergy.

earth. The Christian clergy, I think, were expected to participate in this sacralizing endeavor.

The obvious problem was that the relationship between church and state, between Christianity and culture might work the other way around. The church risked being secularized and becoming no more than a department of state. The danger was by no means unperceived by fourth-century Christians, and in various ways they sought to combat it. One way involved tightening the rules for catechetical instruction and protecting the sacraments of the church from profanation. Another involved enlisting the support of that protest movement, monasticism. What is often overlooked, however, is that there was a persistent demand for "liberty of religion" not merely on the part of the Donatists but also on the part of the Nicenes against Arian emperors and on the part of Ambrose against orthodox emperors. "Liberty of religion" did not mean, as we might suppose, toleration. It meant the rights of the Christian church.[44] The church appears to have realized that it was for the first time obliged to take a public and corporate role in society and to have been concerned to maintain its integrity and independence in defining that role.

THE CLERICAL IDEAL IN THE FOURTH CENTURY

We find Gregory, Chrysostom, and Ambrose in agreement that the clerical order is distinct from and superior to the laity of the church. Just as God through his providential ordering has distinguished the ruling parts from those ruled in the body, so he has ordered the church by distinguishing shepherds from sheep. It would be a great evil and anarchical if all Christians were rulers and, equally, if all Christians refused ordination.[45]

---

44. I am greatly indebted to an as yet unpublished manuscript by Lester L. Field, Jr., entitled "Liberty, Dominion, and the Two Swords: On the Origins of Western Political Theology (180-398)." Mr. Field skillfully shows how the old martyr rhetoric that defended the church by attacking the state was adapted in the fourth century to the new situation in which church and state remained distinct but not necessarily opposed.

45. Gregory of Nazianzus, *Oratio* 2.3-4, PG 35.409B-412A.

The separate character of the ordained ministry in the church fulfills the type of the Old Testament, and the clergy are the counterpart of Israel's priesthood. Like the Levites, Christian clergy are to have no share in earthly possessions (Num. 18:23). Instead, the Lord is their portion.[46] The association of the ordained ministry of the church with priesthood and sacrifice has been fully established by the beginning of the third century.[47]

Chrysostom thinks of the Christian priesthood not merely as the fulfillment of Old Testament types but also as a heavenly order:

> For the priestly office is indeed discharged on earth, but it ranks amongst heavenly ordinances; and very naturally so: for neither man, nor angel, nor archangel, nor any other created power, but the Paraclete Himself, instituted this vocation, and persuaded men while still abiding in the flesh to represent the ministry of angels. . . . For if no one can enter into the kingdom of Heaven except he be regenerate through water and the Spirit, and he who does not eat the flesh of the Lord and drink His blood is excluded from eternal life, and if all these things are accomplished only by means of those holy hands, I mean the hands of the priest, how will any one, without these, be able to escape the fire of hell, or to win those crowns which are reserved for the victorious?[48]

For Chrysostom, perhaps more than for Gregory and Ambrose, the great honor and dignity of the priesthood are associated

---

46. Ambrose, *De officiis* 1.50 (NPNF 2.10, p. 41). The reference to the Lord's portion is, of course, taken from Psalm 16:5. See also Paulinus' *Life of Ambrose* 41, in which he refers to "priests and deacons, whose portion is God" (The Fathers of the Church, vol. 15, p. 58). Also see Jerome, Letter 52.5: "For since the Greek word *kleros* means 'lot,' or 'inheritance,' the clergy are so called either because they are the lot of the Lord, or else because the Lord Himself is their lot and portion." Jerome goes on to cite Psalm 16 and makes the comparison with the priests and Levites of the Old Testament (NPNF 2.6, p. 91). Gregory of Nazianzus supplies a long discussion based on Old Testament passages that relate Christian clergy to the priests and prophets of Israel (PG 35.468ff.).

47. It seems unlikely that the association was made as long as early Christianity and Judaism were seeking to define the ways in which they differed. See Dix's discussion on pp. 34ff. in *Jurisdiction in the Early Church*.

48. *On the Priesthood* 3.4-5; NPNF 1.9, pp. 46-47.

with the sacraments of baptism and the Eucharist.[49] No matter how the function of the clergy is understood, there can be no doubt that priests receive a special status and are set over the church.

It is tempting, but I think inadequate, to see in this lofty view of the priesthood no more than a hierarchical view of the church. However exalted they are, the clergy remain part of the body of Christ. People must be obedient to the bishop, Ambrose says, "for the rule of truth is, to do nothing to advance one's own cause whereby another loses ground, nor to use whatever good one has to the disgrace or blame of another." Differences exist between rich and poor, saints and sinners; but the important fact is that "we are one in Christ."[50] And, says Chrysostom, that unity can be preserved in health only if the members of the body fulfill their proper function.[51] A major source of the church's weakness is that commonplace and inexperienced men are ordained because of "the inconsiderate and random way in which prelates are chosen and appointed." The head ought to be the strongest part of the body; if it is not, "it becomes feebler itself than it really is, and ruins the rest of the body as well."[52]

Thus the exalted status of the clergy, particularly of the bishop, is necessary for the health of the body of Christ. But we can go one step further. Christ's example of humility in emptying himself to take on the form of a human being (Phil. 2:6-7)

---

49. Ambrose exploits the Old Testament typology and says, "The shadow is in the law, the image in the Gospel, the truth in heaven. In old times a lamb, a calf was offered; now Christ is offered. But He is offered as man and as enduring suffering. And He offers Himself as a priest to take away our sins, here in an image, there in truth." A little later Ambrose speaks of the "Levites": "Thou, then, art chosen out of the whole number of the children of Israel, regarded as the firstfruits of the sacred offerings, set over the tabernacle so as to keep guard in the camp of holiness and faith" (De officiis 1.48, 50; NPNF 2.10, pp. 40, 42). Ambrose's emphasis appears to be upon the clergy as guardians and patrons of the church. Gregory of Nazianzus says virtually nothing about the sacraments and emphasizes the role of the priest as a teacher for salvation.

50. Ambrose, De officiis 2.24; NPNF 2.10, p. 62. Cf. De officiis 1.33; NPNF 2.10, p. 29.

51. See also Jerome, Letter 52.9; NPNF 2.6, p. 94.

52. On the Priesthood 3.10; NPNF 1.9, p. 50.

shows us how the members of the body ought to treat one another.[53] Speaking of King David, Ambrose says it is "no small thing, especially in the case of a king, so to perform humble duties as to make oneself like the very lowest."[54] Gregory of Nazianzus makes the same point when he portrays Paul as the model for Christian priests: "For he does not seek his own, but he seeks the good of his children, whom he has begotten in Christ through the Gospel (1 Cor. 4:15). This is the definition of all spiritual authority, everywhere to overlook one's own for the profit of others."[55] In this way the status of the clergy is tied to their place in the church, and the paradox is established that true power expresses itself in service and humility.

Let me now turn from the character and status of the priesthood to its function, and let me use the term "priesthood" the way the fourth-century church fathers did — to mean both the episcopate and the presbyterate.[56] Of course, we have already seen that priests were responsible for administering the sacraments of the church, but the two functions with which I shall be concerned in the discussion that follows are those of the teacher and of the patron. The three treatises I am examining place considerable emphasis upon the first of these functions. Indeed, Ambrose comes close to identifying the priesthood with the task of teaching. He observes, "[I] can no longer now escape from the duty of teaching which the needs of the priesthood have laid upon me." And he laments that his sudden ordination has obliged him to teach before he has learned.[57]

Ambrose says little else about teaching, largely because he is preoccupied with the moral and spiritual character of the teacher. But Chrysostom tells us that part of the teaching office of the priest has to do with the defense of Christian doctrine against Greeks, Jews, and heretics.[58] In this way the priest

---

53. Ambrose, *De officiis* 3.3; NPNF 2.10, pp. 69ff.
54. *De officiis* 2.7; NPNF 2.10, p. 49.
55. *Oratio* 2.54; PG 35.464BC.
56. See the notes in SC 272, pp. 72-73, 112-13, 142.
57. *De officiis* 1.1; NPNF 2.10, p. 1.
58. Cf. L. William Countryman, "The Intellectual Role of the Early Catholic Episcopate," *Church History* 48 (1979): 261-68. On p. 268 he says, "In summary, the intellectual work of the early Catholic clergy, particularly

wages war on Satan and protects his flock from Satan's followers.[59] One can imagine not only catechetical instruction and ordinary preaching but also public debates like those Augustine used in his attempts to put down Manichaeism and Donatism.[60] The positive dimension of teaching, however, is far more important. And here we may think of the priest as preacher. Gregory of Nazianzus judges his willingness to use Greek philosophy as an argument for his inability to preach to the people.[61] What he says implies that the priest's teaching must be made available to simple people. Chrysostom does not disagree, but insists that the preacher "not be unskilled in the knowledge and accurate statement of doctrine."[62] Paul is the model preacher, and we should esteem his gifts in speaking more valuable than his ability to work miracles.[63] The preacher faces the difficult task not only of struggling to compose his message so that it will be both true and persuasive but also of learning to be indifferent to praise, slander, and envy.[64]

The aim of teaching and preaching is "to educate others to virtue."[65] One way of understanding this is to appeal to the

---

of the bishops, under the early Empire was an essential aspect of the social function which these officers were fulfilling. By defining doctrine, they reinforced and defended the boundaries of the Catholic church as a sub-society of the Roman world." Countryman, of course, is concerned with the pre-Constantinian period, but if we omit his last phrase, what he says remains true of the priests of the fourth century.

59. On the Priesthood 4.3-4; NPNF 1.9, pp. 64-65.

60. See, for example, his biographer's accounts: Possidius, Life of Augustine 6, 13-14 (The Fathers of the Church, vol. 15, pp. 80, 88ff.).

61. Oratio 2.7; PG 35.416A.

62. On the Priesthood 4.6; NPNF 1.9, p. 67.

63. On the Priesthood 4.7-8. Chrysostom's view of miracles, like that of the young Augustine, treated the gospel and apostolic miracles as important to establish the authority of the gospel. He denied that miracles any longer took place.

64. On the Priesthood 5.1-4; NPNF 1.9, pp. 70-71.

65. Gregory of Nazianzus, Oratio 2.14; PG 35.424A. Cf. Robert Wilken's assessment of Origen's teaching and his school in Alexandria: "The teachers of Alexandria were not interested solely in conveying knowledge or transmitting intellectual skills. They were interested in moral and spiritual formation." ("Alexandria: A School for Training in Virtue," in Schools of Thought in the Christian Tradition, ed. Patrick Henry [Philadelphia: Fortress Press, 1984], p. 19.)

common understanding of Christ's work as the conquest of Satan and of the Christian life as a moral and spiritual warfare by which Christians appropriated Christ's victory for themselves. The teacher is, as it were, the general who commands Christ's army in this conflict. Chrysostom's treatise concludes with a long and moving passage in which he describes the assembling of a mighty army and asks whether some young country lad would not flee if asked to take command of it. How much more, then, when the battle is against spiritual foes, would one shrink from taking charge and find one's soul paralyzed "unless it happen to be very noble, and to enjoy in a high degree as a protection to its own courage the providential care of God."[66]

Another way of construing the aim of teaching is to use the metaphor of a physician. The priest must heal sick souls, Chrysostom points out, and "how shall they to whose lot falls the care of the body [of Christ], which has its conflict not against flesh and blood, but against powers unseen, be able to keep it sound and healthy, unless they far surpass ordinary human virtue, and are versed in all healing proper for the soul?"[67] One basic difficulty that attaches to the task of healing is that one can only persuade. "For it is not possible for any one to cure a man by compulsion against his will."[68] Another is that different people require different remedies, and it is difficult to discern what will best restore someone to health.[69] Chrysostom's emphasis is upon the moral reformation that should be effected by the priest's teaching, but he may also envisage the priest's power to administer the discipline of the church. Ambrose at one point uses the metaphor of the physician this way. What he has in mind is the bishop's power of excommunication: "Thus it is a good bishop's desire to wish

---

66. *On the Priesthood* 6.12-13; NPNF 1.9, pp. 81ff. The words I have cited are on p. 82. Immediately before employing the soldier metaphor, Chrysostom uses the example of a beautiful bride and an unworthy bridegroom. For the war with Satan, see also *On the Priesthood* 2.3.

67. *On the Priesthood* 4.2; NPNF 1.9, p. 64.

68. *On the Priesthood* 2.3; NPNF 1.9, p. 41.

69. *On the Priesthood* 2.3-4; NPNF 1.9, pp. 40-41. See also *On the Priesthood* 4.3 and 6.4.

to heal the weak, to remove the spreading ulcers, to burn some parts and not to cut them off; and lastly, when they cannot be healed, to cut them off with pain to himself."[70] Here the metaphor describes the priest not so much as teacher but more as judge or patron.

Gregory of Nazianzus provides us with a more sophisticated understanding of the priest's teaching function, and the Christian-Platonist spirituality he elaborates obviously is central to his understanding both of the Christian life and of the priesthood.[71] For Gregory,

> [the aim of spiritual healing is] to give wings to the soul, to snatch it away from the world and give it to God, to preserve what is made in God's image if it remains, to guide it if it is in danger, to save it if it has fallen, and to cause Christ to dwell in their hearts through the Spirit (Eph. 3:17). In sum, the purpose is to make him who has a rank on high God and a participant of blessedness on high.[72]

It is easy enough to see that the priest is meant to assist people to their destined salvation, a goal understood simultaneously as the ascent of the soul to God (as in Plato's *Phaedrus*) and as divinization, since God the Word became human that we might be made divine. Gregory continues by arguing that this destiny is willed for us by the whole of Scripture, and that the Incarnation has fulfilled this will. God's beneficent dispensation toward us became the "new mystery" revealed in the narrative of Christ's life beginning with his birth from the Virgin and completed by his victorious death and resurrection.[73] The true healing, then, is that of the Incarnation, and "we are ministers

---

70. *De officiis* 2.27; NPNF 2.10, p. 64.

71. Like Chrysostom, Gregory of Nazianzus uses the physician metaphor as a way of speaking of the healing the Christian teacher must effect, and he mixes the metaphor with that of spiritual warfare (*Oratio* 2.19-21; PG 35.428ff.).

72. *Oratio* 2.22; PG 35.432B.

73. *Oratio* 2.24-25; PG 35.434ff. It seems to me of considerable importance that Gregory not only integrates the Platonic themes with Christian teaching but also treats the Incarnation as a narrative rather than a theological puzzle.

and assistants of this healing, so many of us as preside over others."[74]

I have used the word "patron" to describe the second function of the fourth-century priest I wish to discuss. By this term I mean the priest's role in caring for the poor, in administering the discipline of the church, in judging Christians, and in representing the church's interests in the wider society. I find it interesting that the three treatises under consideration say relatively little about this function. Ambrose's treatise may be excepted to a degree, but I can find no real discussion of the function in Gregory's *Oration* and little in Chrysostom's treatise. If I am correct, the phenomenon is quite surprising, because many scholars would argue that in the fourth century the teaching role of the priest was eclipsed by his role as patron and magistrate.[75] Of course, the function itself is by no means novel. Bishops were expected to care for the poor, to provide hospitality for strangers, and almost certainly to judge disputes among Christians in accordance with Paul's instructions in 1 Corinthians 6. What seems novel is the degree to which the

---

74. *Oratio* 2.26; PG 35.436A. Maintaining the healing metaphor, Gregory goes on to speak of the difficulty of finding the right cure, of the necessity of healing people's beliefs as well as their moral character, and of the particular difficulty involved in erasing erroneous beliefs from the tablets of the mind before sound doctrine can be written on them.

75. See W. Telfer, *The Office of a Bishop* (London: Darton, Longman & Todd, 1962), chapter 7, "Bishops as Magistrates." Telfer traces the development before the fourth century, and he sees it as especially characteristic of the West. See especially pages 140-41: "It was, however, just as the ancient world was passing away in the West that the magistracy of bishops became a predominant feature of their office." See also Henry Chadwick, *The Role of the Christian Bishop in Ancient Society* (Berkeley, Calif.: The Center for Hermeneutical Studies, Protocol of the 35th Colloquy, 1979). Chadwick says, "The patronage role assumed by fourth-century bishops meant or could mean power" (p. 8). In his response, Peter Brown says, "In a society where membership of the community was expressed most clearly in terms of the patron-client relationship . . . the care of the poor by the Christian bishop was far more than a laudable form of economic relief. . . . It redrew the boundaries of the Late Roman urban community" (p. 20). For patronage in an earlier period, see Charles A. Bobertz's 1988 Yale dissertation entitled "Cyprian of Carthage as Patron: A Social Historical Study of the Role of Bishop in the Ancient Christian Community of North Africa."

function began to predominate in the fourth century. Let me suggest that the ideal proclaimed by Gregory, Chrysostom, and Ambrose stems from the pre-Constantinian tradition, while the practice that emphasized patronage and judicial functions was not accepted on equal terms in theory.

In any case, we can learn something about what was happening from a passage in Possidius' *Life of Augustine*. He cites 1 Corinthians 6:1-8 and goes on to note how Augustine acted upon Paul's exhortation, sometimes spending all day hearing cases: "This work, which, however, took him away from better things, he regarded as an obligation. His greatest pleasure was always found in the things of God, or in the exhortation or conversation of intimate brotherly friendship."[76] The church had clearly become not only big business but also a forum for litigation.[77] And the same tone of slight resentment implied by Possidius' words is to be found in an interpretation Chrysostom gives to Christ's command to Peter: "Feed my sheep" (John 21:15-17). Chrysostom points out that Christ might have said to Peter, "If thou lovest me practice fasting, sleeping on the ground, and prolonged vigils, defend the wronged, be as a father to orphans, and supply the place of a husband to their mother."[78] Christ's actual command envisages the cure of souls and must take precedence over asceticism and, remarkably, over the care of orphans, widows, and those who have been wronged. The priest is to be a moral and spiritual teacher first, and only secondarily a patron.

Chrysostom does, however, take the priest's responsibilities as patron with utter seriousness. He treats these duties as

---

76. Possidius, *Life of Augustine* 19; The Fathers of the Church, vol. 15, p. 97.

77. Henry Chadwick, in discussing the Roman synod of A.D. 378 that defended Pope Damasus, points out that the synod not only insisted that bishops were exempt from the civil courts but also argued that a bishop "has a higher moral standing as a judge because he is bound by his conscience to acquit the innocent and to condemn the guilty; he will not need to tear the flesh of innocent witnesses under judicial torture because his charismatic office enables him to judge the moral character of the defendant" (*Priscillian of Avila: The Occult and the Charismatic in the Early Church* [Oxford: Clarendon Press, 1976], pp. 128-29).

78. *On the Priesthood* 2.2; NPNF 1.9, p. 40.

reasons for his refusal of ordination and points out that "super-
intending widows, . . . the care of virgins, [and] the difficulty
of the judicial function" each holds "a different kind of anxiety,
and the fear is greater than the anxiety."[79] The discussion that
follows specifies these anxieties and adds to the list of the
priest's tasks hospitality to strangers and the care of the sick
and the poor. All these responsibilities and the expectations that
surround them expose the priest to slander and backbiting:

> And talking of patronage, let me disclose another pretext for
> fault-finding. For if the bishop does not pay a round of visits
> every day, more even than the idle men about town, unspeak-
> able offence ensues. For not only the sick, but also the whole,
> desire to be looked after, not that piety prompts them to this, but
> rather that in most cases they pretend claims to honor and
> distinction.[80]

What Chrysostom says helps explain why I have chosen the
category of "patron" as a rubric under which to discuss the
charitable and judicial functions of the priest.

The rhetorical context in which Chrysostom places his
discussion is somewhat misleading; it does not seem to me that
he wishes to deny the importance of the priest as patron. That
this is so finds support in his comparisons of the monk and the
priest. The monk is not obliged to deal with demands made
upon him by other people and is free from the difficulties and
dangers that beset the active life of the priest. "For the recluse
has but himself to fear for." And even if he is obliged to care
for others, his task is made easy by the fact that he is free from
"worldly concerns," including a wife and children.[81] The monk
has no difficulty sitting at the helm of his ship in a safe harbor,
but the priest must guide the ship in storms on the open sea.[82]
The fact that the priest must preserve the spiritual and moral
ideals of the monk in the context of the world means that his
office is not only more difficult but also more honorable.

Most of Ambrose's references to the priest as patron are

---

79. *On the Priesthood* 3.16; NPNF 1.9, p. 55.
80. *On the Priesthood* 3.17; NPNF 1.9, p. 58.
81. *On the Priesthood* 6.3; NPNF 1.9, p. 75.
82. *On the Priesthood* 6.6; NPNF 1.9, p. 77.

found in Book 2 of *De officiis* and so reflect the basic structure of the treatise, a structure that Ambrose borrows from Cicero. Book 1 examines duties derived from what is virtuous; Book 2 examines duties derived from what is useful. Book 3 then treats the relationship of virtue and utility.[83] In a sense, however, Ambrose employs the Ciceronian conventions only to demolish them. He insists that "we measure nothing at all but that which is fitting and virtuous, and that by the rule of things future rather than of things present; and we state nothing to be useful but what will help us to the blessing of eternal life; certainly not that which will help us enjoy merely the present time."[84] Ambrose translates the classical categories of virtue and utility into Christian terms by orienting them to the age to come, and he can think of them as faith and works or as contemplation and action. His insistence that the two be united further collapses the apparent structure of his treatise. Works are necessary, he says, but unless they are built upon the foundation of faith, they are without value: "The higher one builds, the greater is the fall; for without the protection of faith good works cannot stand."[85] Virtue and utility end by being the same thing. Nothing can be virtuous without being useful, and nothing useful is vicious.[86]

We can, I think, conclude that Ambrose takes a more immediately positive view of the priest's patronage than Chrysostom. In any case, the duties he outlines cohere with what we have already found Chrysostom discussing. The priest must care for virgins, widows, and the poor; he must show hospitality to strangers. He must defend people in court, especially the poor and weak. The bishop must administer ecclesiastical discipline, even if it means excommunication.[87] Ambrose adds to the list of responsibilities the ransoming of captives. He defends his own use of the church plate for this purpose, insisting that

---

83. This structure is indicated by *De officiis* 1.9, 2.1, and 3.2; NPNF 2.10, pp. 5-6, 43, and 68.

84. *De officiis* 1.9; NPNF 2.10, p. 6.

85. *De officiis* 2.2; NPNF 2.10, p. 45.

86. *De officiis* 3.2; NPNF 2.10, p. 68.

87. See *De officiis* 1.11, 1.20, 2.15-16, 2.21-22, 2.25; NPNF 2.10, pp. 7, 15, 54-56, 59-61, 62-63.

the freedom of captives is more important than gold.[88] He also elaborates on the necessity of protecting money that widows have entrusted to the church and attacks clergy who behave like fortune hunters.[89] Both the duties and the ways in which they must be discharged receive consideration.[90]

However, as I have already suggested, the emphasis of the three treatises under consideration is upon the character of the priest who serves as teacher and patron. The faults of priests who fail to attain the ideal are in part the product of inexperience or youth. According to Chrysostom, the reason so many commonplace and inexperienced men become priests is to be found in "the inconsiderate and random way in which prelates are chosen and appointed."[91] And Ambrose speaks of his refusal to ordain a man who used unseemly gestures and walked arrogantly. He also regards jests as immodest and attacks as undignified those who curry favor by going to parties and visiting widows and virgins. As clergy, he points out, "no duty to make ourselves agreeable to men has been laid upon us."[92] It is difficult to regard youth or inexperience as a character flaw, and Ambrose's complaints are hard to take with utter seriousness. But the worry is that the young priest will have an unformed character, and that careless behavior will express a vicious character.

The word we find used for the character fault that prevents priests from being what they should be is "vainglory." The word "ambition" also expresses what the church fathers mean: "For they certainly would be deserving of the greatest punishment who, after obtaining this dignity through their

88. *De officiis* 2.28; NPNF 2.10, p. 64. Cf. 2.15.

89. *De officiis* 2.29, 3.9; NPNF 2.10, pp. 65ff., 76ff.

90. One other function that might be discussed is the role Christian priests play as ambassadors, particularly in parlays during war. On this point, see Ammianus Marcellinus XX.7,9, XXIX.5,15, XXXI.12,8-9, and XXXI.15,6.

91. *On the Priesthood* 3.10; NPNF 1.9, p. 50. Cf. the argument by Gregory of Nazianzus from his own youth and inexperience, his faulty knowledge of Scripture, and his moral imperfection (*Oratio* 2.49; PG 35.457B).

92. *De officiis* 1.18, 20, 23; NPNF 2.10, pp. 12ff. The words cited are on p. 16.

own ambition, should then either on account of sloth, or wickedness, or even inexperience, abuse the office."[93] Vainglory can be a lust for money or for power, and it is the greatest possible obstacle to virtue.[94] It is, says Chrysostom, a rock "more dangerous than that of the Sirens," for it holds a vast multitude of wild beasts:

> They are wrath, despondency, envy, strife, slanders, accusations, falsehood, hypocrisy, intrigues, anger against those who have done no harm, pleasure at the indecorous acts of fellow ministers, sorrow at their prosperity, love of praise, desire of honor . . . , doctrines devised to please, servile flatteries, ignoble fawning, contempt of the poor, paying court to the rich. . . .[95]

Chrysostom goes on for ten more lines, and we obtain a glimpse into one dimension of clerical life in the fourth century.

Both Chrysostom and Ambrose, however, distinguish vainglory from a proper ambition for office. Ambrose believes "one should strive to win preferment, especially in the Church, only by good actions and with a right aim."[96] And Chrysostom reminds us that Scripture says, "If any man desireth the office of a bishop, he desireth a good work" (1 Tim. 3:1). He avoids contradicting himself by saying he has not attacked those who desire the work of a bishop, only those who desire authority and power.[97] The real issue has to do not with how people behave but with their motives. In other words, the cautionary moral to be drawn from considering unworthy priests is the realization that character is decisive. According to Chrysostom, the reason that the wrong people become priests is that those responsible for the appointment "do not all look to one thing,

---

93. Chrysostom, *On the Priesthood* 4.1; NPNF 1.9, p. 62.

94. See Ambrose, *De officiis* 1.28, 1.30; NPNF 2.10, pp. 23, 26. See also Gregory of Nazianzus, *Oratio* 2.41, 51; PG 35.450, 461.

95. *On the Priesthood* 3.9; NPNF 1.9, p. 49. In this same passage Chrysostom goes on to say, "The divine law indeed has excluded women from the ministry, but they endeavor to thrust themselves into it; and since they can effect nothing of themselves, they do all through the agency of others." We can remind ourselves that Chrysostom did not live in the twentieth century.

96. *De officiis* 2.24; NPNF 2.10, p. 61.

97. *On the Priesthood* 3.11; NPNF 1.9, p. 50.

which ought to be the only object kept in view, the excellence of the character. . . ."[98] Ambrose almost certainly means the same thing when he remarks that it is useless to look for a spring in the mud.[99]

It is, of course, not enough to speak of character or virtue. We must explain what we mean by those words; the fathers of the church probably had a far clearer idea of what they meant by the terms than we do. The reason? They employed the conventions of Greek philosophy and thought of character in terms of widely accepted structures. At one level, the ideal character is formed by the acquisition of the four cardinal virtues: prudence, justice, fortitude, and temperance. Ambrose, more clearly than the other two, has this in mind. Emphasis on these virtues dominates part of his discussion in De officiis (1.25-50). In part he does no more than repeat conventional themes. To have one of the virtues is to have them all.[100] The virtues must be understood as ways of describing living according to nature.[101] "Virtue is the only and the highest good."[102] These themes and others Ambrose derives from Cicero, but also from Platonism, which had incorporated much Stoic and Aristotelian moral philosophy.

What is more remarkable, however, is that Ambrose sets his discussion of the virtuous character in a Christian context. As the highest and only good, virtue "richly abounds in the fruit of a blessed life . . . by means of which eternal life is won. . . . A blessed life is the fruit of the present, and eternal life is the hope of the future."[103] By relating the virtues to Christian hope, Ambrose redefines them. It is essential that the

---

98. On the Priesthood 3.15; NPNF 1.9, p. 53.

99. De officiis 2.12; NPNF 2.10, p. 52. See also De officiis 2.17; NPNF 2.10, p. 57: "Such, then, ought he to be who gives counsel to another, in order that he may offer himself as a pattern in all good works, in teaching, in trueness of character, in seriousness. Thus his words will be wholesome and irreproachable, his counsel useful, his life virtuous, and his opinions seemly."

100. De officiis 1.25; NPNF 2.10, p. 20: "Note here [in Abraham's sacrifice of Isaac] all these four virtues in one act." Cf. 2.9 and 2.14.

101. De officiis 1.46; NPNF 2.10, p. 37.

102. De officiis 2.5; NPNF 2.10, p. 46.

103. Ibid.

virtues be built upon a true foundation, and "[that] foundation is Christ." This means that faith is essential; and although Ambrose does not elaborate his point, his implication is that the active life of virtue depends upon the contemplative life and the religious vision of God. And Ambrose Christianizes his discussion of the virtuous character in yet another way. Instead of using examples from classical history as Cicero had done, he draws upon Scripture and finds in the biblical narratives illustrations of the ideal he proposes. "A succession of old-time examples set down in such small compass," he says, "may offer much instruction."[104]

Chrysostom's understanding of virtuous character is much the same as Ambrose's. Fortitude is the virtue he emphasizes in Book 3. It is not merely ascetical discipline that tests the priest's fortitude of soul, but also "insult, and abuse, and coarse language, and gibes from inferiors, whether wantonly or justly uttered, and rebukes idly spoken both by rulers and the ruled." When attacked in this way, fortitude can be corrupted into anger.[105] Here Chrysostom employs the stock idea that vices and virtues are the opposite of one another. Fortitude can become anger; love can become lust. The virtuous life, then, consists in transforming the vices into virtues. The idea depends upon the Stoic notion of the mind as the governing principle of the passions and the body. When the mind fulfills its role as governor, virtues result; when the passions overwhelm the mind, vices result. The difficulty of the priestly life is that its circumstances test the mind, and "the emotions of the mind when chafed and irritated, are naturally more exasperated, and those who possess them are driven to commit greater sins." Accordingly, it is difficult for the priest to maintain "the balance of the mind."[106]

Like Ambrose, Chrysostom brings his understanding of

---

104. *De officiis* 3.22; NPNF 2.10, p. 89.

105. *On the Priesthood* 3.13; NPNF 1.9, p. 51.

106. *On the Priesthood* 6.8; NPNF 1.9, p. 78. See also *On the Priesthood* 6.12; NPNF 1.9, p. 80: "He who makes them [the passions of the soul] weak, places them in subjection to right reason; but he who nourishes them carefully, makes his battle with them harder, and renders them so formidable that he passes all his time in bondage and fear."

the virtuous life in a moral sense into relation with the spiritual life. The office of the priest, he says, requires "the virtues of an angel": "For the soul of the Priest ought to be purer than the very sunbeams, in order that the Holy Spirit may not leave him desolate, in order that he may be able to say, 'Now I live; and yet no longer I, but Christ liveth in me' (Gal. 2:20)."[107] Discussing the purification of the soul, of course, is a way of speaking about the acquisition of moral virtue. But virtue points beyond itself to the spiritual unity of the priest with Christ in the Holy Spirit. What Chrysostom implies is the dialectical unity of contemplation and action. Similarly, perfect teaching results when "the teachers both by what they do and by what they say . . . , bring their disciples to that blessed state of life which Christ appointed for them." Practice and doctrine belong together.[108] The priest needs "much understanding, and, before understanding, great grace from God, and uprightness of conduct, and purity of life and superhuman virtue."[109] Spiritual union with Christ is both the cause and the product of moral virtue, and the dialectic of contemplation and action is presided over by God's grace.

Gregory of Nazianzus says little about the virtues and instead emphasizes the union of contemplation and action. Priests are to be "higher than the many in virtue and in familiarity with God." The moral and the spiritual are united.[110] Paul's instructions about bishops and presbyters (1 Tim. 3:2-3; Titus 1:7, 9), as well as Jesus' instructions to his disciples (Matt. 10:8-9), make it clear that living the life of the gospel involves both the moral life *(tropon)* and the spiritual life *(logon)*.[111] His chief concern, however, is with the importance of the spiritual life, and he understands this as the spiritual sacrifice Paul speaks of in Romans 12:1.[112] "One must first be purified, and then make pure," he says; "first be made wise and then make wise; become light and then enlighten; be close to God and then

---

107. *On the Priesthood* 6.2; NPNF 1.9, p. 75.
108. *On the Priesthood* 4.8; NPNF 1.9, pp. 68-69.
109. *On the Priesthood* 3.7; NPNF 1.9, p. 49.
110. *Oratio* 2.3; PG 35.409B.
111. *Oratio* 2.69; PG 35.477C.
112. *Oratio* 2.95; PG 35.497A.

bring others to him; be sanctified and then sanctify."[113] God's grace and election alone make this possible, "shepherding the shepherds and guiding the guides."[114]

CONCLUDING REFLECTIONS

The major point I have sought to demonstrate is that the clerical ideal of the fourth century revolves primarily around the character of the priest. The ideal character is defined in both moral and spiritual terms and in the conventions of the prevailing Christian Platonism of the time. But I should wish to add that character is never separated from the life meant to flow from it, specifically from the functions the priest is obliged to fulfill. Those functions and the circumstances attending them produce a number of tensions that characterize the priestly life. The priest must belong to a local community and yet be a part of the universal church. He is set over the community hierarchically, but must in humility and service build up the whole body of Christ. He must be a teacher and at the same time act as patron for his flock.

These tensions, it seems to me, reflect what I should regard as the fundamental problem of the fourth- and fifth-century church.[115] A theology of freedom, revolving around a

---

113. *Oratio* 2.71; PG 35.480B.

114. *Oratio* 2.117; PG 35.513B.

115. See my study of miracles in the Roman imperial church entitled *The Fear of Freedom* (University Park: Pennsylvania State University Press, 1989). I had completed the manuscript before reading Elaine Pagels' volume entitled *Adam, Eve, and the Serpent* (New York: Random House, 1988); but what is interesting is that in some respects her conclusions agree with mine. Take, for example, her comment on p. xxv: "From these explorations I came to see that for nearly the first four hundred years of our era, Christians regarded *freedom* as the primary message of Genesis 1–3. . . . With Augustine . . . this message changed." I am not sure I would make Augustine responsible for the change, and I would argue that the more important change is the one effected by the Constantinian Revolution. Moreover, I find myself unpersuaded that the change stems from sexual attitudes or that Augustine's doctrine of original sin is tied in any limited way to sexuality. And I find myself questioning some of Pagels' interpreta-

Christianized version of the late antique quest for virtue, predominated in catechetical instruction, in the homilies of the period, and in the theological treatises we possess. On the other hand, the cult of the saints and, to some degree, the holy man as patron appear to have occupied center stage in the corporate and cultic life of the church. That life implied, I think, not a theology of freedom but one of power. What people were being taught from the pulpit was that God would help them use their freedom to pursue virtue. What they were learning in the cultic life of the church and beginning to be taught by the theology of the mature Augustine was that God's power and grace would deliver them.

In examining the three treatises about the priestly ideal, we find, it seems to me, the predominance of the theology of freedom. It is in this context that the emphasis upon character and virtue makes most sense. The role of the priest in patronage seems to me far more coherent with what I have called a theology of power. It is clear that at least Chrysostom and Ambrose believe that character is equally decisive for the patron, and I should like to believe this myself. At the same time, all three figures recognize that it is in the area of power that the greatest threats may be found to the development and preservation of Christian character. It is easy enough to correlate virtue with membership in a community and with the persuasive role of the teacher. It is harder to fit virtue into a scheme of things that is hierarchically ordered and requires the exercise of power. Yet this is, I think, precisely what the three figures I have examined all recognize in their own way. They are unwilling to abandon their ideals of moral and spiritual virtue. They see the difficulty of applying those ideals to a changed situation, but they insist nevertheless that this is what must be done.

---

tions of Chrysostom's and Augustine's stances toward the Empire. Nonetheless, although I have approached the issue from a completely different perspective, I am pleased to find points of contact with Pagels' interesting and provocative work.

Class, Profession, and Morality: Moral Formation in American Protestant Seminaries, 1808-1934

E. Brooks Holifield

In 1832, Enoch Pond joined the faculty of the Congregationalist theological seminary in Bangor, Maine. There he presented detailed lectures on the finer points of pastoral duty and ministerial ethics and etiquette. His lectures on clerical ethics, consisting largely of exhortations to cultivate character, piety, prudence, and gentility, promoted a dual ideal: "But I would," he said, "that every minister of Christ should be, not only a holy exemplary man, but in his manners a gentleman — a *Christian gentleman*."[1]

Pond's exhortations provide a clue for understanding a long tradition of moral formation in Protestant divinity schools in America. He thought himself to be proposing durable lessons in clerical demeanor drawn from the deep reservoirs of Christian tradition, but his maxims also displayed his alertness to the intricacies of class and status in antebellum society and especially his sensitivity to recent changes in the social location of the clergy in America. The early patterns of moral guidance for seminarians embodied a hidden ambiguity. At one moment

---

1. Pond, *The Young Pastor's Guide: Or, Lectures on Pastoral Duties* (Bangor, Maine: E. F. Duren, 1844), p. 21.

the seminaries could recommend ancient standards of Christian behavior; at another they could display a sublime confidence in the rules of decorum prevalent among the elevated classes of nineteenth-century society. They combined the two sets of standards with little sense of any possible tension between them.

Later generations of seminary teachers found it easy to dismiss some of Enoch Pond's prescriptions but hard to discover any alternative to his practice of intermingling ancient Christian formulations with the cultural standards prevailing in polite society. But by the early twentieth century, this ambiguity began to elicit a sense of unease. For one thing, the venerable methods of moral formation seemed no longer invariably effective. For another, the earlier confidence in a harmonious synthesis between Christian ethics and the cultural proprieties of the refined classes began to fade.

I.

Even before the end of the eighteenth century, Protestants began to think about building theological seminaries to educate their ministers, and everyone assumed that disciplines of moral and spiritual formation would accompany the academic training. Within two decades after the founding of Andover Theological Seminary in 1808, eighteen schools provided theological instruction, usually in biblical studies, systematic theology, church history, and sacred rhetoric. The schools supplemented their formal instruction by promoting exercises in piety. The faculty at Andover required students to attend early morning and evening prayers every day; students at Harvard were to be in the chapel for morning prayers at sunrise. But no one thought that formal chapel services would suffice: the rules at Andover informed students that the school also expected them to practice private devotions daily, to observe occasional days of fasting, and to attend weekly conferences with faculty members. Students at the General Theological Seminary of the Episcopal Church in New York were to "maintain every day stated periods of pious reading, meditation and devotion; and occasional special seasons."[2]

Seminary faculties conveyed clear expectations about the cultivation of piety and morality. At Bangor Seminary, for example, Enoch Pond gave his students precise instructions for cultivating the religious and moral affections. His lectures in pastoral theology encouraged the devotional study of the Bible, sacramental piety, frequent religious meetings, spiritual conversation, and secret prayer. The faculty at other seminaries made similar efforts to create nurseries of piety, and they both admonished and suspended students who displayed "levity or indifference in regard to practical religion." General Theological Seminary was typical in requiring entering students to present evidence of their "religious and moral character" and to pledge that they would "uniformly cultivate religious and moral dispositions and habits" during their period of theological study.[3]

Students not only accepted this regimen but also formed their own societies to promote moral growth. The Moral Society of Yale College, for example, formed in 1797, gradually became an organization exclusively for theological students, who used its meetings to advance in rhetorical skills, debating acumen, and ethical insight. They held exercises on ethical topics every three weeks, debating the fittingness of everything from the celebration of Christmas to temperance, capital punishment, civil disobedience, and slavery. At Yale and elsewhere, such societies exacted from their members sacred pledges to observe biblical rules of morality. At Yale this meant admonitions and

---

2. Leonard Woods, *History of the Andover Theological Seminary* (Boston: James R. Osgood, 1885), p. 304; Henry K. Rowe, *History of Andover Theological Seminary* (Newton, Mass.: Thomas Todd, 1933), p. 36; Willard L. Sperry, "'A Beautiful Enmity': The Student History in the Nineteenth Century," in *The Harvard Divinity School*, ed. George H. Williams (Boston: Beacon Press, 1954), p. 152; *The Constitution, Act of Incorporation, and Statutes of the General Theological Seminary* (New York: Protestant Episcopal Press, 1832), p. 16.

3. Woods, *History of the Andover Theological Seminary*, p. 301; Pond, *The Young Pastor's Guide*, p. 292; *The Constitution, Act of Incorporation, and Statutes of the General Theological Seminary*, pp. 14-15.

expulsions for members who used profane language, played cards, or tippled to excess.[4]

Despite the fervent atmosphere of the seminaries, their faculties frequently had to answer complaints that instruction was too academic, with insufficient attention to everyday pastoral duties, the cultivation of the affections, and the practice of piety. Partly in response to their critics, the schools encouraged students to undertake pastoral labors in neighboring churches. But they also instituted the lectures in pastoral theology, and it was in those lectures that they attended most explicitly to theories and techniques of moral formation.

At Andover, pastoral theology was a part of church history; at Princeton, founded in 1812, it fell within the scope of ecclesiastical history and church government. By the time the Harvard Corporation formed its theological faculty in 1819, it seemed useful to plan for a distinctive chair of "Pulpit Eloquence and Pastoral Theology," which came into being eleven years later. Eventually every seminary offered instruction in pastoral topics. The courses provided training in preaching, pastoral conversation, and methods of leadership, but they always devoted a portion of their time to instruction in ministerial morality.

Before long, the pastoral theologians began to publish their lectures, along with supplementary texts on the topics of their courses. In 1827 Samuel Miller, a teacher at Princeton, published his *Letters on Clerical Manners and Habits*. In 1844 Enoch Pond released his *Young Pastor's Guide; or, Lectures on Pastoral Duties*, derived from his lectures at Bangor Seminary. The Episcopal Bishop of Virginia, William Meade, published in 1849 *Lectures on the Pastoral Office*, a collection of the lectures that he had delivered to the seminary students in Alexandria. These are but three examples of a popular genre of nineteenth-century religious literature. Seminary faculties also had their

---

4. John T. Wayland, *The Theological Department in Yale College, 1822-1858* (New York and London: Garland Publishing, 1987), pp. 292, 298; Conrad Wright, "The Early Period (1811-40)," in *The Harvard Divinity School*, p. 64.

students read and recite from European texts like the *Pastoral Theology* of the Swiss minister Alexander Vinet, and they encouraged them also to read domestic productions like *Thirty-Four Letters to a Son in the Ministry* (1842), written by the Presbyterian minister Heman Humphrey while he served as the president of Amherst College.

The textbooks and lectures in pastoral theology challenged students with a clerical moral ideal by outlining their duties to themselves, to others, and to God. The tripartite outline was a commonplace in the moral-science courses that students were expected to have mastered in college, so the seminary lectures had a familiar aura. The difference was that the seminary courses applied the collegiate maxims specifically to the duties of the ministry. The teachers urged seminarians to fulfill their duties to themselves by preserving their health, cultivating their minds, examining their consciences, and stirring the affections of their hearts. Duties to others included restraint from evil-speaking, abstention from envy, the avoidance of undue ambition, and the tempering of a meddlesome spirit. "More than all," added Enoch Pond, the minister who indulged in "too great liberties with the other sex" risked losing "all respect for his character." And then came the minister's duties to God: faith, love, piety, and a passionate concern for the saving of souls.[5]

In addition to the three kinds of duties, the pastoral theologians developed what became a standard list of character traits. A portion of the lectures sometimes consisted of simple descriptions of such virtues as gravity, humility, prudence, zeal, and honesty, along with similar descriptions of the vices that ministers should avoid: avarice, ambition, excess, and fretfulness. Often the theologians took care to exhibit the biblical roots of their lists of virtues and vices. James Spencer Cannon, who taught pastoral theology in the Dutch Reformed Seminary in New Brunswick, turned to the New Testament for descriptions and illustrations of each of the virtues that he urged his seminarians to embody. At least some of the pastoral theologians sought to isolate a distinc-

---

5. Pond, *The Young Pastor's Guide*, p. 330.

tive Christian ethic as the nucleus of their ideal of clerical formation.[6]

Yet the textbooks and lectures ranged far beyond the New Testament in their advice and admonition. They tried to inculcate a new set of manners so that graduates would "never say or do anything, which would be offensive to the best bred families in [their] congregation." Samuel Miller warned young ministers against paring their fingernails, picking their teeth, or combing their hair in public. He told them how to conduct themselves at the dinner table. Reminding them that spitting tobacco endangered both refined feelings and delicate health, he urged them not to spit on floors or carpets and to seek spitting boxes if they could not forego using tobacco during their clerical visits. Heman Humphrey exhorted them to keep their feet off the mantle pieces and their cigar smoke out of other people's faces. And he also included advice about chewing tobacco. The minister, he said, should never be "at a loss to know what to do with his *quid,* in a lady's drawing room."[7]

Not all the pastoral theologians ventured to be as explicit as Miller and Humphrey in their descriptions of possible clerical indelicacy, but all would have subscribed to the ideal of clerical gentility that undergirded the lessons in etiquette. The pastoral theology courses encouraged young ministers to learn what Enoch Pond called "easy and gentlemanly manners." Humphrey offered a description of the ideal minister that every pastoral theologian could easily have accepted: "Every clergyman," he said, "ought to be a gentleman; not a man of show and ceremony, but a real gentleman in his manners, in his conversation, in all his habits and feelings."[8]

Humphrey was candid about the reason for attending to matters of etiquette. Only clerical gentility, he said, would en-

---

6. Cannon, *Lectures on Pastoral Theology* (New York: Board of Publication of the Reformed Protestant Dutch Church, 1859), pp. 29-55, 602-7.

7. Samuel Miller, *Letters on Clerical Manners and Habits: Addressed to a Student in the Theological Seminary at Princeton, New Jersey* (New York: G. and C. Carvill, 1827), pp. 54-66; Humphrey, *Thirty-Four Letters to a Son in the Ministry* (Amherst: J. S. and C. Adams, 1842), p. 345.

8. Pond, *The Young Pastor's Guide,* p. 20; Humphrey, *Thirty-Four Letters,* p. 345.

sure access to the higher classes in the Protestant congregations. Only gentility would make the minister welcome in refined society. The pastoral theologians assumed that most ministers would have little difficulty with "the poor and uneducated," though they did advise them to put aside haughtiness and superiority with their inferiors. "If you live to be a minister," Miller told them, "a large part of your social and professional intercourse will be with those who, according to popular language, are your *inferiors*." And he wanted ministers to serve those people without supercilious condescension. But first he wanted ministers to learn their manners.[9]

The elementary character of the instruction in clerical etiquette provides a clue to the way the pastoral theologians regarded at least some of their students. Samuel Miller remarked that a regrettable number of nineteenth-century theology students and ministers seemed totally ignorant of the world, "unacquainted with the most obvious and established proprieties of life." The exhortations in the pastoral theology courses suggest that more than one seminary faculty felt it necessary to educate students who shared that ignorance of the proprieties.[10]

When the Baptist minister Francis Wayland published his book entitled *The Apostolic Ministry* (1853), he urged young men not to choose the ministry merely as a "profession" for the "sake of worldly advantage." Anyone who reads clerical laments about low salaries and other temporal discomforts in nineteenth-century America might find it surprising that Wayland had to warn against choosing the ministry as an avenue to "worldly advantage," but he obviously felt that his admonition served a purpose. And indeed, he was addressing young men for whom the ministry did often serve as a route to upward social mobility.[11]

In the background of exhortations about clerical etiquette stood a transition in the social location of the ministry. The wealthy had always contributed less than their share of sons to

---

9. Humphrey, *Thirty-Four Letters*, p. 345; Miller, *Letters on Clerical Manners and Habits*, p. 42.

10. Miller, *Letters on Clerical Manners and Habits*, p. 16.

11. Wayland, *The Apostolic Ministry* (Rochester: Sage and Brother, 1853), p. 35.

the ministry in America. By the early nineteenth century the offspring of the privileged classes seemed less inclined than ever to enter the pulpit. In the early eighteenth century, for example, about 50 percent of Yale graduates entered the ministry; by 1821 the number fell to 33 percent; by 1861 it fell still further to 15 percent. Burton Bledstein has discovered that in other representative colleges the declension in numbers remained steady during the antebellum period: from 30 percent in 1820 to 25 percent in 1840 to 20 percent in 1860. By 1835 the law rivaled the ministry as the professional choice of graduates at the elite schools.[12]

The demand for ministers remained high, however, and the leaders in the churches recognized that they could fill the pulpits only if they opened the ministry to worthy young men who in earlier generations would have entertained no realistic hope of entering a profession. In the small towns and the countryside, the nineteenth-century revivals had drawn a host of young converts into the churches. They provided a natural pool for clerical recruitment. But they also came from the homes of families that would never have been able to afford the cost of education, families in a social stratum that had been largely excluded from the learned professions.

As early as 1712, scholarships had been available for young men planning to enter the ministry. In 1722 Harvard College offered as many as 24 scholarships, and in the following decade Bishop George Berkeley established a small scholarship endowment at Yale. But by the nineteenth century those scholarships had declined, so in 1811 clerical leaders in Connecticut founded the Connecticut Education Society, designed to pay the bills for pious young men at Yale. In 1815, a larger band of ministers formed in Boston the American Education Society, designed to preserve the ideal of an educated ministry. They were mainly urban Congregationalists worried by the

---

12. James W. Schmotter, "Ministerial Careers in Eighteenth-Century New England: The Social Context, 1700-1760," *Journal of Social History* 9 (1975): 251; Burton J. Bledstein, *The Culture of Professionalism: The Middle Class and the Development of Higher Education* (New York: W. W. Norton, 1976), pp. 37, 198.

possibility that the rural and small-town churches of New England might follow the example of Baptists and Methodists and fill their pulpits with uneducated exhorters. But they soon cast their sights beyond New England and began to share a vision that Lyman Beecher had given them in his 1814 address to the Charitable Society for the Education of Indigent Pious Young Men for the Ministry of the Gospel.[13]

A powerful Congregationalist minister in Litchfield, Connecticut, Beecher warned that "illiterate men, however pious, cannot command the attention of that class of the community whose education and mental culture is above their own," and he predicted an imminent decline of civilization unless the churches could provide at least one competent, educated pastor for every thousand souls in America. Rejoicing that the revivals had attracted young men to the faith, he warned that too many of these converts were "by their poverty, shut out from the vacant vineyard of the Lord." Beecher wanted to open that vineyard. A population as large as that of the United States needed, he said, 8,000 educated ministers; it had only about 3,000, along with about 1,500 illiterate preachers. The challenge was to recruit and educate almost 5,000 young men.[14]

The American Education Society started slowly, but after its reorganization in 1825 it moved with impressive success toward Beecher's goal. By 1830, it supported 500 young men a year in colleges and seminaries, and it soon had branches in every section of the country. It also served as a model for similar denominational societies. By the end of the 1830s, the Board of Education of the General Assembly of the Presbyterian Church supported about half as many students as the AES. The Northern Baptist Education Society supported about 50 a year. By 1848 Lutherans organized a Young Men's Society to support indigent students at Concordia.[15]

---

13. David F. Allmendinger, Jr., *Paupers and Scholars: The Transformation of Student Life in Nineteenth Century New England* (New York: St. Martin's Press, 1975), p. 48.

14. Beecher, *An Address of the Charitable Society for the Education of Indigent Pious Young Men for the Ministry of the Gospel* (n.p.: n.p., 1814), pp. 5-15.

15. Allmendinger, *Paupers and Scholars*, p. 67; Donald M. Scott, *From*

Not everyone rejoiced at the new arrangements. The AES sponsored students from "the common walks of life," not from "the higher class of society." Most of its scholarship recipients came from small towns and rural areas and from families without much education; they went to college not at Yale or Harvard but at the smaller provincial schools closer to their agricultural communities. And they sometimes had a hard time adapting themselves to the standards of etiquette that their mentors assumed as normative for a minister. By 1861 the AES had to contend with critics who disseminated unfavorable stereotypes: "With many men," complained one AES official, "the prevailing notion of an Education Society student is, that he is a heavy, coarse-featured, and coarse-minded individual. . . . Others seem to think that for some reason this class of students are [sic] apt to fail in notions of Christian propriety — that they are proverbially liable to disgrace their sacred profession, and bring reproach upon the cause of Christ by their misconduct." The Society acknowledged a few "solitary cases" of unworthiness among its students, but it defended the character of the vast majority and even insisted that they were preferable to "the sons of early wealth and ease." It also instituted rigorous reviews to assure that candidates showed "suitable traits of character for the ministry."[16]

No evidence suggests that the influx of indigent scholars diminished the moral standards of schools that educated ministers. It is true that external discipline collapsed during the early nineteenth century in the American colleges. Harvard had to expel 43 of the 70 members of the class of 1823. And violent and disorderly conduct disrupted many other schools during

---

Office to Profession: The New England Ministry, 1750-1850 (Philadelphia: University of Pennsylvania Press, 1978), p. 58; Carl S. Meyer, *Log Cabin to Luther Tower: Concordia Seminary* (St. Louis: Concordia Publishing House, 1965), p. 26.

16. *Twenty-First Annual Report of the Directors of the American Education Society, 1837* (Boston: Perkins & Marvin, 1837), p. 43; *Forty-Fifth Annual Report of the Directors of the American Education Society* (Boston: T. R. Marvin & Son, 1861), pp. 15-16; Joseph Harvey, *Address to the Friends of Religion in Behalf of the American Education Society* (Andover: Flagg & Gould, 1825), p. 2.

the 1820s. Students carried weapons and used them against both teachers and other students. Princeton endured six insurrections between 1800 and 1830; students at the University of Virginia launched armed attacks on the homes of professors, murdering one of them; students at Yale killed one tutor and maimed another. It is also true that seminaries occasionally had to discipline and suspend theological students for unethical behavior. During the 1840s, for example, Harvard Divinity School dismissed students for "immoral conduct," "deception and fraud," and "illicit aids in examination." But indigent scholarship students hardly set the tone of student life at Harvard, Yale, and the University of Virginia, and no one ever suggested that students on AES scholarships broke the rules more than any other students. The AES official Joseph Harvey was probably accurate when he acknowledged "some instances of misconduct" among the scholarship students but claimed that on the whole they exercised a salutary moral influence on other students. Yet the indigent scholars did pose a problem for the seminaries.[17]

The changes in the social origins of the seminarians help us to understand the ideal of moral formation implicit in the pastoral theology lectures. In forming ministerial character, the seminaries had not only to deepen piety but also to alter customs and habits that were acceptable in one social class but taboo in another. In his lectures at Bangor Seminary, Enoch Pond was open and explicit about his intention to change the behavior of students with "rustic, boorish habits." Samuel Miller believed that the minister's "delicacy ought to be quite as scrupulous and pure as that of the most refined lady." He clearly saw it as a challenge when he encountered a rough farmboy from the backwoods with a quid of tobacco in his cheek.[18]

The pastoral theologians made no clear distinctions be-

---

17. Sperry, " 'A Beautiful Enmity,' " p. 161; Bledstein, *The Culture of Professionalism,* pp. 214-45; Harvey, *Address to the Friends of Religion,* pp. 12-13.

18. Pond, *The Young Pastor's Guide,* p. 20; Miller, *Letters on Clerical Manners and Habits,* p. 104.

tween etiquette and ethics, between the manners acceptable to the elevated classes and the moral dispositions that embodied the central themes of the Christian tradition. All the maxims blended together. Samuel Miller came close to defending the position that refined etiquette served as evidence of the sanctified heart: "My object," he said, "is to recommend those manners which become the *Christian Gentleman;* which naturally flow from the meekness, gentleness, purity, and benevolence of our holy Religion." But standards of propriety in a culture are subject to change, and by the later nineteenth century the seminaries were subtly modifying their ideals of moral formation.[19]

II.

After the Civil War a new generation of pastoral theologians took up the task of expounding the themes that guided moral formation in the seminaries. They continued to seek a wider circle of clerical readers by publishing their lectures as books. The list of such volumes is large: *Pastoral Theology* (1885) by the Congregationalist James M. Hoppin at Yale; *The Pastor Amidst His Flock* (1890) by the Congregationalist G. B. Willcox at Chicago Theological Seminary; *The Pastor* (1880) by the Episcopal theologian Gregory Thurston Bedell; *The Christian Pastorate* (1871) by the Methodist Daniel Kidder at Drew; *Pastoral Theology* (1877) by the Presbyterian Thomas Murphy in Philadelphia; *For the Work of the Ministry* (1907) by the Baptist T. Harwood Pattison at Rochester Theological Seminary. These and a host of similar publications carried the older themes into a postwar society.

The reader of these books is struck by the continuities that link them to their predecessors. They sometimes acknowledged their indebtedness to the honored worthies of the past. Thomas Murphy made use of copious notes he had taken as a student under Archibald Alexander at Princeton. The Episcopalian Gregory Bedell, writing in 1880, confessed that he knew of no

---

19. Miller, *Letters on Clerical Manners and Habits*, p. 19.

rules for the cultivation of clerical manners that could supersede those in Samuel Miller's *Letters on Clerical Manners and Habits*. The books suggest that the structure of the pastoral theology courses remained largely unchanged. Instructors taught students how to preach, how to visit and offer counsel, how to handle the administrative tasks of their churches, and how to behave.[20]

They continued to exalt the ideal of clerical gentility. Baptist students at Rochester learned from their teacher Harwood Pattison that "the very fact that a man is a minister of Christ should make him a gentleman," and he was echoing a commonplace. Pastoral theologians continued to outline the same lists of virtues and vices that had appeared in the older courses, the only difference being their somewhat greater attention to the theme of clerical character. Convinced that "a right ministerial character" came only through the sustained cultivation of habits of goodness, they offered exhortation and advice about character formation. The Methodist Daniel Kidder told students to immerse themselves in the study of exemplary characters in Scripture, history, and biography as a way of building character.[21]

Class consciousness still subtly informed the ideal of moral formation. The American Education Society reported in 1892 that "the ranks of our ministry are recruited more and more from those who are without means of their own to pursue a regular course of instruction." The society's report acknowledged that the average American preacher had for the most part come from poor families in "smaller and less thriving towns." But by that time the society had decided that a humble background constituted a recommendation for ministry: "The possibilities of a strong, effective character, all things considered, are more often found with the poor than with the rich." The 1892 report observed that a large proportion of

---

20. Murphy, *Pastoral Theology* (Philadelphia: Presbyterian Board of Publication, 1877), p. 4; Bedell, *The Pastor: Pastoral Theology* (Philadelphia: J. B. Lippincott, 1880), p. 586.

21. Pattison, *For the Work of the Ministry* (Philadelphia: American Baptist Publication Society, 1907), p. 443; Kidder, *The Christian Pastorate* (Cincinnati: Hitchcock & Walden, 1871), p. 208.

distinguished pastors had come from the lower economic classes.[22]

In 1908 David Spence Hill conducted an unsystematic but diligent survey of seminaries and reported that more than two-thirds of the schools offered free tuition to all students while others provided financial aid based on economic needs. Hill feared that the free tuition would encourage habits of dependence — a fear shared by William Rainey Harper at the University of Chicago. But the financial practices of the seminaries indicated that the social patterns that had emerged in the early part of the century continued to mark clerical education. For someone with "wealth, social standing, and brilliant worldly prospects," observed one minister, "it was a coming down . . . to enter the ministry." But for people without privileged backgrounds, the ministry still served as an avenue of social mobility, and this pattern continued into the twentieth century. From 1929 through 1933, the Conference of Theological Seminaries conducted, under the leadership of the Yale educational psychologist Mark May and the Union theologian William Adams Brown, an intensive study of 63 Protestant seminaries. Their report, published in 1934, revealed that most seminarians still came from low-income families in small communities. Their parents had, on average, two years of high-school education.[23]

Pastoral theology classes in the late nineteenth and early twentieth centuries therefore offered the familiar basic lessons in etiquette. Students still learned useful hints about table manners, refined conversation, and deportment. "Never spit," warned the Baptist Harwood Pattison. "Nothing excuses the habit of expectoration." He advised his students to learn good manners by "noticing what are the customs of the best people."

---

22. *Eighteenth Annual Report of the American College and Education Society, 1892* (Boston: Rapid Printing, 1892), pp. 9-11.

23. Hill, *The Education and Problems of the Protestant Ministry* (Worcester, Mass.: Clark University Press, 1908), p. 66; Andrew L. Stone, *Responsibility of the Church* (Boston: T. R. Marvin & Son, 1860), p. 7; Brown, *The Education of American Ministers*, vol. 1: *Ministerial Education in America* (New York: Institute of Social and Religious Research, 1934), pp. 110-11; Harper, "Shall the Theological Curriculum Be Modified, and How?" *American Journal of Theology* 3 (1899): 52.

When the Methodist Nolan Harmon published his *Ministerial Ethics and Etiquette* in 1928, he still insisted that it should "almost go without saying" that every minister should be a gentleman. But the authors of the 1934 report on American Protestant seminaries lamented, after surveying 1,530 students and interviewing a number of them, that although the researchers found no serious moral problems, they still encountered ample evidence of social deficiencies: "What is needed," the report concluded, "is not so much formal discipline as counsel on those matters of personal decorum in which men with faulty social background are deficient."[24]

Despite such continuities with the past, the seminaries reflected the cultural changes of postwar America. The Civil War had led American intellectuals to discard many of the "feeble sentimentalities" of the early nineteenth century. It produced in American life a vocabulary of toughness, realism, masculinity, and efficiency. The postwar industrial economy intensified the new evaluations of power and forcefulness by glorifying the barons of industry who built the factories, railroads, and steel companies. Popular expressions of Darwinian thought, images of masculinity derived from the playing fields of the English public schools, a growing admiration for sports figures in American culture, and a vague popular consciousness of the power embodied in new technology all coalesced by the 1890s in a veritable cult of virility, which preachers in England and America promptly translated into the new religious vision of "muscular Christianity." A host of preachers spoke in a vocabulary that resonated with technological metaphors, Darwinian images, and anecdotes derived from the football field.[25]

---

24. Pattison, *For the Work of the Ministry*, pp. 443, 446-47; Harmon, *Ministerial Ethics and Etiquette* (Nashville: Abingdon Press, 1928), p. 11; Brown, *The Education of American Ministers*, vol. 1, p. 150. (In the 1987 edition of *Ministerial Ethics and Etiquette*, Harmon added that every woman in ministry should be a lady.)

25. John Higham, "The Reorientation of American Culture in the 1890s," in *Writing American History: Essays on Modern Scholarship* (Bloomington: Indiana University Press, 1970), pp. 77-100; George M. Frederickson, *The Inner Civil War: Northern Intellectuals and the Crisis of the Union* (New York: Harper & Row, 1968), pp. 68-110, 211-13; William E. Winn, "*Tom*

The cultural changes found expression in the promulgation of new moral imperatives for seminarians. They were to embody "ministerial manliness," and this required a moral commitment to "physical cultivation" and decisiveness of character. Earlier pastoral theologians had advised seminarians to care for their health, but in the late nineteenth century the image of healthy manliness connoted a panoply of moral virtues: freedom from slavish fear, simplicity of character, the courage of conviction, the overcoming of timidity, and the capacity for self-denial. James Hoppin told students at Yale that good health and a sound physical organism were "moral powers in the work of the ministry." Antebellum seminaries had conjoined piety and mannered refinement; their successors seemed intent on linking ministerial morality to an image of vitality and robustness.[26]

The accent on a muscular ministry paralleled a growing discomfort with the older double standard of ministerial morality. In the antebellum seminaries, both students and faculty seem to have agreed that the minister was bound to a standard of morality and decorum higher than that of any other person or profession. This point of view continued to have earnest supporters in the later part of the century. "Because he is a minister he is expected to show a loftier standard of life than other men," said Harwood Pattison, "and this expectation he must not disappoint." More than one of the pastoral theologians taught their students that it was necessary to impose such a double standard on those individuals charged with renovating and improving the characters of others. But discomfort with the double standard emerged as early as the 1870s.[27]

In 1876, for example, William Taylor, the minister of the

Brown's School Days and the Development of 'Muscular Christianity,'" Church History 29 (1960): 64-73.

26. Humphrey, Thirty-Four Letters, p. 348; Hoppin, Pastoral Theology (New York: Funk & Wagnalls, 1885), p. 178; Pattison, For the Work of the Ministry, pp. 36-41; G. B. Willcox, The Pastor Amidst His Flock (New York: American Tract Society, 1890), p. 14; Kidder, The Christian Pastorate, pp. 245-46.

27. Pattison, For the Work of the Ministry, p. 507; Kidder, The Christian Pastorate, p. 204; Harmon, Ministerial Ethics and Etiquette, p. 20.

Broadway Tabernacle in New York City, announced that it was wrong to suppose that the minister should be "more sedate, subdued, and holy than another Christian." Taylor's was not an isolated voice, and the critique of the double standard gradually made its way into a few of the seminaries. The pastoral theologian G. B. Willcox at Chicago Theological Seminary told his classes that nothing in the clerical profession could be considered "more sacred than in any other." "No more thorough self-surrender is required of a minister than of any other man," wrote Willcox in 1890. "He is nowhere called to live nearer to God than a merchant or physician or farmer."[28]

The opponents of the double standard worried that its excessively rigid formulations had separated the clergy from the people. They disliked the image of clerical isolation and fussiness, the stereotype of the minister as "out of touch with life, aside from the stream of daily struggle and need." They feared that seminaries produced young ministers who often failed "to touch the life of common, daily temptation." In his textbook on pastoral theology entitled *The Christian Pastor and the Working Church* (1898), the Social Gospel theologian Washington Gladden presented the ideal of a minister immersed in the busy life of the community, resolutely refusing to withdraw from familiar intercourse with people. Even seminary teachers who defended the double standard put a new emphasis on the need for ministers to keep in touch with the grimy life of the world that surrounded them.[29]

The ideal of involvement in the world came partly from seminary faculties drawn toward some of the themes of the Social Gospel. When Francis Greenwood Peabody initiated in 1883 his course on social ethics at Harvard Divinity School, he represented the turn from an ethic of individual purity to one

---

28. William M. Taylor, *The Ministry of the Word* (New York: Anson D. F. Randolph, 1876), p. 268; Willcox, *The Pastor Amidst His Flock*, p. 14; Bedell, *The Pastor*, p. 21.

29. F. L. Godkin, "The Clergyman of Today," *The Nation*, 26 Oct. 1899, p. 311; George Hodges, *The Theological Seminary and Modern Life* (Cambridge, Mass.: Caustic-Claflin, 1905), p. 14; Gladden, *The Christian Pastor and the Working Church* (New York: Charles Scribner's Sons, 1903), p. 176; Pattison, *For the Work of the Ministry*, p. 512.

of public duty. The Social Gospel Progressives almost invariably retained an elevated sense of private morality, but they also shifted the angle of vision. And some of the pastoral theology courses betrayed the influence of this shift in moral consciousness. They adapted but reinterpreted an older image of the minister as a public person by urging their students to exercise "grave responsibility of a public nature." The faculty at Union Theological Seminary in New York City, for example, arranged in the 1890s for theological students to work in settlement houses and public institutions in order to learn about public powers and social ethics.[30]

All the older agencies of moral and spiritual formation in the seminary remained intact. Throughout the nineteenth century faculties continued to require daily worship; students continued to form theological societies to discuss ethical questions and prayer groups to cultivate the spiritual life. Between 1929 and 1933 the researchers for the Conference of Theological Seminaries visited the campuses of 12 seminaries and observed that student prayer groups remained active in 11 of them, that almost 50 percent of the schools sponsored devotional retreats, and that seminaries still encouraged students to seek counsel from members of the faculty. Union Theological Seminary in New York City provided an apt symbol of the moral tone of Protestant seminaries in the 1920s when the faculty, for reasons of propriety, turned down student requests for dances in the refectory.[31]

Seminaries continued to exact pledges of moral probity. They asked entering students to vow that their deportment would conform to the dignity of the ministerial office, to promise that they would pursue "gravity, industry, and soberness of life," to affirm that they would always treat others with respect, or to avouch that they would "uniformly cultivate religious and moral dispositions." Throughout the 1920s students signed

30. Hoppin, *Pastoral Theology*, p. 218; Robert T. Handy, *A History of Union Theological Seminary in New York* (New York: Columbia University Press, 1987), p. 109.

31. Meyer, *Log Cabin to Luther Tower*, pp. 3-54; Mark A. May, *The Education of American Ministers*, vol. 3: *The Institutions that Train Ministers* (New York: Institute of Social and Religious Research, 1934), p. 433.

such declarations as a prerequisite for entry into many of the American seminaries.[32]

By the early twentieth century, however, a few seminary faculties received petitions from students complaining about the rules. The petitions claimed that chapel requirements were legalistic and the services perfunctory. As early as 1903, laments could be heard that the devotional life of the seminary was dying. By 1934, only 17 of the 63 seminaries discussed in the May-Brown report required chapel attendance, and in some schools only about 30 percent of the students bothered to attend. Equally telling about the changing ethos were student assertions that the programs provided by the seminaries offered little help with "personal problems such as sex, or the more complex matters of social duty." When asked to evaluate the seminary activities designed to help them with moral problems, the students replied that the least helpful were the chapel services. Although the schools encouraged faculty members to offer counsel and conversation, students said that they saw faculty members as unapproachable or uninterested in their moral problems. Some students found courses that provided useful moral guidelines; others found help in books; still others said that they relied on conversations with friends. But most claimed that they received the greatest help from private devotions and meditation.[33]

The authors of the 1934 report lamented the deficiencies because they found students particularly liable, almost as soon as they entered the seminary, to "the vices and peculiar moral problems of 'professionalism.'" The lament was familiar. Donald Scott has recently traced the transition of the ministry in New England from its status as a public office, in which ministers were normally bound to lifetime tenures in local communities that paid them from public funds, to its modern form

---

32. Mark A. May and Frank K. Shuttleworth, *The Education of American Ministers*, vol. 4: *Appendices* (New York: Institute of Social and Religious Research, 1934), pp. 249-53.

33. Meyer, *Log Cabin to Luther Tower*, p. 127; Brown, *The Education of American Ministers*, vol. 1, pp. 158, 164; May, *The Education of American Ministers*, vol. 3, pp. 448, 450, 453.

as a professional career, in which ministers provide specialized services to a self-selected clientele as they move upward through a series of congregations offering ascending degrees of remuneration and status. Different denominations in different regions underwent the transition at different times. Scott believes that the change was complete among New England Congregationalists by the 1850s. In 1853 Francis Wayland worried about its effect on New England Baptists. By the 1890s, in any case, some of the pastoral theologians included in their lectures on ministerial morality earnest exhortations against the temptation of considering one parish merely as a stepping-stone to another that offered greater "personal, professional success."[34]

By the time Mark May and William Adams Brown published their study of seminary education in 1934, however, some of the seminaries had found more to approve than to deplore in the image of the minister as a professional. William Rainey Harper at the University of Chicago had helped to popularize a notion of theological education as a program of professional ministerial preparation grounded in the premise that "specialism in the ministry is as necessary as specialism in any other profession." From this perspective, the problem of moral formation resolved itself partially into a matter of courses insuring that graduates would not "enter the profession ignorant of the particular types of moral problems to which [their] profession lays [them] open."[35]

Not everyone agreed with the view that seminaries should suddenly devote more of their attention to problems of ministerial morality. When Robert Kelly, working for the Institute of Social and Religious Research, published in 1924 his study entitled *Theological Education in America,* he complained

34. Brown, *The Education of American Ministers,* vol. 1, p. 165; Scott, *From Office to Profession,* pp. xi, 1-9; Wayland, *The Apostolic Ministry,* p. 35; Willcox, *The Pastor Amidst His Flock,* p. 35.

35. Harper, "Shall the Theological Curriculum Be Modified, and How?" p. 59; Glenn Miller and Robert Lynn, "Christian Theological Education," in *Encyclopedia of the American Religious Experience,* 3 vols., ed. Charles H. Lippy and Peter W. Williams (New York: Charles Scribner's Sons, 1988), 3:1644.

that "goodness rather than intelligence is often held up as an end of theological teaching" in the seminaries, with the result that the ministry too frequently represented narrow visions of the good more fervently than it embodied intelligent presentations of religious insight. But May and Brown, writing a decade later, urged the seminaries to assume as a "major responsibility" the task of cultivating the private and corporate devotional life and the moral character of theological students.[36]

The reports written by May and Brown suggested some of the reasons that such an ideal now seemed hard to attain. The denominations had come largely to accept the image of the ministry as a career, and in most of them seniority or popular success overrode other considerations in the filling of pulpits. Seminary faculties had moved toward specialization, with faculty members dividing into a multiplicity of departments and seeking academic achievement within restricted fields. Seminaries made little provision for "the systematic oversight and discipline of the individual religious life." Moreover, the schools assumed that their students already had a firm religious and moral grounding, so that they could be largely trusted to look after these matters for themselves. The report noted one modest change that serves as a symbol of the transitions: courses in pastoral theology now placed the emphasis on theories of pastoral skill and practice, ignoring the earlier traditions of guidance in the cultivation of the religious and moral life.[37]

One reason for the emergence of clinical pastoral education in the early twentieth century was the hope that long-term supervised encounters with men and women in crisis in hospitals, prisons, and social agencies might resolve problems that the seminary no longer effectively addressed. When the Harvard physician and ethicist Richard Cabot issued his "Plea for a Clinical Year in the Course of Theological Study" in 1925, he

---

36. Kelly, *Theological Education in America: A Study of One Hundred Sixty-One Theological Schools in the United States and Canada* (New York: George H. Doran, 1924), p. 235; Brown, *The Education of American Ministers*, vol. 1, pp. 165, 167.

37. Brown, *The Education of American Ministers*, vol. 1, p. 154; May, *The Education of American Ministers*, vol. 3, p. 435.

suggested that a clinical year could offer unique training in the formation of moral judgment. He thought of moral growth as the consequence of attending unblinkingly to the real — "Thou shalt grow by learning Reality" — and this aim of moral formation informed the early years of clinical education. But the clinical movement soon found it as difficult as the seminaries to define the moral criteria that should guide the formation of students.[38]

One dimension of the change went unnoticed in the 1934 report, for at that time it was barely visible. When the seminaries first turned their attention to moral formation in the early nineteenth century, they fastened their ethical vision to a program of etiquette defined by the gradations of social class. Even when they modified their moral ideals in the later part of the century, they still accepted uncritically the moral images popular in the wider culture. But by the 1930s, some theologians and ministers felt it quaint to reiterate the familiar homilies about gentility or masculinity. By that time, theologians were on the verge of rediscovering the ancient problem of the tension between Christ and culture. The theological critique of culture religion removed one of the props that had supported the older ideal of moral formation.

The theologians of the Social Gospel had already called into question the subservience of churches and seminaries to narrow norms of cultural respectability. By the 1930s the issue assumed more subtle forms. In 1932 H. Richard Niebuhr translated Paul Tillich's critique of Western culture, *The Religious Situation* — an argument that genuine religion was antithetical to the illusion that cultural values were God's values. Throughout the decade the theological Realists — Tillich, H. Richard Niebuhr, Reinhold Niebuhr, George Richards, and others — complained that the church had, in H. Richard Niebuhr's phrase, "adjusted itself too much rather than too little to the world in which it lives." They warned that excessive attachments to cultural ideals — which presumably would include notions like gentility and masculine vitality — betrayed

---

38. See my book entitled *A History of Pastoral Care in America: From Salvation to Self-Realization* (Nashville: Abingdon Press, 1983), pp. 235-37.

an identification of the Christian gospel with the assumptions of a particular social class. When that warning took hold in the seminaries, the older synthesis of ethics and etiquette seemed suspect.[39]

It hardly suffices, however, merely to call into question an outmoded formulation of a cultural and religious synthesis. The Realist theologians themselves recognized that the Christian gospel always found embodiment in cultural forms. It would be hard to know how to affirm the moral imperatives of the Christian tradition without incarnating them within manners and forms specific to cultural traditions. The antebellum synthesis faltered because it pursued too uncritically the amalgamation of Christianity and one stream of American culture. Faced with a change in the social composition of the ministry and disturbed by its implications, the antebellum seminaries leaped too quickly toward norms of genteel refinement that offered the prospect of acceptance and respectability among the powerful. But surely the solution is not merely to disdain cultural forms. One can even argue that certain patterns of etiquette and manners might indeed embody the deeper dimensions of Christian ethics in a given time and place.

In any case, the longer story suggests that if the seminaries of our own time are intent on engendering moral depth within their students, they must remain alert not simply to the complexities of Christian ethics but also to the intricacies of social class, to the forms of interaction among students and between students and faculty, to patterns of corporate and private worship, to the implicit criteria that inform the work of faculties, and to the unspoken norms prevailing within the American denominations. No simple matter. But Enoch Pond probably could have told us that.

---

39. H. Richard Niebuhr, "The Church Against the World," in *Theology in America*, ed. Sydney Ahlstrom (Indianapolis: Bobbs-Merrill, 1967), p. 597.

Spiritual Formation for Ministry: Some Roman Catholic Traditions — Their Past and Present

John W. O'Malley, S.J.

Among the various aspects of preparing young people for ministry, spiritual formation has been for centuries and remains today an overriding concern among Roman Catholics. Today this concern manifests itself in official documents emanating from the Holy See, from episcopal conferences, and from the superiors of religious orders of men and women — all of which in some way or other reflect ideals and agenda set by the pertinent documents of Vatican Council II. The concern is equally as manifest, however, in the spontaneous interest that students preparing for ministry have in courses on spirituality and in programs of formation. In Roman Catholicism today, no one questions in principle the importance of spiritual formation, and at least for priesthood candidates it has impressive systemic support. Of course, this does not mean that in many ways the situation is not confusing and that there are not many questions begging for resolution.

Given my own training and experience, I believe that the best service I can at the moment render in relationship to the issues addressed by this conference is to try to set the contemporary situation in its broadest historical context. What I have to say is divided, therefore, into three parts: first, a description of the historical origins of modern Roman Catholic traditions of spiritual formation, from the thirteenth century until Vatican II; second, an analysis of the changes that occurred in these traditions from the time of Vatican II until the present, especially in the United States; and third, a presentation of a few contemporary issues concerning formation in Roman Catholic institutions.

I apologize for the breathtaking sweep of the first part of my essay, but I feel it is essential to review that history and keep it in mind if we are to understand the present. (As I review these ancient traditions, I am struck by their tenacity.) Moreover, I have in my title indicated that I am addressing only some traditions, thus warning the unwary of the gross limitations of my undertaking. I make a special apology for the disproportionate attention I give in that section to the Society of Jesus; it happens to be the tradition with which I am most familiar. My undertaking in its entirety is thus not the presentation of the results of a study controlled by a rigorous methodology but is, rather, an interpretative essay, with all the perils inherent therein.

I believe that the most striking feature of what I have to say is that, in contrast with divinity schools not in the Roman Catholic tradition, our schools assume not only that spiritual and moral formation is crucial in the preparation of future ministers but also that it can and should be promoted in formal ways by the institutions in question. A "fundamental option" has been taken. Unlike their counterparts in other Christian traditions, therefore, every Roman Catholic school has a more or less elaborate set of offices and structures related to spiritual formation. Accordingly, the questions and problems that Roman Catholics have regarding spiritual formation are on the *formal* level quite different from those arising in schools where such offices and structures are not in place. On other levels — for example, that of the actual needs of students who come to divinity schools — the questions and problems are similar or identical.

I. THE ORIGINS OF SOME IMPORTANT TRADITIONS

The thirteenth century was surely a critical turning point for the issues with which we are concerned. With the creation of that absolutely new entity, the university, it marked the beginning of the end of the apprenticeship system for the training of ministers. What happened was not simply that the texts of ancient Greek philosophy, especially so-called natural philosophy or science, were recovered in the West and now confronted Christian revelation, but that out of this confrontation, and to a large extent as a result of it, a whole new style of learning was produced, along with an institution to advance it. The style of learning was the "professional" style, and the institution was the university. The university was the first step in displacing the haphazard, varied, and informal learning situations that had long held sway.

No more apt designation could be devised for this professionalized style of learning than "scholastic" — that is, academic and scientific. In this system, theology for the first time was practiced apart from ministry and divorced from affect and from that compelling correlate of affect, spirituality. The complaints of contemporary and subsequent critics of these aspects of scholastic theology and all its academic counterparts through the ages have sometimes been exaggerated but have without doubt hit upon the most vulnerable aspect of the enterprise. The classroom replaced the monastic chapel and the episcopal *cathedra* as the place where theology was done.

I play with Dom Jean Leclercq's title for his classic study of monastic culture in the Middle Ages when I say that in the universities the "love of learning" persisted, but the "desire for God" was generally replaced by a desire for the doctoral degree.[1] The thirteenth century invented academic degrees — that is, credentials — which are what mark a person as a professional, set off from others not by what the person is but by what he or she has achieved in an objectively measured and publicly recognized way.[2]

Just as the universities were coming into being, so were

---

1. Leclercq, *The Love of Learning and the Desire for God*, trans. Catharine Misrahi (New York, 1961).

2. See my essay entitled "The Jesuit Educational Enterprise in Historical Perspective," in *Jesuit Higher Education* (Pittsburgh, 1989), pp. 10-25.

the Dominican and Franciscan orders.[3] The ministry of the Dominicans was a response to the Albigensian heresy that the local clergy was impotent to address. The Albigensians were a radically alienated group who condemned the life-style and wealth of the clergy. In order to deal effectively with the Albigensians, Dominic insisted that his friars be theologically learned (and hence he founded his convents in university cities) but that they also take a vow of poverty. That vow for the Dominicans was not, therefore, simply a continuation of earlier ascetical ideals but had a clear relationship to ministry. By preaching in poverty, the Dominicans had a better chance of being heard.

Saint Francis' romance with Lady Poverty may in some ways seem to antedate and be more independent of his own early ministry, if we may thus speak of it, but here too the fusion of spirituality and ministry is early. Both these orders soon established novitiates where, as soon as a candidate entered the order, the spiritual ideas began to be inculcated as a basis for the entire future life of the friar and his ministry. No matter how academic the theology might be that the friar learned, he already had undergone spiritual formation in the novitiate, and after his training there he continued in an atmosphere congenial to its flowering in the convent.

Moreover, through subsequent propagandistic documents like the *Little Flowers of St. Francis* of the fourteenth century, the idea became widely accepted that the friars were responding to a direct and personal call from God in their life-style and ministry, and that the effectiveness of their preaching was directly related to the holiness of their lives. On a different level, St. Thomas and St. Bonaventure had already developed the idea for the friars in their defenses of their orders against detractors.[4]

Preaching was the principal ministry of the friars, and its purpose was, especially for the Franciscans, some form of conversion of life. Despite the legitimacy of the criticisms that have

3. On the Dominicans, Franciscans, and Jesuits and their relationship to ministry, see my essay entitled "Priesthood, Ministry, and Religious Life: Some Historical and Historiographical Considerations," *Theological Studies* 49 (1988): 223-57, especially pp. 231-43, with bibliography.

4. See the article entitled "vocation" in *Dictionnaire de théologie catholique*, cols. 3162-64.

been leveled against the "penitential" aspect of the preaching of the friars in the late Middle Ages, that kind of preaching did indicate the centrality of the conversion reality in the Christian vision of the friars.

In the sixteenth century the Jesuits built upon, codified, and further articulated traditions of formation practiced by the Mendicants. With the Jesuits, however, I can begin to be more specific because I know the history better. As I see it, the Jesuit contribution to spiritual formation for ministry consists particularly in the codification of some instruments of formation whose elements derived from earlier traditions. The Jesuits were only one group among many who engaged in this activity during the so-called Counter Reformation, but for our purposes they can be taken as emblematic.

First of all, the *Spiritual Exercises* marked the creation of the retreat as we know it today. Although the practice of spending a period of time alone in contemplation is older than Christianity itself, there existed no widely recognized program for it until Saint Ignatius. Even during Ignatius' own lifetime, the purpose of the *Exercises* was variously interpreted — to teach prayer, to enable discernment of God's will, to lead to and sustain conversion. But in each of these cases, what we have is the creation of an instrument for spiritual formation.

The second contribution is the importance that the Jesuits attached to spiritual direction and the amount of reflection they gave to it and promoted. Obviously the Jesuits were not alone in an enthusiasm that effected an entirely new phase in the development of an instrument of spiritual formation which, again, is older than Christianity itself. Another factor was the insistence on direction by Teresa of Ávila in her many and widely diffused works toward the end of the century. In any case, by the early part of the seventeenth century there was a deeply rooted persuasion that spiritual progress was impossible without recourse to direction, whether this was given inside the confessional or in other settings.[5]

When the Jesuits adopted the idea of a novitiate for their

---

5. See the article entitled "Direction spirituelle" in *Dictionnaire de spiritualité*, 3:1002-1214, especially 1108-33.

recruits, they were obviously following in an earlier and well-established tradition.[6] However, the first Jesuits prided themselves on the fact that, to a degree not found even in the Mendicants, their novitiates were intended to impart a spiritual foundation that was geared to ministry. As Jeronimo Nadal noted in an important tract addressed in 1572 to Saint Charles Borromeo, other religious orders trained their novices for their duties in choir, liturgy, and convent regimen, whereas the Jesuits trained theirs from the very beginning in a pastoral spirituality.[7]

We perhaps have to ascribe some self-serving exaggeration to Nadal, but what is clear is that the idea of a programmatic training in spirituality directed toward ministry had not only been born but had also been firmly institutionalized and articulated into a coherent program. This I would consider a third Jesuit contribution. Key features in that training were ongoing spiritual direction, the making of a month-long retreat, training in methods of prayer, a program of spiritual reading, and more or less supervised experience in various services to others, like nursing in hospitals and even some preaching.

A fourth contribution of the early Jesuits was the idea found again and again in the *Constitutions* and other foundational documents that efficacy of ministry depended to a large extent on the degree to which the minister was united with God. The Jesuit was to be *instrumentum Deo coniunctum,* which is simply an application of the idea of instrumental causality found in scholastic theology.[8] Loyola also used instru-

---

6. See Manuel Ruiz Jurado, *Origenes del noviciado en la Compañia de Jesús* (Rome, 1980).

7. See *Monumenta Nadal IV,* Monumenta Historica Societatis Jesu (Madrid, 1906), p. 175.

8. See Ignatius Loyola, *The Constitutions of the Society of Jesus,* ed. and trans. George E. Ganss (St. Louis, 1970), p. 332 (X.2 [813]): "For the preservation and development not only of the body or exterior of the Society but also of its spirit, and for the attainment of the objective it seeks, which is to aid souls to reach their ultimate and supernatural end, the means which unite the human instrument with God and so dispose it that it may be wielded dexterously by His divine hand are more effective than those which equip it in relation to men. Such means are, for example, goodness and virtue, and especially charity, and a pure intention of the divine

mental causality to validate for the Jesuits the use of human learning and skills in ministry, but the primacy clearly belongs to the spiritual.[9]

Undergirding this idea of "an instrument conjoined to God" was the persuasion that the Jesuit was "called." Call or vocation, in the sense of an inward inspiration from God toward a certain way of life, permeates the ascetical tradition that predates the Jesuits. The Jesuits did not, therefore, invent the idea, but they gave it a lucid articulation that related it directly to ministry. The transhistorical immediacy of it could hardly be more boldly formulated than by Nadal, the most influential Jesuit contemporary of St. Ignatius: "Our vocation is similar to the vocation and training of the apostles: first, we come to know the Society, and then we follow; we are instructed; we receive our commission to be sent; we are sent; we exercise our ministry; we are prepared to die for Christ in fulfilling those ministries."[10] Accordingly, by the end of the sixteenth century, if not earlier, the idea that ministry was not so much a profession as it was the fruit of vocation was being widely disseminated and accepted.

What each of these contributions of the Jesuits assumes is the primacy of personal appropriation and internalization of religious values — some degree of conversion, if you will. There was, however, another aspect of Jesuit "formation" that codified deportment into sets of rules, the most important being the Jesuits' "Rules of Modesty," which date from the earliest years of the order. Eyes were to be cast down, frowns on the forehead were to be avoided, clothing was to be clean, every

---

service, and familiarity with God our Lord in spiritual exercises of devotion, and sincere zeal for souls for the sake of glory to Him who created and redeemed them and not for any other benefit. Thus it appears that care should be taken in general that all the members of the Society may devote themselves to the solid and perfect virtues and to spiritual pursuits, and attach greater importance to them than to learning and other natural and human gifts. For they are the interior gifts which make those exterior means effective toward the end which is sought."

9. See ibid., pp. 332-33 (X.2 [814]).

10. Nadal, *Orationis observationes*, ed. Miguel Nicolau (Rome, 1964), p. 138, #379.

gesture and action was to be edifying. In other words, there was such a thing as proper behavior, and there were conventional standards to which the minister should be trained to conform.

These two aspects of spiritual formation — conversion of heart and external conformity to norms of behavior — are not intrinsically incompatible, but the danger of taking the second as a reliable sign of the first cannot be discounted, as contemporary experience amply demonstrates. The Jesuit rules had their counterparts in other orders of men and women, and are, for better or worse, one of the important traditions in Roman Catholic formation. They can possibly be viewed as another manifestation of the impulses behind the various sumptuary laws and codes for the higher clergy that were common in the Middle Ages.

That brings us to the local or diocesan clergy, as distinct from the members of religious orders to which we have devoted our attention up to this point. From the thirteenth century down to the present, there have been many points of intersection between the diocesan and the religious clergy, and a great deal of reciprocal influence. However, we are dealing here with two truly distinct traditions that should never be lumped together if we wish to understand them properly.[11]

Although these traditions differed in many ways, perhaps the most palpable difference was the relationship of the diocesan clergy to the benefice system — that is, what was known among Anglican clergy even in the nineteenth century as "a living." A "living" (or benefice) was a revenue attached to the cure of souls in some given church, chapel, hospital, or

---

11. See my essay entitled "The Houses of Study of Religious Orders and Congregations: A Historical Sketch," in *Reason for the Hope: A Study of the Futures of Roman Catholic Theologates*, ed. Katarina Schuth (Wilmington, Del., 1988), pp. 29-45. See also the booklet containing papers from the Assembly of the Conference of Major Superiors of Men (CMSM) entitled *Our Search for God as Religious* (Ottawa, 1984), and the papers delivered by Marcello de Carvalho Azevedo to the meeting of Superiors General of religious orders of women, 1985, published with permission by the Religious Formation Conference under the title *Formation: Religious Life in Contemporary Culture* (Washington, n.d.).

other ecclesiastical institution. The cure of souls entailed clearly defined duties. Presumably, if one were able to perform the duties, one could have the living. In other words, in the Middle Ages inspired vocation had nothing to do with fulfilling this ministry and at least into the seventeenth century in Roman Catholicism never seems to have played a significant role in thinking or actions pertaining to the beneficed cure of souls, which is where the ordinary ministry of the church was performed.[12] No spiritual formation was seen as needed for this ministry, in contrast with the entirely different appreciation for spiritual formation that we have seen in the religious orders. (The vow of poverty was the counterstatement to the benefice system.) The "professional" training that the universities offered lent indirect support to this assumption.

Certainly there was an ancient and deep-rooted persuasion that the minister should practice what he preached, and priests were expected to uphold by their example accepted standards of decency and morality. By the sixteenth century many people were convinced that all too many priests were in fact violating those standards, and they attributed the rapid spread of the Protestant Reformation to the immoral lives that both higher and lower clergy were accused of living. The high standards of religious commitment that the religious orders insisted upon for their own members who engaged in ministry surely helped exacerbate criticism of the diocesan clergy, no matter how feebly those standards were sometimes translated into the lives of the religious.

The famous decree of the Council of Trent of 1563, which

---

12. I know of no really satisfactory study of the history of this question for the diocesan clergy, although elements of it can be gleaned from articles under the heading of "vocation" in the *Dictionnaire de théologie catholique*, and in both the old and the new editions of the *Catholic Encyclopedia*. The article in the *Dictionnaire* provides the most information, but a bias is detectable. Perhaps the most revealing part of the article is that which deals with the early twentieth century, cols. 3171-74. However, see also John Blowick, *Priestly Vocation* (Dublin, 1932). Luigi M. Rulla has studied aspects of the psychology of vocation in his several publications, from *Depth Psychology and Vocation* (Rome and Chicago, 1971) to *Anthropology of the Christian Vocation* (Rome, 1986).

mandated the creation of seminaries for candidates for the
diocesan priesthood, made no provision for what we would
today term the study of theology, nor for what we have been
describing as spiritual formation. It was a little more concerned with training in certain basic pastoral skills. But the
major educational concern behind the decree seems to have
been the creation of an atmosphere in which these young men
would be sheltered from the corruptions of the world and
trained in deportment deemed appropriate to the clergy. In
other words, the decree was concerned with moral education
and practice.[13] In this regard, however, the seminary was a far
cry from the novitiates and houses of study (*studia*) of the
religious orders. Moreover, the Tridentine decree looked especially to "the sons of the poor" and never envisioned the
seminary as the place where training for the priesthood would
exclusively take place — it was surely not intended for the
higher clergy. The persuasion that all candidates for priesthood must be trained in a seminary is a much more recent
development.

Not until the next century in France did the so-called
French School of Pierre de Berulle, Jean Jacques Olier, and St.
Vincent de Paul try to elaborate a spirituality specifically for
diocesan priests that would be an integral part of their training.[14] The seminary programs inaugurated in France by these
eminent individuals had a different structure than the more
lowly institution that Trent seemed to envision. In 1642, for
instance, Olier established his famous seminary in Paris at the
church of St. Sulpice, the largest parish in the city, of which he
was the pastor. The seminarians did their course work at the

---

13. For the decree, see *Conciliorum Oecumenicorum Decreta*, ed. Giu-
seppe Alberigo et al., 3rd ed. (Bologna, 1973), pp. 750-53. For an English
version, see *The Canons and Decrees of the Council of Trent*, trans. and ed.
H. J. Schroeder (Rockford, Ill., 1978), pp. 175-79. See also Joseph M. White,
"How the Seminary Developed," in *Reason for the Hope*, pp. 11-28.

14. See White, "How the Seminary Developed," pp. 12-13; Edward J.
Ciuba, "The Impact of Changing Ecclesiological and Christological Models
on Roman Catholic Seminary Education," *Theological Education* 24 (1987):
57-72; and Eugene Walsh, *The Priesthood in the Writings of the French School:
Berulle, de Condren, Olier* (Washington, 1949).

university, whereas the seminary served as a residence where they were guided in spiritual and moral formation in ways that made use of the current instruments for such formation. As Joseph White observes in this regard, "Some seminaries were no more than retreat programs for candidates educated elsewhere, often at a local university." He adds almost immediately, "The emphasis on spiritual training did not assign much importance to theological study as a preparation for ministry."[15] To that extent this French model differed from the somewhat similar one utilized by the Jesuits in Rome for their correlative institutions for the diocesan clergy — the German College, the Venerable English College, and even the *Seminario Romano* — where considerable emphasis was placed on study.

Nonetheless, what the Sulpician model underscores is how by the seventeenth century the primacy of spiritual formation as preparation for ministry was beginning to be stressed also for the diocesan clergy. For our purposes the Sulpician model is of special importance, for in 1791 four Sulpician priests opened St. Mary's Seminary in Baltimore, the real beginning of seminary education in the United States. The Vincentians, disciples of St. Vincent who had a similar program, arrived a little later. These two groups would be extremely influential in the development of the Roman Catholic seminary system in this country.

Whereas members of religious orders had in their canonized saints numerous "role models" for their ministry, the diocesan clergy could not so easily specify such models of spirituality. This situation began to be remedied in the middle of the nineteenth century: it was then that the humble Curé d'Ars, Jean-Baptiste-Marie Vianney (1786-1859), began developing a growing reputation for sanctity and efficacious ministry. By 1905 he was beatified, by 1925 canonized, and by 1929 declared the patron of parish priests. Since the Curé had been a notoriously poor student of theology, the success of his ministry had to be attributed to his personal holiness.[16] Whatever else

---

15. White, "How the Seminary Developed," p. 13.
16. For perceptive comments on the Curé and the style of spirituality he inspired, see Thomas Franklin O'Meara, "The Crisis in Ministry Is a Crisis of Spirituality," *Spirituality Today* 35 [1985]: 20-21.

might be said about the impact that the cult of the Curé had upon the formation of diocesan priests, it surely helped reinforce in many circles the persuasion that the most important aspect of formation for ministry was spiritual formation.

At least by the beginning of the twentieth century, it was generally assumed that candidates for the diocesan priesthood were responding to a "vocation," though the term was somewhat ambiguously used. In order to resolve the ambiguity in the face of a specific controversy in France, Pope Pius X (1903-14) constituted a commission of cardinals, whose decision he ratified in 1912. The cardinals decided that a vocation to the (diocesan) priesthood did not necessarily and ordinarily consist in an internal invitation by the Holy Spirit. Rather, it consisted in the free election of the candidate by a bishop, who based his action upon the candidate's having an honest intention and the physical and spiritual qualities suitable for ministry.[17]

During his pontificate, Pius X issued in his own name several documents in which he delineated ideals of the Catholic priesthood, influenced surely by ideas derived from the traditions of the French School, and his example was followed by his successors through Pius XII (1939-58). These documents have been translated into English and gathered into two volumes entitled *The Catholic Priesthood*.[18] Despite the decision of 1912, these documents insist with ever-increasing clarity after that date that vocation is an inward inspiration from God, and the idea took firm hold. Moreover, in these documents spiritual formation is a major — perhaps the dominant — theme. The divine call and spiritual formation are heavily depended upon by the documents of Vatican II on "the ministry and life of priests" *(Presbyterorum ordinis)* and on "the training of priests" *(Optatam totius)*, as is clear from the number of times they are referred to.

Pius X also initiated the codification of canon law, which was not finally published until 1917. Canons 1352-1371 deal

17. See the article entitled "vocation" in *Dictionnaire de théologie catholique,* 3171-74.

18. *The Catholic Priesthood,* 2 vols., ed. Pierre Veuillot (Westminster, Md., 1958-64).

with seminaries. The canons prescribe that every seminary is to have, besides at least two confessors, a spiritual director, and that every seminarian is to spend some time each day in "mental prayer," go to confession and hear an exhortation "de rebus spiritualibus" every week, and go on a retreat of some days every year. These and similar prescriptions about the spiritual, liturgical, and moral formation of the seminarians found their specific warrant in the documents on priesthood issued in the names of the recent popes.

Our survey has thus brought us practically to the eve of Vatican Council II. Before we move on to that momentous event, perhaps we should briefly cast a glance backward to see some of the traditions that were created during this period whose influence would continue to be important. First, the development of the university marked the beginning of a dichotomy between theological formation and spiritual formation that was new and that would persist into the present. Second, the religious orders from the very beginning developed full-fledged programs of spiritual formation they deemed consonant with their ministerial goals, as was made especially clear by the Jesuits. Third, certain instruments for spiritual formation like retreats and spiritual direction received clearer formulation during this period than they had had before, and they gradually achieved a normative status. Fourth, the spiritual formation of the diocesan clergy followed less smooth and less clear paths than did that of any given order, but by the beginning of the twentieth century the importance of spiritual formation for them was vigorously promoted by the Holy See. Fifth, behind this insistence on the importance of a profound spiritual life for the minister, one sometimes detects a correlative anti-intellectualism. Finally, in both the religious and the diocesan traditions an emphasis on conventional deportment and conformity to certain external norms or discipline competed somewhat with the insistence on interiorization, which is in one way or another the presumed goal of all spiritual formation.

Before moving on, I must call attention to a huge lacuna in my survey. Even during this period, priests were in fact not the only people doing ministry. From the seventeenth century onward, and especially from the nineteenth century onward, innumerable orders and congregations of women religious were founded to teach catechism, to run schools, and to nurse the sick and aged. For lack of space and competence, I am unable to deal with the history and present reality of this phenomenon, except to suggest that for these women spiritual formation has been for various reasons perhaps even more central and more effectively operative than for their male counterparts.

II. FROM VATICAN II TO THE PRESENT

On October 28, 1965, the Second Vatican Council issued its decree on the training of priests, *Optatam totius*.[19] This brief document discusses three aspects of the training of priests — spiritual, intellectual, and pastoral, with the spiritual given pride of place. About six weeks later, on December 7, just as the Council drew its proceedings to a close, it issued a related document "on the ministry and life of priests," *Presbyterorum ordinis*.[20] Although this document treats a number of issues related to the priesthood, from the priest's relationship to the local bishop to monetary compensation and retirement pensions, it is permeated with issues relating to spirituality and the spiritual life of the priest. In it "spirituality" includes but surely goes beyond what we ordinarily mean by "character formation."[21] It in fact urges the practice of "poverty, chastity and obedience" so fervently that one at moments might be drawn into the illusion that it was intended primarily for members of religious orders, which is not the case. Those priests would presumably find their place in the Council's treatment of re-

---

19. See *Documents of Vatican II*, ed. Austin P. Flannery (Grand Rapids, 1975), pp. 707-24.

20. See ibid., pp. 863-902.

21. The ambiguities in both these terms are pointed out repeatedly in the supplementary number (#1, 1988) to *Theological Education* entitled *Theological Education as the Formation of Character*. The philosophical and theological issues underlying the whole enterprise of spiritual formation are exposed and ably debated by George Lindbeck, David Tracy, Douglas John Hall, Jane I. Smith, and Robert P. Meye.

ligious life, *Perfectae caritatis* (October 28, 1965); unfortunately, the generic nature of the document is not of much help in this regard. One might say, however, that spirituality is the almost unique theme of that document.

In any case, all three of these documents must be framed against the background of *Lumen gentium,* the dogmatic constitution on the church, the pivotal pronouncement of Vatican II.[22] That document culminates in chapter 5, "The Call to Holiness." All ministers in the church are called upon to teach and exemplify the holiness of life that Jesus preached "to each and every one of his disciples without distinction."[23] One could easily infer that this is the scope and ultimate end of all ministry in the church, so that a more authoritative and sweeping warrant for programs of spiritual formation would be difficult to find.

In 1971 the Congregation for Catholic Education issued its so-called Basic Plan *(Ratio fundamentalis)* as an attempt to reduce the principles of *Optatam totius* and other conciliar documents to more practical form. The *Ratio* was meant to guide episcopal conferences as they further specified the principles in what came to be known in the United States as the *Program for Priestly Formation.*[24] In the *Ratio* personal and spiritual formation is described and enjoined before intellectual and pastoral formation, and the *Program,* now in its third edition (1981), follows suit. The *Program* includes many things under personal and spiritual formation, including a listing of virtues especially appropriate for the priest-minister and a call for conversion of heart. It also includes a section on "community life." Perhaps most significant, the *Program* calls upon the whole faculty to collaborate with the director of spiritual formation or with the team of which the director is the head. "No faculty member," the document states, "may feel that this high responsibility lies outside of his or her interest or labor."[25]

---

22. See ibid., pp. 350-426.

23. Ibid., p. 397.

24. The *Ratio,* as well as other official documents subsequent to it, can be found in *Norms for Priestly Formation* (Washington, 1982), pp. 15-60.

25. *Program for Priestly Formation,* 3rd ed. (Washington, 1981), p. 27.

In 1980 the Congregation for Catholic Education issued a document entitled "Circular Letter Concerning Some of the More Urgent Aspects of Spiritual Formation in Seminaries,"[26] and in 1984 the American bishops further underscored their interest in the matter by publishing in their own name a booklet entitled *Spiritual Formation in the Catholic Seminary.*[27] The pertinent section of the new Code of Canon Law promulgated in the previous year also stressed the importance of spiritual formation (#239-247).

These official documents are important for a number of reasons. They demonstrate the importance attributed to spiritual formation and the insistence upon it in the highest quarters.[28] They give some indication of what instruments are to be used to accomplish it and give some description of its goals. In some contrast with previous statements, they clearly indicate that this formation must be adapted to the needs of seminarians as we find them today, and they correlatively support using the

---

26. Reprinted in *Norms for Priestly Formation,* pp. 207-23.

27. In the same year the bishops issued *Liturgical Formation in the Seminaries: A Commentary,* and in 1985 they issued *Pastoral Formation and Pastoral Field Education in the Catholic Seminary.* Under the auspices of the bishops (U.S.C.C., Washington), a number of studies have been published over the course of the years relating to ministry and priesthood, and therefore related indirectly to our topic. I am indebted to Howard J. Gray, S.J., for the following list of them: Andrew Greeley, *The Catholic Priest in the United States: Sociological Investigations* (1972); Eugene C. Kennedy and Victor J. Heckler, *The Catholic Priest in the United States: Psychological Investigations* (1972); *The Program of Continuing Education of Priests* (1972); *Spiritual Renewal of the American Priest,* ed. Gerard T. Broccolo (1973); *The Report of the Bishops' Ad Hoc Committee for Priestly Life and Ministry: Authority, Evaluation, Ministry, and Scholarship* (1974); *As One Who Serves: Reflections on the Pastoral Ministry of Priests in the United States* (1977); *Recommendation and an Inquiry about Alcoholism among Catholic Clergy* (1978); *Fullness in Christ: A Report on the Study of Clergy Retirement* (1979); *Growing Together: A Conference on Shared Ministry* (1980); *The Priest and Stress* (1982); *A Reflection on Human Sexuality and the Ordained Priesthood* (1983); *The Continuing Formation of Priests: Growing in Wisdom, Age, and Grace* (1984); *The Health of American Catholic Priests: A Report and Study* (1985); *Vocations and Future Church Leadership* (1986); *A Shepherd's Care: Reflections on the Changing Role of Pastor* (1987).

28. This might be the appropriate place to call attention to the document entitled "Spiritual Formation in Theological Education" published by the World Council of Churches (Geneva, 1987).

findings of modern psychology and related disciplines in current formation programs. They call, above all, for an integration of the three aspects of formation almost universally recognized — the academic, the pastoral, and the spiritual-personal. Finally, these documents are meant for *all* candidates for priesthood, even for those who are members of religious orders — a significant departure from previous traditions in this regard.

In the principles they propound, these documents stand solidly within the traditions of Roman Catholic formation for ministry. They do this to such an extent that one must be familiar with the actual history of Catholic seminaries and theological schools in this country to appreciate how very different the situations are to which these principles are being applied and how differently they are being translated into action. In the years immediately following the Council, a number of those institutions moved to the cities from secluded locations in the country, they joined in consortia with Protestant divinity schools, they substantially revised their curricula in accordance with what they believed was mandated by the Council, and they reformulated and restructured their programs of formation. Perhaps the most far-reaching change of all was that a significantly large number of them began to train for ministry both men and women who were not candidates for the priesthood.[29]

Accordingly, to understand what is actually happening in spiritual formation for ministry today in Roman Catholicism, we must descend from the exalted level of official documents to concrete reality. In recent years there have been some important studies of that reality. The most highly publicized was the visitation of all phases of training for priesthood candidates, both diocesan and religious, that was mandated for the United States in 1981 by Pope John Paul II. We still do not have a comprehensive report of the results of this venture, although a partial one has been published.[30] Moreover, that study dealt

---

29. These and other changes in the theologates of religious orders and congregations I have described in "The Houses of Study of Religious Orders and Congregations," pp. 38-45. I do not know of a similar study for diocesan institutions.

30. See *Origins* 16/18 (16 Oct. 1986): 313-25, especially pp. 320-21 dealing with "Spiritual/Liturgical Formation" and "Celibacy."

exclusively with programs for candidates for the priesthood, even in those institutions that also train others for ministry.

Katarina Schuth has, however, recently published her *Reason for the Hope: A Study of the Futures of Roman Catholic Theologates*.[31] Her study, done in collaboration with David Nygren, was funded by the Lilly Endowment, and is the Catholic counterpart of John C. Fletcher's *The Futures of Protestant Seminaries*, also funded by Lilly and published in 1983. Between 1985 and 1988, Schuth, sometimes accompanied by Nygren, visited twenty out of a possible fifty institutions and conducted over four hundred interviews with faculty, administrators, and students. Her study includes diocesan seminaries and the theologates of the religious orders.

The information she gathered through interviews was supplemented by information from questionnaires and other methods of data gathering and analysis. Her book tells us more than we have ever known before about what is going on in Catholic training programs for ministry. Perhaps most important for our purposes, she has interviewed every director of spiritual formation in the institutions visited, and Part IV of her book contains a long section entitled "Total Formation Program."

I will try to highlight some of the more important results that she reports in this section. I must remind you at the outset, however, that these results derive not simply from information or reflections provided by people directly involved in spiritual formation but from all the people interviewed. I must also remind you that Schuth's study, like the study mandated by John Paul II, looks directly at priesthood candidates, but it also takes into serious account the fact that many of these institutions are training others alongside those candidates, and Schuth tries to assess the impact of that factor.

One final caution: like Schuth's study, what I say subsequently blurs the distinction between institutions that train candidates for the diocesan clergy and those related to the training of members of religious orders. Many of the issues are the same, but many are different. The ministries, or at least the settings for ministry, toward which spiritual formation looks are

---

31. See note 11 above.

often notably different, which sometimes results in different appreciations of priesthood itself. Consequently, there exists a pluriformity difficult to capture in such a summary presentation.

One of the things that Schuth reports, however, is that in both kinds of institutions the spiritual and personal dimensions of formation are being stressed even more than in the past. By and large, programs are geared to help the seminarian internalize religious values, especially through regular prayer and meditation, and at the same time relate these values to the public nature of ministry in the church. The relationship between one's spirituality and one's ministry does not always seem easy for these students to establish. Schuth reports that students often show minimal interest in the broader mission of the church and in social justice issues. This situation is doubtless due to a number of factors operative in contemporary American culture, but it may also be related to the fact that many students now come to theology with very little former involvement with the church.

Of the fifty-three schools that Schuth studied, practically all designate a person who is responsible for spiritual formation. Titles vary a great deal, and they tend to reflect both the organization of the institution and also the philosophy that underlies the program. For instance, "spiritual director," a title used in twenty schools, suggests one-on-one work with students, a rather straightforward continuation of the tradition of the spiritual director developed in the sixteenth and seventeenth centuries, whereas "director [or dean] of formation" suggests a team approach and an effort at coordination of all activities encompassed by formation, which we assume in most or all cases includes spiritual direction as one of its component parts.

Perhaps somewhat related to the different philosophies of formation suggested by these titles is another distinction that Schuth draws. She observes that there is a general recognition that, in diocesan seminaries and even in the houses of study of the religious orders, formation before Vatican II was too easily satisfied with inculcating compliance with external discipline. Recognition of the inadequacies of that approach does not automatically supply a clear alternative to it. Nevertheless, Schuth

is able to distinguish two general models that are widely operative and function somewhat in that capacity. In the brief space
at my disposal, I cannot do much more than suggest their
contours.

The first she calls the "integration model." Its ultimate
goal is an internalized locus of control, where one realizes the
effect of one's actions in relationship to public ministry. The
language associated with this model includes descriptions of
personal development, psychological strengths, and various
forms of internalized discernment. Schuth's study sees this
model as running the risk of encouraging an individualistic,
privatized, or therapeutic spirituality — or even substituting
psychology for spirituality. This risk manifests itself, for example, in an unclear demarcation between spiritual direction
and psychological or vocational counseling.

The "identification model," in contrast, urges the student
to emulate a certain "master image," often depicted by the
standard of "Christ the Priest," a term that recurs in documents
on seminary training. When this model is operatively in place,
Schuth notes that, although interiorization is the goal, more
attention is paid than in the "integration model" to external
observance of role expectations, such as perceived prayerful-
ness and even attendance at certain functions. Among other
risks that this model runs, Schuth notes over-identification with
role, premature cognitive commitment, and over-dependency
of the individual on external factors. As one student put
it, "They want you to become a priest before you become a
person."

Most institutions seem to operate somewhere between the
extremes of these two models. They increasingly take into account that some students come to them as seekers rather than
fully committed believers and that all students come at different stages of psychosocial and faith development.[32] They are
beginning to formulate profiles of what can reasonably be
hoped for as the student moves through the years of theological

---

32. Influential here, of course, have been Bernard J. Boelen, *Personal
Maturity* (New York, 1978) and James W. Fowler, *Stages of Faith* (San Francisco, 1981), as well as Fowler's other publications.

training. This process calls for a delicate mix of realism, savvy, and perseverance in ideals on the part of those charged with formation.

Moreover, the needs of students as a group seem to change with some frequency. Adaptation to those changing needs and to operative modifications of the mission of the institution induces a certain fluidity in programs that often means they are not as fully developed in reality as they seem to be on paper. This seems to be truer when programs are trying to meet the formational needs also of students who are not candidates for ordination.

Despite the divergences in philosophy and in implementation of programs of spiritual formation, and despite the seeming instability of some of them, Schuth reports considerable agreement on many of the essential instruments that such programs employ. Perhaps first on the list is spiritual direction, which seems to be as highly esteemed by students for ministry as it is by faculty and administration.[33] Canon law requires that seminarians go on an annual retreat. In contrast with spiritual direction, however, retreats were taken with less seriousness and commitment by a fair number; others, however, saw them as important occasions for spiritual growth. The divergence here is surely due in part to how the retreat was conceived, proposed, and conducted.

Virtually every formation program includes a series of events like faith sharings, spiritual talks, discussion of vocation, and discipleship. Regular — if not daily — participation at the Eucharistic liturgy is expected in these programs, and those liturgies invariably include a brief homily by the celebrant on the text from the gospel of the day. Many schools have public morning and evening prayer, either the Liturgy of the Hours or something related to it, and attendance is generally required. At intervals workshops or seminars are provided on prayer and meditation, and sometimes on other topics like alcoholism, sexuality, and faith development.

---

33. Although it deals principally with Protestant institutions, see the recent article by Forster Freeman, "Spiritual Direction for Seminarians," *Theological Education* 24 (1987): 44-56.

As must be clear by now, *Reason for the Hope* contains an immense amount of information and analysis pertinent to the topic before us. At this point I can do no better than to send you to it for full elaboration of topics that I can do little more than mention here. However, I would like to elaborate on one aspect of contemporary spiritual formation among Roman Catholics in the United States that must not be overlooked. I am referring to developments since Vatican II in some of the traditional instruments of spiritual formation.

In the decades preceding Vatican II, spiritual direction maintained "on the books" the secure place it had long enjoyed, but by general admission the actual practice of it was all too often merely perfunctory and done by people who had little aptitude or training for it. In fact, the only training that was obtainable, even for those few who thought it might be desirable, was some form of apprenticeship at the feet of a "master of the spiritual life." Moreover, the only writings that were available about spiritual direction were certain classic texts from bygone centuries, which in fact seem to have been rather seldom consulted.

That situation has changed dramatically in the past two decades in the United States. At regular intervals there now appear books and especially articles — many of high quality — that reflect upon the findings of theology, psychology, and practical experience as they relate to spiritual direction. Perhaps more important, centers and internships have been established for those who want to develop skills in spiritual direction, skills which are being ever more satisfactorily defined. One of the best-known and best-developed of such centers is the Center for Religious Development in Cambridge, Massachusetts. Also being explored are the advantages of "group spiritual direction" — a new venture — for certain people at certain times.

Retreats have also undergone similar developments, especially in their classic form based on the *Spiritual Exercises* and variations thereon. Before Vatican II all retreats were "preached" — in other words, the director exhorted an audience of listeners or presented to them a series of points for meditation. In some settings this has now been replaced by the "directed retreat," a situation in which the retreat participant meets privately with the director once a day over the course of several days or even weeks. This much more delicate procedure has led to the creation of internships for the training of retreat directors, a phenomenon unknown twenty years ago. There is obvious potential for spiritual formation in these directed retreats, especially when they last for a full month. Such retreats are used in some programs preparing individuals for ministry; in addition, seasoned ministers who are doing sabbatical programs are encouraged to take such retreats.

These developments in spiritual direction and in retreats have enhanced traditional Catholic interest in various forms of meditation or mental prayer. As is well known, those forms have been influenced in recent years by confrontation with non-Christian traditions along the same lines. Moreover, the whole enterprise of spiritual formation is supported by a number of publishing ventures related to it, such as the "Classics of Western Spirituality" series published by Paulist Press, and by periodicals such as *The Way, Human Development, Spirituality Today, Review for Religious,* and *Studies in Formative Spirituality.* In other words, a variety of resources is now available for those who would undertake for themselves or for others spiritual formation for ministry.

III. ISSUES FOR THE PRESENT AND THE FUTURE

Accordingly, at the present moment there can be little doubt that spiritual formation is in many ways alive and well in Roman Catholic institutions in the United States that train young people for ministry. This is a conclusion we can draw from Katarina Schuth's study, and it is consonant with my own experience of these institutions and with what I hear from others. By and large, spiritual formation has impressive institutional support in word and deed. It has been articulated into programs, and these programs are under the direction of dedicated personnel. It has an impressive array of instruments at its disposal. It is periodically reviewed and even refashioned, and it is a topic of lively and seemingly constructive discussion among faculty, administration, and students.

Nevertheless, given the kinds of institutions involved,

given the range, complexity, and delicacy of the issues with which spiritual formation must deal, and given the status of certain questions within the Roman Catholic community today, we should not be surprised that some concerns remain outstanding. In fact, by the nature of the case, spiritual-personal-moral formation is one of those perennial questions in every educational enterprise that begs definitive solution.

In what follows, I single out eight concerns for special mention and some discussion. The amount of space I devote to them should not be taken as indicating their relative importance or complexity. Indeed, in some cases brevity indicates precisely that they are very important and highly complex.

1. In spiritual and moral formation today, sexuality has to be an issue for every church, but it has a special complexity in Catholicism because celibacy is required of the priest.[34] Moreover, the structural ramifications of this discipline result in peculiar problems of role definition regarding ministry, both during formation and afterward. Every minister of the gospel is somehow "set apart," but none more obviously in contemporary society than the vowed celibate.

2. Related to the issue of celibacy is a whole range of other issues about how authority is exercised in the church and the kind of "loyalty" which that authority seems to demand. Not all ministry students are equally convinced of the validity of certain church teachings or discipline, yet they know that open disagreement will not be tolerated. In a few seminaries, "laying down the law" seems to be the first and last word on many issues, including celibacy.

In Roman Catholicism, as in some other confessions, the number of "church teachings" seems to be growing. Many of them touch issues that are the object of public controversy in the press, like birth control and abortion, and can hardly be avoided in active ministry today. Ministry in the Catholic Church has begun to be defined as including ever more centrally the role of spokesperson for official positions, even

---

34. See the document entitled "A Guide to Formation in Priestly Celibacy" issued in 1974 by the Congregation for Catholic Education, in *Norms for Priestly Formation*, pp. 153-205.

though assuming such a role may not have been a very important factor in the individual's original understanding of his vocation.

The psychological ramifications of these and similar phenomena are challenges to any program of formation. Duplicity, double-talk, and unresolved angers are among the most obvious. Such ramifications become intertwined with problems widespread in American society today deriving from unstable and dysfunctional family backgrounds — problems that range from low self-esteem and distrust of authority to preoccupation with status and personal fulfillment without reference to the needs of church, society, and the proverbial person in the pews.

3. Behind the scenes, moreover, a debate is being waged over the respective merits of the freestanding seminary and the so-called collaborative theologates (university-based schools, unions, etc.). The former proposes the advantages of a "holistic" model — that is, a program of intellectual, pastoral, and spiritual formation carried on in a single institution with a single purpose: education of the seminarian.[35] The other model proposes the advantages of interaction with other traditions and institutions.

We are dealing here with a debate over milieu that has obvious and important repercussions for spiritual formation. At present, about half of the diocesan clergy are trained in freestanding institutions, the model that now seems to be favored by more bishops than a decade ago, whereas almost all the members of religious orders are trained in collaborative theologates — a bifurcation surely related to long-standing different traditions in the diocesan and religious clergy pertaining to church, ministry, and spiritual formation.

4. Formation programs are marked by a persistent tension between conformity to expectations and personal appropriation of religious values, a tension that is deeply rooted in tradition and that is in fact perhaps simply endemic to the human situation. It deserves further notice here only because in

---

35. See Howard Bleichner, Daniel Buechlein, and Robert Leavitt, "The Preparation of a Diocesan Priest: The Experience of the Holistic Model of Priestly Formation" (St. Meinrad, Ind., 1988).

diocesan seminaries the members of the faculty vote upon the suitability of candidates for ordination. Built into the system, therefore, is a factor that militates against spontaneity and free expression, that makes it imperative to distinguish clearly between what canon law calls the internal and the external fora, especially in the relatively small community of the seminary, where multiple relationships ("enmeshments") between individuals almost inevitably develop. The issue is also present, though in different and seemingly less pressing ways, in the schools where members of religious orders are trained. Despite attempts to design formation programs in which interiorization of values is paramount, subtle pressure to perform for the sake of the vote is difficult to eliminate. The result is that there are still cases where within a few years after ordination a "model seminarian" has clearly become a dysfunctional priest.[36]

5. Even the recognition of a distinction between spiritual, academic, and pastoral formation raises the question about integration among them. According to Schuth, this is a concern in almost all the programs she studied.[37] Perhaps expectations among both students and faculty are too high here. In some ways the displacement of neo-scholastic theology from the curriculum cleared the way for better integration, for the peculiar assumptions of that system about the academic nature of the theological enterprise made it almost impossible to relate classroom work to spirituality or ministry. There seems to be no doubt that the more biblical emphasis in the curriculum that has prevailed since Vatican II, as well as understandings of systematic theology that relate it more effectively to praxis, are aids in overcoming this dichotomy.

However, faculty members have been trained in Ph.D. programs, and they tend to teach the way they themselves were taught. They probably need to do more reflection about how both the style and the content of their teaching can be made more congruent with the pastoral character of even the academic program. In any case, what is clearly needed today are structures in programs of spiritual formation, especially in diocesan insti-

36. See Schuth, *Reason for the Hope*, p. 153.
37. See ibid., pp. 164-65.

tutions, that make connections with ministry and especially with the study of theology. Just as urgent, from the other side, is the need to develop ways of teaching theology that make connections with spirituality and ministerial practice.

Not all the blame for whatever deficiencies exist in this regard can be laid at the door of organization, personnel, and pedagogy. Among candidates for ministry in the "mainline" churches, Roman Catholics in the United States have a notable reputation for anti-intellectualism. The very emphasis on spiritual formation and the models that are at least implicitly held up as "good priests" sometimes seem to give this deplorable tendency quasi-official support.

6. A related concern has arisen that may seem curious to those who are not Roman Catholics: how to provide for diocesan seminarians a "spirituality" that they would find appropriate and helpful for their lives as priests. This concern does not make much sense until one has some understanding of the history of this issue as I have briefly sketched it. In contrast with their counterparts in religious orders, diocesan priests often feel that the spiritual life to which they are exhorted from all sides does not have clear contours.

The sense of being somewhat adrift in this area has ancient roots, as we have seen, but even thirty years ago many were able to find satisfaction in spiritual writings and programs centered on the ideal of "Christ the Priest." However, the results of contemporary scholarship dealing with priesthood and ministry in the New Testament, new understandings of liturgy, competing ecclesiological models, and the reality of lay ministers in the church have all taken their toll on this ideal.[38] The very identity of the priest seems unclear to many. When that is, for whatever reason, the case, programs of spiritual formation for priesthood must necessarily falter.

Attempts are being made to construct a spirituality (or

---

38. See Ciuba, "The Impact of Changing Ecclesiological and Christological Models on Roman Catholic Seminary Education." Students, faculty, and formation personnel in seminaries must at the same time take account of official documents like the one issued on 25 March 1988 by the Congregation for Catholic Education, Vatican City, entitled "The Virgin Mary in Intellectual and Spiritual Formation."

spiritualities) appropriate for the diocesan priest.[39] Problems inherent in these attempts — of which the substitution of indoctrination for formation is only one — become evident simply by listing what would seem to be the constitutive elements of such enterprises. Those elements are the construction (and prescription?) of a set of beliefs about the nature of priesthood, a daunting undertaking today; the construction (and prescription?) of a set of feelings appropriate to those beliefs; and the construction (and prescription?) of a system of behavior that will express and foster those feelings.

7. This brings us to the men and women who are training for ministry in the Catholic Church who are not candidates for ordination. In many parts of the United States, as well as elsewhere in the world, the shortage of priests is already acute and in the foreseeable future can only become more so.[40] The implications of this situation are staggering. Women religious and lay women and men are doing what only priests used to do in Roman Catholic ministry just a few years ago, and they are duly appointed to these tasks by pastors and bishops.

In view of this situation, these individuals are in ever larger numbers seeking M.Div. degrees and other forms of certification and training. As yet they tend to receive little financial support in this endeavor, but the well trained have no difficulty finding a position and a welcome, especially if they are willing to move to some part of the country where the shortage of priests is more keenly felt. Most Catholic seminaries and schools of theology matriculate these women and men. While for various reasons some institutions professedly do not admit them into the M.Div. program, they give them training in theology and in pastoral skills that is practically the equivalent of that program.

In many instances, therefore, the training of these individuals as "professionals" meets contemporary standards.

---

39. See, for example, Robert Morris Schwartz, "On Christ and the Church: An Ecclesial Spirituality for American Priests founded on the Magisterium of the Bishops of the United States," Ph.D. dissertation, Gregorian University, Rome, 1987. See also the supplementary volume (#47) to *The Way* entitled *Spirituality and Priesthood* (Summer 1983).

40. See the study by Dean Hoge, *Future of Catholic Leadership: Responses to the Priest Shortage* (Kansas City, Mo., 1987).

But in the long-standing debate in the United States about whether seminaries and schools of theology are training people for a profession or for a vocation, Catholics have stood with the latter, no matter how defined.[41] Certainly today the whole apparatus of spiritual formation for ministry in the Catholic Church somehow rests on the assumption that the individual has, or possibly has, a genuine call from God to do ministry in the church. Spiritual formation provides resources to the individual to test the genuineness of the call, to further interiorize it, and to articulate the serious commitments that are implied in it. For ministry students who are not candidates for ordination, those resources are at present practically absent or at least not available in a programmatic form, even though some institutions are beginning to address the problem.

As you can see, the problem has immense ramifications for all aspects of the questions we have been discussing. If a spirituality for the diocesan clergy, for instance, is still in need of articulation, a spirituality for "lay ministers" is an even more complex enterprise. Virginia Sullivan Finn has recently published a well-received book on the topic. She has been one of the first to perceive and to begin to think through the issues that are involved in this and other aspects of the emerging reality often now referred to as "collaborative ministry."[42] She is not alone in addressing these issues, however.[43]

---

41. On the debate, see Ellis L. Larsen and James M. Shopshire, "A Profile of Contemporary Seminarians," *Theological Education* 24/2 (1988): 35.

42. Finn, *Pilgrim in the Parish: A Spirituality for Lay Ministers* (New York, 1986). See also her "Formation for Non- Ordained Ministry," *The Way*, Supplement 56 (Summer 1986), pp. 39-53; "Lay Ministry and Lay Musicians," *Pastoral Music* 10/1 (Oct.-Nov. 1985): 14-21; "The Web of the World: Psychological and Sociological Aspects of Sharing Ministry Responsibly," in *Growing Together: Conference on Shared Ministry*, co-sponsored by the National Conference of Catholic Bishops' Committee on the Laity and the United States Catholic Conference, Department of Education/Young Adult Ministry (Washington, 1980), pp. 29-44; and "A Plea for Collaborative Ministry," in *One Body, Different Gifts, Many Roles: Reflections on the American Catholic Laity*, published by the Bishops' Committee on the Laity, National Conference of Catholic Bishops (Washington, 1987), pp. 24-28.

43. See, for example, the other contributions in *Growing Together* and in *One Body, Different Gifts, Many Roles*, as well as Mary Moisson Chandler, *The Pastoral Associate and the Lay Pastor* (Collegeville, Minn., 1986).

She and others have been at least implicitly encouraged to think along these lines by the American bishops themselves. Just over a decade ago the bishops issued a set of pastoral reflections entitled "Called and Gifted: Catholic Laity, 1980."[44] That document has a section entitled "The Call to Ministry," which is immediately preceded by the section entitled "The Call to Holiness." Perhaps even more significant, just a few years ago the Pontifical Council for the Laity, Vatican City, issued a publication entitled "The Formation of the Laity." While this document of some fifty-seven pages never ascribes "ministry" to the laity, its premise is a formation for what it calls "missionary presence in the world," or "a new evangelization," or "witness and prophecy." Accordingly, although this document does not directly and explicitly address formation for ministry, it is related to it. It concludes with "twelve theses" about formation of the laity that are pertinent for the more specific formation with which we are here concerned. Nonetheless, Catholic officialdom emits almost contradictory signals about the relationship of the laity to ministry.

Be that as it may, many students who are not candidates for ordination are eager for spiritual formation, at least when they are working on their degree in a Catholic institution. This is a change in attitude from just a few years ago. Even so, in addition to grappling with the ambivalence that the institution they are attending evidences toward the issue, these students must still wrestle with ambivalence within themselves. They do not, in any case, want to participate in programs designed primarily for candidates for the priesthood or members of religious orders, for those programs do not, in their opinion, take seriously what is now sometimes called the lay vocation.

How devise a program that does? Moreover, most formation programs envision a situation in which the students live at the institution. How devise a program that takes into account a more dispersed living situation, a program that takes into account spouses and children? Certain aspects of feminist theology add further complications known to us all. How assess them soberly and then take them into account in practical ways?

---

44. Published in *Origins* 10/14 (27 Nov. 1980): 367-73.

8. Many more questions could be raised about the formation of lay ministers, but I will conclude by mentioning a concern about spiritual formation that is pertinent for others as well as for them. As I have been implying all along, today Catholic seminaries and similar institutions have a large number of people engaged directly in the task of spiritual formation. Almost all of these people have degrees beyond the M.Div., although the fields vary widely. According to Schuth, however, only about 25 percent of those she studied felt that their preparation was adequate for the work they were expected to do.

In fact, the years since Vatican II have seen the development of programs designed wholly or partially to help people who have been given the task of spiritual formation. Among these are programs at the Gregorian University in Rome, at Duquesne University in Pittsburgh, and at the Institute for Religious Formation in St. Louis; Creighton University in Omaha has a summer program along these lines. Professional training is, therefore, now available, and at first glance the only problem would seem to be convincing those in authority that these programs must be taken advantage of.[45]

But in fact this situation simply confronts us once again with the basic duality that underlies the formation question. Are future ministers responding to an inner call, or are they entering a profession? Catholicism has, at least in the present century, generally opted for the former answer, and that fact helps account for the amount and quality of the emphasis it places on spiritual formation. No one, I assume, would for that reason discount the advisability of professional formation for the *formatores*, but does such formation really address the heart of the matter?

If formation is somehow connected with conversion of heart, with inner appropriation of the message of the gospel,

---

45. There is a growing body of literature dealing directly or indirectly with the philosophy and practice of spiritual formation. See, for example, the volumes of Adrian L. van Kamm, *Formative Spirituality* (New York, 1983-), the supplementary volume (#56) to *The Way* entitled *Formation for Ministry* (Summer 1986), and especially the supplementary volume (#1, 1988) to *Theological Education* entitled *Theological Education as the Formation of Character*, described above in note 21.

as the idea of vocation implies, it comes face to face with the mystery of the human personality — with all its richness and poverty, its resilience, resistance, and vulnerability. How does one touch that mystery and help it unfold into freedom and goodness?

As one tries to facilitate that unfolding, professional skills can surely be a help — at least in preventing the worst malpractice, especially in the substitution of control for guidance. But the mystery is not susceptible to recipe. It seems to be most deeply touched by factors that are evocative, not prescriptive; that are aesthetic, not cognitive; that are inspirational, not clinical. These factors find best expression in poetry, music, dance, painting, and liturgy — all of which, except the last, are notably lacking in most seminary situations, and even liturgy is often beset with ritual routine.[46]

In the history of Christian spirituality, the disciple has best been formed by sitting at the feet of someone who embodies the wisdom that is being striven for, of someone who by his or her life communicates what it means to live the human mystery in tranquillity and in surrender to God's will, of someone who has taken up his or her cross and become a disciple, of someone who has had a profound experience of God's love. I believe that in some form or other that is what spiritual formation in its deepest expression is all about.

If that is true, we cannot get around the conclusion that no one assumes the task unto himself or herself and then undertakes a program of professional training for it. One first needs to be recognized and sought after as having that wisdom and integrity, that indefinable something, and only then might one seek means to enhance ways of making it helpful to others.

Gregory the Great speaks of the cure of souls as the *ars artium*, the art surpassing all others.[47] His description can surely be applied to spiritual formation. It is not a skill; it is an art. Art springs from something inside the artist that skills enhance but

---

46. See the perceptive comments by Don E. Saliers, *Worship and Spirituality* (Philadelphia, 1984), pp. 41-56.

47. *On Pastoral Care* (Regulae pastoralis liber), I.1, PL 77, 14: ". . . ars est artium regimen animarum."

can never create. If we concede that virtue, wisdom, and love of God cannot be taught, we must still yield to the evidence that they can be called forth by others — but only by those whose art springs from their own inner goodness.

We have to take this fact into account when we speak about formation for the *formatores*. If we do, we shall wonder less why spiritual formation so often seems to be an intractable problem that constantly eludes our efforts to program and contain it in tidy fashion. That consideration leads me to my final point — one that is humbling and resoundingly obvious yet utterly necessary to state: in today's world, if ever, programs in seminaries and divinity schools are only one factor among many that form our future ministers, and these programs are far from being the most powerful.

Chasing Schleiermacher's Ghost: The Reform of Theological Education in the 1980s

Merle D. Strege

Students should constantly be reminded that the rule in human life is [that] . . . whoever grows in learning and declines in morals is on the decrease rather than the increase. This is even more valid in spiritual life, for since theology is a practical discipline, everything must be directed to the practice of faith and life.[1]

Christian Theology, accordingly, is the collective embodiment of those branches of scientific knowledge and those rules of art, without the possession and application of which a harmonious Guidance of the Christian Church, that is a Christian Church-Government, is not possible. . . . The said branches of knowledge, when they are acquired and possessed without reference to the government of the Church, cease to have a theological character, and become assignable to those sciences to which, according to the nature of their contents, they respectively belong.[2]

---

1. Spener, *Pia Desideria*, trans. and ed. Theodore G. Tappert (Philadelphia: Fortress Press, 1964), pp. 104-5.
2. Schleiermacher, *Brief Outline of the Study of Theology*, trans. William Farrar (Edinburg, 1850; reprint edition by American Theological Library Association, 1963), p. 93.

Thus spoke two reformers of theological education, Philip Spener and Friedrich Schleiermacher. Their juxtaposition here introduces to the contemporary discussion of that topic certain questions that are long-standing and still pertinent: What is theology? What is the goal of the theological curriculum? Is theological education a matter of training minds or forming character? Since the 1983 publication of Edward Farley's *Theologia*, these questions and related ones have been addressed in a growing body of literature. These more recent publications are of such numbers and topics as to suggest a persistent uneasiness about, if not dissatisfaction with, theological education today.

Recent critics of American theological education focus their attention primarily on the structure of the theological curriculum. More precisely, it is the curriculum's lack of any material unity that critics find to be the root cause of the problem. Farley, the most persistent voice, charges that the curriculum is "fragmented."[3] Others describe this incoherence as the "pernicious organization of [the] curricula in terms of academic disciplines,"[4] or an aggregation of courses widely distinguished from one another by the methodologies distinctive to each.[5] This line of criticism has telling implications for a discussion of the role of character formation in theological education. In fact, it is not too much to say that discussions of curricular reform set the agenda for considerations of moral formation in the seminaries.

---

3. This, of course, is the point of *Theologia: The Fragmentation and Unity of Theological Education* (Philadelphia: Fortress Press, 1983). But Farley has put the issue in stronger terms than any other critic. Cf. "The Reform of Theological Education as a Theological Task," *Theological Education*, vol. 17, no. 2 (Spring 1981): 93-117. In that essay Farley contends that in its present form "theological education is now in a historical cul-de-sac."

4. Joseph C. Hough, Jr., and John B. Cobb, Jr., *Christian Identity and Theological Education* (Chico, Calif.: Scholars Press, 1985).

5. Charles M. Wood, *Vision and Discernment: An Orientation in Theological Study* (Atlanta: Scholars Press, 1985).

THE PROBLEM OF THE CURRICULUM

Farley offers a detailed and complex historical account of the process by which the theological curriculum has entered into its present state of disarray. Schleiermacher plays a central role in this story because of his attempt to unify the curriculum by means of what Farley calls the "clerical paradigm." This paradigm served as the foundation of what subsequently became a functionalist approach to theological education. This functionalism, Farley contends, is at the heart of the contemporary dilemma of theological educators.

Schleiermacher rightly understood that in the new German universities the study of theology was undertaken as a positive science. While he approved of this development, he also recognized that without the unifying principle of "church government" — that is, the ministry — the theological sciences would become precisely that: sciences governed by the general standards of *wissenschaft* and the specific methods of each discipline. Accordingly, he insisted that it was the socially important institution of the ministry that not only justified the presence of theology in the university curriculum but also prevented the increasingly specialized disciplines of the theological curriculum from degenerating into a collection of isolated specializations. Schleiermacher further reformed the curriculum by revising the traditional fourfold curriculum (Bible, dogmatics, history, and pastoral work) into a threefold division: historical theology (under which biblical study was subsumed), philosophical theology, and pastoral theology. This latter proposal was never widely implemented, but the unification of the curriculum in the institution of the ministry became standard.

It is important to distinguish the clerical paradigm from its later functionalist interpretations. The social setting of theological education was shifting further away from the church toward the university. Schleiermacher's proposals might have served temporarily to bridge the gap growing between them. But the ministry itself came to be understood increasingly as a range of professional activities. Nowhere is this description more accurate than in the United States. "The ministry" has been replaced by "this ministry" or, worse, "my ministry," by which the speaker means his or her activities: the minister is what the minister does. Functionalist accounts of the clerical paradigm open the door to seminary coursework intended to enlarge the expertise of ministers in the wide variety of activities that increasingly define the profession. Thus functionalism has a centrifugal effect on the theological curriculum.

The shift in the social setting of theological education from church to university brought with it another development that has contributed materially to the fragmentation of the curriculum. Nineteenth-century German universities enthusiastically practiced the historical method. The critical-historical consciousness it produced made an "irreversible impact" on theological reflection[6] by completing the emancipation of theologians from the traditional "way of authority."[7]

While it may be appropriate to describe the shift from confessional authority to critical-historical consciousness as an "emancipation," the accompanying exchange of university for church as the locus of theological education has not been an unmixed blessing. In the German universities of the previous century, education became *wissenschaft*. The disinterested pursuit of knowledge became its own justification. The new American universities of the late nineteenth and early twentieth century effected a growing partnership with what Burton Bledstein calls the culture of professionalism. In this partnership, education came to mean the acquisition of skills requisite for a successful career. In neither its German nor its American forms has the university developed in a manner particularly well-suited to the moral formation of ministers. Moreover, universities themselves have become so diversified that their inhabitants no longer are able to converse meaningfully with one another across disciplinary boundaries. Each discipline develops its own methodology and hence its own language. Without a "common tongue," the university not only is no longer unified but also loses its capacity to reflect upon a common goal and loses concern for contributing to the develop-

---

6. Ibid., p. 9.
7. Farley, "The Reform of Theological Education as a Theological Task," p. 97.

ment of good human beings.[8] Furthermore, the openness of the undergraduate curriculum itself aids and abets the "consumerist morality" of our culture, thus reinforcing the character and values of students and frustrating the university's attempts to change them if it so desired.[9] Not only does theological education shaped by the university enjoy the freedom of the critical principle, but to the degree that it is so ordered, theological education also suffers from the university's defects.

I do not mean to suggest that the shift from church to university has produced only negative repercussions for theological education. But we ought to understand all the effects of the curriculum's changed social setting. In ways both positive and negative, the university has profoundly influenced the shape of theological education. Not the least of these effects has been the alteration of what stands for authority in making theological judgments. But we should not be too hasty in accepting the supposition of both Farley and Charles M. Wood that the rise of critical methodologies in the university signals the end of traditional authority in theological education. Surely they are correct in saying that the Enlightenment brought about the demise of confessional authority where theological education conformed to the new intellectual standards institutionalized in the university. But that observation need not automatically pre-empt all discussion about authority.

The reason Farley makes such a point of the collapse of the house of authority has to do with the kind of theological education that confessional authority made possible. This particular form of education Farley labels "theologia." By this term he expresses a formational notion of theological education: "'Theologia,'" he says, "is a state and disposition of the soul

---

8. This point is eloquently and insightfully made by Wendell Berry in "The Loss of the University" in *Home Economics* (San Francisco: North Point Press, 1987), pp. 76-97.

9. Christian colleges and universities are not exempt from this criticism, as Stanley Hauerwas has pointed out in "How Christian Universities Contribute to the Corruption of Youth," in *Christian Existence Today: Essays on Church, World, and Living in Between* (Durham, N.C.: Labyrinth Press, 1988).

which has the character of knowledge."[10] This knowledge was commonly regarded as practical rather than theoretical. So when Spener said, "Theology is a practical discipline," he cited a maxim accepted by Protestant scholastics and pietists alike.[11] *Theologia* was knowledge attending unto God and salvation. As such it possessed the character of *sapientia* more than *scientia*. Farley argues that the earliest instruction in *theologia* took the form of a Christian paideia, the unity and goal of which was the saving knowledge of God. The notion of *theologia* as wisdom persisted even after medieval theologians made the new universities their home. They augmented this Christian paideia with their belief that *theologia* could be "promoted, deepened and extended by human study and argument."[12] Such a position could be maintained because Scripture remained authoritative for medieval theologians.

The coming of the Enlightenment and the rise of the critical principle undercut the traditional ground of authority and left the study of theology on the horns of a dilemma. The Enlightenment's critical methodologies reworked the theological disciplines into Schleiermacher's positive sciences and left them without the material unity that *theologia* had provided. To unify them in *theologia* would seem to require the abandonment of critical scholarship and mean theology's eviction from the university. Thus Schleiermacher attempted to escape the dilemma by unifying the curriculum in the professional ministry. *Theologia* as a unifying principle, not to mention as an invaluable component of the curriculum in its own right, was lost to theological education because the confessional church authority that sustained it could not survive in the world of the Enlightenment.

---

10. Farley, *Theologia*, pp. 35-36.

11. "*Theologia habitus practicus est* [was] a common assertion of orthodoxist theologians in the seventeenth century" (*Pia Desideria*, p. 105, note 22).

12. Farley, *Theologia*, pp. 36-37.

The Lost Unity of the Theological Curriculum and Moral Formation

Farley's description of *theologia* as the one-time material unity of the theological curriculum and his reference to *theologia* as a Christian paideia suggest that the issue of the moral formation of seminarians must be seen in connection with the problem of an incoherent curriculum. But this means that proposals to improve seminarians' moral or spiritual formation must do more than add a formation component to the program. Measures limited to adding such components would only further the incoherence. The problem of the curriculum's lost unity is addressed in very different ways in recent discussions on theological education. It is interesting that some of these approaches take up and refurbish aspects of Schleiermacher's theological or curricular agenda.

One approach to the problem proposes to unify the theological curriculum in the Christian identity of the professional minister. In this view the seminary is a professional school, but its goals must transcend training men and women in managerial expertise. Theological education must prepare people for professional leadership in the church, so expertise must be qualified by theological understanding. This theological understanding is the means by which the professional minister guides the church in developing its own identity. Because theological schools exist for the training of a professional ministry, "the understanding of what it is to be a Christian community in the world will be the aim of its research and pedagogy."[13]

To seek, à la Schleiermacher, the unity of theological education in the notion of a professional ministry is a perilous move. At least in the United States, the idea of a "professional" has been largely reduced to a functionalist meaning that segregates professional activity from a person's character. Given this social reality, it is difficult to see how contemporary proposals to unify theological curricula in the idea of a professional ministry can escape Farley's charge of functionalism any more

13. Hough and Cobb, *Christian Identity and Theological Education*, p. 19.

successfully than previous attempts. But perhaps there is a professional activity unique to the ministry that overcomes this challenge. Joseph Hough and John Cobb suggest that such an activity does indeed exist. In their view the professional ministry is characterized by the model of the minister as "Practical Theologian." The professional minister practices a theological method that leads to the theological understanding by which the church is led to discover its Christian identity. The practical theologian unites vision with critical reflection *on* practice *in* practice.

The problem of theological education turns, then, on the question of Christian identity. There is much to commend in a proposal that approaches the reform of the theological curriculum from such a perspective. For one thing, it calls to our attention the fact that the formation of Christian identity is a project for both the seminary and the church. Thus we are justified in asking whether they may have similar goals. But even more to the point, claims that theological education centers in the formation of Christian identity raise the question of character, or at least it would seem that the question of the moral formation of the ministry ought to be raised in such a discussion.

That Hough and Cobb do not address Christian identity in these terms is a major disappointment. For them this identity seems to be the achievement of a certain point of view on the history of God's dealings with the world. This point of view rises in the church but is not bound by it. Thus Hough and Cobb seek the presence of Christian identity outside the church as well as within its borders, although they acknowledge that, outside the church, Christian identity does not transmit well across generations.

Christian identity, as Hough and Cobb describe it, is a point of view that we choose. Identity is achieved by the self as it owns the internal history of the Christian tradition. But such a view neglects the powerful ways in which traditions or narratives shape the self into a particular kind of person long before that person ever reaches a point of "choosing" an identity for himself or herself. And these traditions or narratives are multifaceted in their effect, as the writers of *Habits of the Heart* point out:

The stories that make up a tradition contain conceptions of character, of what a good person is like, and of the virtues that define such character. But the stories are not all exemplary, not all about successes and achievements. A genuine community of memory will also tell painful stories of shared suffering that sometimes creates identities deeper than success. . . . And if the community is completely honest, it will remember stories not only of suffering received but of suffering inflicted — dangerous memories, for they call the community to alter ancient evils.[14]

It also appears that the formation of Christian character becomes a much more difficult project for those whose theological agenda calls them to mediate between church and world. One might argue that the minister as practical theologian by his or her profession bridges church and world. But when the distinction between them collapses, the theological understanding that leads to the development of Christian identity loses touch with the story of those people called by God and set apart as witnesses of what God has done for the world. Yet this story is the fountain out of which rises the church's character. Moreover, as the church embraces more of the world which God indeed loves, less of the church's witness to that world is distinctively Christian. With less to say that is distinctively Christian, the development of Christian identity becomes a highly tenuous project.

Another way of attempting to ground the unity of theological education has been to conceive it as unified in the combination of theory and practice. The former comprises the "classical" part of the curriculum (history, Bible, and theology), and professional courses constitute the latter. Like the fourfold curriculum and the clerical paradigm, the theory-and-practice model arose in the German university. In that context, *wissenschaft* provided a foundation of theoretical knowledge upon which rested professional practice. In certain fields — for example, medicine, but especially law or engineering — the model worked well. But theological education was another

14. Robert N. Bellah et al., *Habits of the Heart* (Berkeley: University of California Press, 1985), p. 153.

matter. The fruits of the knowledge available in a university dedicated to critical scholarship were not readily applicable to the practice of ministry.

A much more promising suggestion for the unification of the theological curriculum has come from Charles M. Wood. He defines theology as "critical reflection into the validity of Christian witness."[15] By "Christian witness" Wood means both the content of the tradition and the activity of witnessing.

According to Wood, theology has three dimensions: (1) to witness to Jesus Christ, (2) to endorse that witness to one's audience, and (3) therefore to be intentional about the content of that witness. Each dimension has its own critical question: the first, whether the witness is authentically Christian; the second, whether it is true; and the third, whether it is appropriately related to its context. These critical questions became the disciplines of the theological curriculum: historical study (which for Wood, again as for Schleiermacher, includes the study of the Bible), philosophical theology, and practical theology. This latter discipline Wood carefully qualifies so as to avoid its confusion with the term as it often is employed in seminaries. Practical theology, as he describes it, "is concerned not only with the pastoral ministry, nor with 'church leadership' in any narrow sense, but rather with the enactment of Christian witness in its entirety — that is, with the entire life and activity of the church as the community of witness."[16] To the disciplines of historical, philosophical, and practical theology Wood adds two others: systematic theology and moral theology. This emphasis on critical reflection, which is the legacy of Schleiermacher's curricular proposals, is the great strength of Wood's program. But one wonders whether such emphasis on critical reflection makes theological education into a completely critical enterprise, in which case it loses relevance for the ministry and becomes "religious studies."

Wood anticipates this criticism by suggesting that these critical capacities are cultivated in the growth of vision and discernment. "Vision" is Wood's metaphor for the ability to

---

15. Wood, *Vision and Discernment*, p. 21.
16. Ibid., p. 48.

make synthetic judgments, to grasp the totality of things as they relate to each other. "Discernment," on the other hand, is his metaphor for our analytic capacity. Theological inquiry is the dialectical relationship between vision and discernment. Critical reflection on the Christian witness advances as a movement between the whole and its particulars.[17] Thus one component of the curriculum may not be designated "visionary" and another "discerning." Each course is a product of the synthetic and the analytic.

Wood's description of vision and discernment as capacities shifts the discussion of the theological curriculum in the direction it must take if moral formation is to be an integral part of the curriculum. For by such terms he introduces the possibility of discussing dispositions as components of theological education. Indeed, the necessity for such discussions is illustrated by Wood's assertion that the disposition for discernment is "the fruit of a certain personal and moral maturity."[18] Wood does not pursue any further the question of how we may come to be so disposed. But he has clearly advanced the discussion of the problem of the fragmented theological curriculum in a way that introduces the notion of moral formation.

Wood defines theological education as essentially "a participation in theological inquiry, ordered to the acquisition of that complex set of intellectual and personal qualities which go to make up what we might still call the theological *habitus.*"[19] In its educational mode, theological inquiry will issue in the judgments that are the outcomes of such inquiry. But they are not the primary aim of inquiry in the seminary. There the proper aim is not the formulation of judgments but the formation of judgment.[20] By focusing on the curriculum's capacity to develop judgment in students, Wood opens the door to considerations of moral as well as intellectual virtues in the education of the ministry.

---

17. Ibid., pp. 67-69.
18. Ibid., p. 75.
19. Ibid., p. 79.
20. Ibid., p. 80.

THE CRITICAL PRINCIPLE, AUTHORITY, AND A CHRISTIAN PAIDEIA

Theological education renders the moral formation of the minister problematic on two counts. First, the critical methodologies employed by the various theological disciplines promote the development of specialists in the use of those methodologies and narrowly framed, specialized fields of knowledge. Although frequently disavowed, *wissenschaftlichkeit* remains a valued trait among all but the most avant-garde critical methods. Thus a powerful interest remains in the content of a seminarian's education. That content, supposedly mastered in a disinterested manner, is carved up among a variety of disciplines united only by their common reliance upon the authority of critical methodologies and their delight at being emancipated from confessional authority. Second, the now universal functionalist clerical paradigm serves to train budding "experts" in the skills they will need as professional ministers. Ministry thereby is reduced to what the minister knows and does rather than who the minister is. Ironically, the person thus prepared for ministry may possess knowledge and skills but not be ready for the kind of theology found in the church.

Theology may be variously described according to the social setting in which it is practiced. In the university, theology is knowledge attained according to the canons of scholarship and skills acquired according to the standards of professional expertise. In the church, theology is preaching, prayer and the devotional life, and praxis.[21] When theological educators are schooled in the canons of scholarship that govern the university, it only stands to reason that theology as limited by critical methodologies will dominate the seminary curriculum. After all, the "classical" or "core" disciplines are considered the meaty part of the theological curriculum. The bones of technique are typically left to the practical fields. But when practices of moral or spiritual formation are introduced into seminaries, they often

---

21. For an illuminating discussion of theology in terms of the sociology of knowledge, see Robert J. Schreiter, *Constructing Local Theologies* (Maryknoll, N.Y.: Orbis Books, 1985), pp. 75-94.

meet the objection that "this is a graduate school." Yet the disciplines of moral or spiritual formation are the very habits of theology in the church setting for which seminarians are ostensibly being prepared. It would seem, then, that we are at an impasse in considering theological education as character formation. The presence of critical methodologies and a functionalist account of ministry combine to inhibit or, more likely, prevent the advance of the idea of the seminary as a school of moral development.

This surely is an odd state of affairs. For how could it be that theological educators have missed what seems an obvious connection? The point appears to have escaped us that not everyone is qualified to engage in theological education. I do not mean only that some are not intellectually or educationally qualified, although that also is true. I mean that others are not morally qualified for theological study in that they lack the moral virtues requisite for critical reflection; they are not honest enough to accept the conclusions of rational argument. In such individuals the virtues are formed according to what Alasdair MacIntyre has termed the goods of effectiveness;[22] to individuals so formed, winning is more important than being right.

It may be objected that while moral virtues may be required for critical reflection in general, there are no special virtues beyond these which could be required of individuals engaging in theological scholarship. Why? Because the canons of scholarship determine the legitimacy of all forms of inquiry. Such conclusions illustrate the manner in which the critical principle has changed forever the landscape of theological scholarship. It invalidated the authority by which *theologia* had been taught and practiced. When *theologia* unified the theological curriculum, moral — even spiritual — virtues were requisite components of preparation for the ministry. That such is no longer the case is not only patently obvious. It is difficult to see how such components ever could be required in theological education as it is presently ordered. One may safely assume

---

22. MacIntyre distinguishes these from the goods of excellence in *Whose Justice? Which Rationality?* (Notre Dame: University of Notre Dame Press, 1988), pp. 30-46.

that theological educators will not soon abandon their critical methodologies. Nor should they. Thus the success of efforts to include moral and spiritual formation within the theological curriculum will depend in some measure upon their ability to ground formation in an account of authority that is at least compatible with the principles of critical scholarship.

A growing body of scholarship opens the possibility that such an account may be more than a utopian quest.[23] I want only to suggest here how a Christian paideia might be compatible with critical scholarship by suggesting an analogy between that project and a similar problem that confronted classical Athens. In order to do so, I must draw heavily on Martha Nussbaum's stimulating analysis of Aristophanes' *The Clouds*.

This classic comedy is presented as Aristophanes' argument that the charges indicting Socrates were correct; he did corrupt the youth of Athens. But the corruption did not lie in the relentless method of questioning that Socrates taught his followers. Rather, the cavalier manner in which Socrates selected his pupils suggests that his unbridled confidence in critical questioning caused him to neglect the question of whether his pupils were ready to use such methods. Thus in teaching all his pupils in the same manner, Socrates acted irresponsibly. Teachers may not simply replace traditional forms of education with critical reflection. Neither may teachers ignore their students' moral readiness, which is requisite for critical reflection. To do so risks the possibility that those so educated will become highly skilled without developing an appreciation of the ends those skills are meant to serve.

---

23. The space available in this essay does not allow for the kind of treatment due each of the following works. They all support notions of authority grounded in tradition in a critically reflective way and thus are suggestive of the project I have in view: MacIntyre, *Whose Justice? Which Rationality?* and *After Virtue*, 2nd ed. (Notre Dame: University of Notre Dame Press, 1984); George Lindbeck, *The Nature of Doctrine: Religion and Theology in a Post-Liberal Age* (Philadelphia: Westminster Press, 1984); and Jaroslav Pelikan, *The Vindication of Tradition* (New Haven: Yale University Press, 1985). In the brief account that follows I am dependent upon another excellent discussion of this theme: Martha Nussbaum, "Aristophanes and Socrates on Learning Practical Wisdom," *Yale Classical Studies* 26 (Cambridge: Cambridge University Press, 1980).

Nussbaum argues that Aristophanes challenges the play's audience to solve the following dilemma: to develop "a form of moral education which combines a Socratic respect for reason with Right's attention to the role of tradition and to the central place of habituation in training the desires."[24] It strikes me that this challenge could be posed to theological educators with equal appropriateness. We are called to practice a form of education that combines respect for critical principles with the role of the Christian tradition and training in the Christian virtues. But what form would such a combination take?

Nussbaum offers Aristotle's conception of education as one response to Aristophanes' challenge. The Aristotelian, says Nussbaum, does not seek the moral formation of students in an unreflective, authoritarian manner. True, the young must be trained to delight in those actions in which the virtuous delight. But education is not encompassed in this early training, nor is this training in the virtues sufficient. The virtuous person must not only act virtuously but do so for good reasons as well. Aristotelian education sought the development of "a virtue that was aware of itself and able to justify itself in argument."[25] Thus a key fixture of Aristotelian education is the person of practical wisdom. But that person's task is not simply the inculcation of an authoritative tradition. Nor does the person of practical wisdom command obedience by virtue of a privileged position or knowledge. As Nussbaum says,

> The "expert" will be special not because he knows something we do not know, but because he sees better and more clearly what we all, collectively know. Thus moral argument and moral change will take place within a climate of reasoned debate, and will represent an attempt to reach the best possible ordered articulation of our moral intuitions.[26]

Nussbaum's model of the Aristotelian educator may not be applied to theologians without an important shift in our

---

24. Nussbaum, "Aristophanes and Socrates on Learning Practical Wisdom," p. 89.
25. Ibid., pp. 89-90.
26. Ibid., p. 91.

understanding of the purpose of theological education. Arguments which find the unity of that education in the ministry narrowly miss the mark, but on an extremely important point. The institution of the ministry is neither the goal nor the unity of theological education. Rather, that goal must be found in the training of ministers. After all, as an institution the practice of ministry can degenerate into a routine of professional activities. In such circumstances the minister has every right to cry, "Who am I when I'm not busy doing ministry?" But, drawing upon an Aristotelian educational model, the seminary could attend to the formation of ministerial character in men and women and in the process solve the problem of a fragmented curriculum.

On such a view a new *theologia* would unify the theological curriculum. As in other forms of paideia, tradition would be expected to play a prominent role. Theological educators would become important mediators of that tradition. But the tradition they would mediate would have received their careful critical reflection. Thus the theological professoriate would need to embody the expertise that knows what the whole community knows. This knowledge would then be put to the service of the whole Christian community about that which concerns the whole Christian community. The product of this reflective activity would also be held up for the evaluation and judgment of a theological community equally interested in *scientia* and *sapientia*. Indeed, it would have to be so, for in this practice of *theologia* the two are mutually dependent.

MORAL FORMATION IN THE SEMINARY, THE CHURCH, AND THE WORLD

In the last two years, *Theological Education*, the journal of the Association of Theological Schools, has focused its attention on matters of spiritual and character formation.[27] Discussions of

---

27. Questions may arise concerning the meaning of spiritual formation vs. character formation. Are we confusing matters by using the terms together? George Lindbeck prefers "spiritual" to "character." But it seems to me that the two terms are closely related to the topic at hand, closely

this topic are helpful, but we will not advance our discussion very far if we do not shape our conversations with the kind of critique made by Farley and others. It also seems to me that many discussions about theological education fail to take account of the students who are subjected to it. Discussions about theological education which proceed only on considerations of the curriculum neglect the obvious but crucial observation that students, their character and abilities, also influence the goals of theological education. As one of my colleagues objects, "You people speak of formation as if these students were some plastic material pliantly waiting for the shaping of the masters' hands." His point is worth the attention of anyone considering the possibility of the formation of theological students. Even a few moments spent reflecting on his concern will bring a note of caution to estimates of the formative ability of a theological curriculum, including one revised along the lines suggested earlier in this essay.

My colleague is quite correct. Theological students are not plastic; they do enter seminary already formed. The paideia of American culture has already shaped their characters in profound ways. This paideia is by no means uniform, given the nation's cultural diversity. The writers of *Habits of the Heart* have, however, noted the salient and common features of white, middle-class American culture. If their estimate is at all accurate, then theological education that seeks the formation of students will have to set itself over against the individualism — whether "expressive" or "utilitarian," to use their terms — of our culture, for it has surely shaped the characters of students entering seminaries. If theological education does not attempt to counter such forms of individualism, then it will be giving to the church ministers who regard the ministry as a means of either self-expression on the one hand or self-fulfillment on the other. Neither alternative seems even remotely connected with the idea that God and the church set apart certain individuals for lives of caring and service.

---

enough that I think we are justified in using "moral," "spiritual," and "character" interchangeably in discussions about theological education as formation. Cf. George Lindbeck, "Spiritual Formation and Theological Education," *Theological Education,* Supplement I, 1988, pp. 10-32.

Others take a darker view. Christopher Lasch, for example, describes the development of the "minimal self,"[28] the character formed by modernity's paideia. The minimal self hopes merely to survive and cultivates those virtues that enable survival by withdrawing from the world. It becomes skilled at individuation and isolation. Work becomes either a job or, at best, a career. But devotion to career means the minimal self loses the capacity to be a neighbor because it never comes to call its domicile home. The minimal self orients itself toward time by attempting to manage the future through expertise, the secular technique of professionals. It is anti-authoritarian, which leads it to understand freedom as autonomy and render life into a succession of choices. The minimal self seeks its survival in terms of this world.

Are those who come to seminary in preparation for the ministry "minimal selves"? Yes and no. The men and women who enroll in the seminary where I teach are, I expect, much like other theological students in this respect. Hints of the minimal self are evident already in the kind of people they have become. But modernity's influence has not worked upon them without a challenge from the church. For the church practices a paideia that intends the formation of a character quite the contrary of modernity's. The extended self of Christian paideia offers not individuation but presence. The extended self understands work as vocation. It understands time as a genuinely narrative temporality wherein the present is a moment on a trajectory from past to future. Because life is understood not as a human right but as a divine gift, it is lived out in a cosmos of meaning and interrelatedness. Accordingly, freedom means not autonomy but rather liberation for love of God and neighbor.

Walter Brueggemann has said that passion and perspective are the poles of education in the Bible.[29] The people of God must form the coming generation in the passion that knows itself to be set against the cultural norms which surround it. But along with passion it must gain a perspective, the wisdom

28. Lasch, *The Minimal Self: Psychic Survival in Troubled Times* (New York: W. W. Norton, 1984).

29. Brueggemann, "Passion and Perspective: Two Dimensions of Education in the Bible," *Theology Today* 42:2 (July 1985): 172-80.

that insists, in the words of James Sanders, "that even the pearls of great price wrung from the agonies of the greatest prophets can also be turned over and scrutinized."[30] The educational mission of the church is this training in passion and perspective. To the degree that the church accomplishes its task, theological students come to study for the ministry possessing characters formed accordingly. But the church does not, of course, complete its task, and thus theological students come to the seminary possessing characters deeply divided between those of modernity and the church. Theological education must entice students to step further in the direction of passion and perspective. In this endeavor the seminary becomes a place for the development of critical reflection and the skills of the profession, but pre-eminently a school of wisdom. We must make our overtures to students fully aware that we will not complete this work, just as the church before us did not complete it. But we must make our overtures in partnership with the church in which the work was begun and to which our graduates will return.

In his autobiographical account of life in and beyond the now-defunct Trinitarian seminary near Phenix City, Alabama, Paul Hendrickson touches the nerve sought by those who see the need for moral formation in seminary. Hendrickson interviewed seminary dropouts and alumni, particularly those in school around 1958, the year he entered. Through this strange collection of priests and former priests, Vietnam veterans and protesters, homosexuals and heterosexuals, alcoholics, welfare workers, lawyers, and practicing and non-practicing Catholics, a common thread runs. As one of Hendrickson's classmates said, "I think you're discovering that you've never left. . . . You're still there. I don't have to search my memory for it either. It's just there."[31]

What was "just there" was a way of educating candidates for the priesthood such that even those who were no longer

---

30. Sanders, *Torah and Canon* (Philadelphia: Fortress Press, 1972), p. 115.
31. Cited by Hendrickson in *Seminary: A Search* (New York: Summit Books, 1983).

priests or who had never been priests had been formed in a particular way. They needed no effort to remember their schooling because it had become a part of them.

Candidates for the Protestant ministry begin their study for the ministry much later in life and have briefer seminary careers than Hendrickson and his classmates. It is extremely unlikely that this will change. From one viewpoint this is unfortunate, for it means that Protestant theological education is neither begun early enough nor of sufficient length to accomplish the moral formation it is increasingly being asked to undertake. But from another viewpoint it may be a good thing that theological education has limited itself in these ways. For if a morally formed clergy is a good to be prized, it may be that theological educators will be forced to draw nearer to the church and the traditions of Christianity than their methodologies have indicated. And the church will have to see itself not as a caretaker of those who come to have their needs met but as the seedbed of the ministry, lay and ordained alike. The moral formation of ministers is a burden that seminaries cannot carry alone. But they might be asked to further the moral growth of those whom the church has set apart for the leadership of a church whose goal is life lived in imitation of the Master.

The Story of an Encounter

Paul T. Stallsworth

On October 13, 1988, some twenty-five professors and pastors from around the country gathered in the Alumni Common Room of the Divinity School of Duke University. They were assembled to participate in a two-day conference entitled "Theological Education and Moral Formation."

After all the participants had been seated around the conference table, Pastor Richard John Neuhaus of New York City, moderator of the conference, asked each participant to identify himself or herself. Dr. Geoffrey Wainwright, a Duke professor, earned a chuckle or two by saying, "I'm Geoffrey Wainwright, a Methodist minister playing at home." Neuhaus went on to note that Professor Stanley Hauerwas, who was preaching in the chapel, would join the conference a bit later. "Hauerwas said that if we were really serious about spiritual formation, we'd all be in chapel," Neuhaus reported with tongue in cheek. "But then I explained to him why he was wrong about that, as about so many other things."

Neuhaus went on to explain the goal of the meeting: "The purpose of this conference is to advance the state of the question. We will have had a successful two days if by tomorrow afternoon we have a firmer understanding of the set of anxieties and the set of hopes about theological education and moral formation that brought us together.

"We'll begin with Dennis Campbell's paper, which lays out the problematic, as they say. Then, to get some historical

132

perspective, we'll move backward, as it were, but in terms of content perhaps forward, to Rowan Greer's paper on the fourth century. Next comes Brooks Holifield's paper on the nineteenth century. Finally, we'll go to the comparative case in which John O'Malley sets the Roman Catholic experience next to the Protestant experience. Throughout this discussion, Merle Strege's paper will be very much in play, because it gives us an overview of the current state of the discussion of theological education and moral formation."

THE CAMPBELL PROPOSAL

Dean Dennis M. Campbell of Duke Divinity School, the first presenter of the conference, began by sketching some of the background of his paper: "Before I became dean of the Divinity School, I hadn't given a great deal of attention to the theology of ministry. So one of the first things I did as dean was to offer a seminar for upper-division M.Div. students on the ministry's theology. That was a very enlightening experience for me, because it had me reading some materials I hadn't attended to before. We did biblical, systematic, and historical work on theology-of-ministry questions.

"As you may or may not know," Campbell continued, "a deanship in a university divinity school involves one enormously in the affairs of the larger university. Therefore, I spend a great deal of my time on fund-raising — probably, believe it or not, 50 percent of my time. I also spend a great deal of time on what I call my 'internal constituency,' which is made up of the board of trustees of the university, the academic council, the provost, the president, and the dean's council. These tasks involve all the complexities of maintaining a presence and a place for theological education within a modern university. In addition, I spend a great deal of time on ecclesiastical relationships. In the case of this school, the relationship is primarily but not exclusively with the United Methodist Church. Our school also has a large number of students from a whole host of other denominations, and particularly those that are nearby make claims on us. For example, the Episcopal bishop of North Carolina, the Lutheran bishop of North Carolina, the United Church of Christ, and others make legitimate claims on our time, energies, and commitments. It is from the combination of all these things that I come to the question of theological education and moral formation."

After alluding to his "growing concern with the reality of American higher education today," Campbell stated, "My conviction is that the starting place for reflection on our task ought to be the nature of ordination. Obviously, there are some in this room who will disagree with me. And there are certainly some in theological education today who will disagree with me. But if it is the case that theological schools are advertising themselves and claiming to be institutions in which serious attention is given to preparation for ordained ministry, then the first question ought to be the nature of ordained ministry. That is, what are the theological components of ordained ministry that should give shape to everything theological schools do? Accordingly, the first part of my paper is simply an effort, in very abbreviated form, to sketch my understanding of ordained ministry. For the most part you will find there a position that is representative, in a fairly sensitive way, of some ecumenical convergences on ordination."

Campbell lamented the relative scarcity of contemporary literature on the theology of ministry and ordination. He noted that although the World Council of Churches' *Baptism, Eucharist, and Ministry* might be turning the situation around, for years ordained ministry has been understood primarily as a profession, like any other profession. Seen as a professional with certain professional competencies, the ordained minister became the "pastoral director" in H. Richard Niebuhr's *Purpose of the Church and Its Ministry*, published in the 1950s.

Campbell, whose understanding of ordained ministry is different from Niebuhr's, said, "We've got to look again at the fundament, which is 'the yoke of obedience,' a phrase I borrow from John Wesley. 'We take upon ourselves with joy the yoke of obedience. We are no longer our own, but Thine,' wrote Wesley. That seems to run contrary to a great deal of the dominant thinking in American society today — even among seminary students. As I work among today's theological students, one of the things that I notice consistently is that they say one of their problems in field settings and in considering vocation is the business about tailoring the self. They are concerned about the church shaping the self rather than the self having control. Also crucial is the question of how one uses one's time on a day-to-day basis in ordained ministry."

Campbell continued by outlining another of his principal points. "In my paper I also address the setting and culture of theological education. Here I really have gone out on a limb. One of the reasons my paper was late was that I became a little unsure about several points. There were times when I thought I should pull back a bit. But I finally decided that, for purposes of discussion, I wouldn't pull back."

Academic Freedoms and Problems

Campbell then bravely ventured out on a limb by engaging the issue of academic freedom. This, he indicated, hit close to home: "Here in North Carolina I've been somewhat troubled that the faculty and some of the students at Southeastern Baptist Theological Seminary in Wake Forest have used the issue of academic freedom to get at their problems regarding authority. I don't want to be misunderstood here: I believe in academic freedom. A faculty must have the freedom to express extraordinary opinions. But for most institutions nowadays — and for most universities — that isn't the primary problem. The other side of the question seems more important in our time: What about the responsibility of faculty members to an institution? What about institutional discipline?

"Last Tuesday morning I represented Duke at the inauguration of a new president at Wake Forest. By no means do I celebrate what has happened there. The framing of the question is what I'm asking about. The question is this: In a theological community or in a theological tradition — say, the Southern Baptist tradition — where is the place for internal critique? It has to be remembered that such a critique is undertaken in the context of a faith community, a community of memory. That understanding of the issue of academic freedom might be more fruitful and less problematic in the long run."

According to Campbell, many theological educators "have bought into certain conventional commitments in higher education. We bought into them in a big way in the late nineteenth and early twentieth century, and we have uncritically continued with them in the middle and late twentieth century. As the history of American theological education has developed and as we look at the current state of higher education, I think not all is well.

"Now," Campbell went on, "let me make a couple of comments about that. I do believe that modern American higher education is relativistic, secular, and materialistic. I don't think one has to work very hard to make that claim. There may be some exceptions out there. But for the so-called major, private-research universities — which is how Duke defines itself — this is the case. Since that is the case, the place of theological education within a relativistic, secular, and materialistic setting is at least ambiguous.

"When I change my hats and meet with Duke's board of trustees or go to the second floor of the Allen Building, where Duke's president and provost and financial officers work, I detest the fact that I have to resort to making the claim for the Divinity School on the market model. Duke University recognizes the place of Duke Divinity School because we rank about fourth among the schools within the university in the amount of money we bring in. That's the truth. We bring in more money annually than the Law School. That's because of church funding and because of very hard work on financial development. When they look at the total amount of money coming in via the Divinity School, the people in the Allen Building are perfectly happy that the Divinity School is here. And they'll continue to be happy — as long as we pay our way. As it is, we more than pay our way, since we now pay the university a good deal of money every year for the privilege of being here. This is what we call our tax, or what some people call our berthing fee, or our port tax. And this is one of the dynamics of the modern university.

"The implications of that, of course, are enormous. It troubles me very much that most of the leadership of private and public higher education espouses values which suggest 'every tub on its own bottom' — and that includes the classics department. Well, can you really have a first-class university without a classics department? Duke, by the way, has a classics department; although it's losing money, we've been able to save it. But you see the point."

Starting Theologically

Campbell then fixed his gaze on the church. Its teaching authority, he said, is "in disarray today. That is, unfortunately, an ecumenically shared experience. About a year ago, Donald Davis and I attended a meeting in Garrison, New York. We both contributed papers — his from an Anglican point of view, mine from a Wesleyan point of view — on the question of teaching authority. Papers were presented by Orthodox, Roman Catholic, Lutheran, Reformed, and Free Church scholars. Everybody there was saying essentially the same thing — that the issue of teaching authority is very much a problem in the ecumenical context today. That presents some real problems for the seminary when you start to ask about moral formation and what that means for students and faculty.

"The question that we're facing in these two days of discussion," Campbell concluded, "is an extremely important one. We won't advance the state of the question about theological education and moral formation unless we face frontally the question of where we begin. From my point of view, we should begin *theologically* with the task of ministry, and specifically with the task of ordained ministry. From the issues of obedience, of discipline, we might fashion a theological curriculum and community that may in fact be in some tension with the modern academic setting. But I believe that one of the functions of a divinity school in a university is actively to provide the witness that the market model is not sufficient for higher education, and that the shaping of values is a part of the education that takes place throughout the university. Indeed, the shaping of values is going on in spite of its denial, and that is one of the things we witness to."

"Thank you, Dennis," said Pastor Neuhaus. "The conference begins very well, thanks to you."

Then Neuhaus joked about the no-smoking rule in the conference room: "Notice, now, that I take out my pipe. There is a dispensation with respect to the usual rules that prevail here. My pipe will be a rare but a decent acknowledgment to this institution's primary source — namely, the Duke family."

One participant who wasn't joking was Dr. David Schuller of the Association of Theological Schools. Said Schuller, "Dennis Campbell's framing of our question ups the ante right off the bat. When we start with ministry, that affects the entire life of the theological seminary. We could say that moral formation is one ingredient that ought to be added to, and perhaps intensified in, the life of a theological institution. But if, on the other hand, we relate moral formation to ordination and add all the implications of moving toward obedience, then we can't simply claim that moral formation is just one factor among others in theological education. Formation becomes foundational. This raises an important question: Is it really possible to undertake moral formation for ordination in an academic setting today?

"Dean Campbell is placing a great challenge before us. He also ought to nail his paper on a church door on the thirty-first of this month, on Reformation Sunday. If he's serious, then we're starting from square one with all of our assumptions about theological education. Then what we're doing here for two days is much more than engaging in a pleasant chat — we're starting all over again. So the question becomes this: Are those involved in theological education honestly ready to enter into this sort of covenant with the churches?"

Campbell responded: "The stakes *are* high, and my paper *is* a frontal challenge to theological schools. On the other hand, there are some mediating positions. Within the last three years here at Duke, for example, we've gone through an extensive curricular revision. To be honest, the revision of the curriculum didn't produce anything radically different. What it did was to establish a course which all seminary students are now required to take. That course deals with — for want of a better word — the theology of ministry. That course is a signal to the school, the faculty, and the church that Duke Divinity School is struggling to find its starting point.

"Vanderbilt's faculty recently underwent a curricular revision as well. Its revision produced a very fine, interesting book that approaches the problem of theology and ministry in a way that diametrically opposes the Duke way. You could almost say that the curricular reflection and revision of Vanderbilt Divinity School starts with the experience of the world as it is commonly perceived, then moves to religious experience, and finally to Christian theology and ministry.

"While Dr. Schuller's analysis is fundamental, there are some ways to address today's problems in theological education — within the university and the church — that are not as radical as he suggests."

Neuhaus then commented to Campbell, "Your statement doesn't seem directly responsive to David's question. David is calling for a revolution, and you seem to be responding by adding a course on revolution."

The Meanings of Obedience

At this juncture Professor Glenn Miller of Southeastern Baptist Theological Seminary addressed the issue of obedience. "In the Southern Baptist tradition," he explained, "we don't have education *for* ministry; we have education *in* ministry. Almost all of our people are in fact ordained when they enter seminary. In our tradition 'the yoke of obedience' means fundamental responsibility to the covenant community or the church universal. That's where we start talking. Although the faculty at Southeastern Baptist Theological Seminary has argued publicly about academic freedom, in our prayer sessions we faculty members ask each other, 'Are you obedient to Jesus Christ?' That's a question that doesn't communicate well to the secular media, but it's kept many of us struggling until three and four in the morning more than once. What does it mean to be 'obedient to Christ in ministry,' to use Baptist terms, or to be 'formed for ministry,' to use more ecumenical terms? That's the right question."

Miller continued, "In every group of Protestant intellectuals that I've ever been with, no matter what issue we start discussing, we always end up discussing the church-culture issue. Unfortunately, we never define *church*, and we never define *culture*. But the question of obedience that Dean Campbell raises is more theologically central for us than the church-culture problem. The question of obedience needs to be heard first and foremost as a question involving a person's relationship to God, to the brothers and sisters in Christ, and what it means to live — in academic culture, or in church culture, or in Kenly, North Carolina — in Christ. The question of obedience can become a frightening question. That's why it's easy to keep dodging it. The problem is this: How does one stand for and in obedience to Christ, and how do we communicate that? That isn't a church-culture problem, but *a* problem — perhaps *the* problem — of the minister's existence."

"The question of obedience strikes me as central," said Professor Roberta Bondi of Emory University's Candler School of Theology. "But Dean Campbell seems to define obedience as obedience to the church. That's where the crunch comes. We need to talk about what it means to be obedient to the church. One of the problems we have at the Candler School of Theology is a student body made up of individuals who are more than eager to be obedient to their district superintendents and their bishops so that they can rise in the hierarchy. This illustrates the need to distinguish between obedience to the hierarchy, obedience to Christian tradition and teaching, and obedience to the church as the body of Christ."

After agreeing with Bondi's comment, Campbell contended, "With regard to United Methodism, I find it interesting that where the clergy really can't get away with being disobedient is in the organization of the congregation. You have to have an administrative board or an administrative council. You have to pay your apportionments to the annual conference. You have to have this and that in your local church organization. Those are the things that are often on the minds of district superintendents and bishops. As for Roberta's comment that we need to distinguish among kinds of obedience, that really never comes up in the life of the churches, does it? So her point is well-made.

"In my paper I don't reduce obedience to doing things that organize the church. That's a regrettable — a very regrettable — development in American institutional religion. I'm interested in obedience related to the questions of the moral fabric of ordination itself, and I'm interested in helping students to think through how that kind of obedience works out. From this perspective there may be legitimate protest, if you will, against a church's hierarchy in the name of obedience."

At this point Professor Richard Hays, a New Testament scholar who was formerly at Yale Divinity School and is now at Duke, entered the conversation. He admitted that he was "profoundly uncomfortable with the proposal that we ought to think about theological education by addressing first the meaning of ordination. To do that already channels our reflection toward a mentality that will lead inevitably to institutional maintenance."

"Even though Dennis' theology of ordination is in terms of radical obedience?" Neuhaus asked Hays.

"Obedience becomes meaningful only when we talk about it in terms of obedience to Jesus Christ," Hays responded. "To know what obedience to Jesus Christ means, we must turn to the New Testament and to materials written long before the formation of the institution that we have come to know as ordination. So to talk about ordination is to talk about secondary concerns."

Campbell spoke next: "I would deny that to talk theologically about ordination is to move inevitably and immediately to 'institutionality.' From the New Testament itself we can see that the church, from the earliest period, was concerned to receive from God through Jesus Christ and the Holy Spirit the gift and the leadership of ministry for the whole people of God. The view that ministry is given to the church and arises within the church is manifest even in the earliest years of the Christian community. Thus leadership in the community of Jesus Christ is not something that develops later, in post–New Testament times, with institutionalization. It is a given, an inherent reality, theologically, within the body of Christ."

Hays challenged Campbell: "But if you were to say, for example, to Jesus or to St. Paul, 'The way we need to straighten things out is by talking about our theology of ordination,' you would be greeted, I would guess, with incomprehension."

"But we're talking about the end of the twentieth century, for better or for worse, and ordination is how the church now talks about leadership," said Neuhaus, ending this exchange. Nevertheless, this was an issue that would not die an early conference death.

Seminary Realities

Professor Russell Richey of Duke kidded that "the first page of seminary catalogs should contain something like a limited warranty." But Richey then turned more serious: "Our conversation presumes that the seminaries must play the decisive role in the shaping and forming of the minister and the priest. Maybe we need to back off and recognize that in most judicatories, seminaries are now understood to be less central to the clerical-formation process than they were twenty years ago. Most judicatories today are mounting much more significant formation efforts before individuals enter the seminary and are following seminary training with continuing education." His point was that seminaries should not consider themselves as part of the order of salvation. "We ought to be self-limiting and aware of what we can and cannot do," he said.

After all, judging from history, Richey continued, "we can see that theological education is variable. The seminary's role vis-à-vis the church and culture has needed to be different things at different times. At times the seminary needs to play a prophetic role. Now, apparently, it needs to play a more priestly and liturgical role. There were times, particularly in the nineteenth century, when the royal role was played, perhaps inappropriately, by Protestant seminaries."

"On the limitations of seminaries," interjected Neuhaus, "we need to face exactly who is attending seminary. Recently I was talking with a faculty member from a Lutheran seminary. She mentioned that there is no way her seminary can have a serious discussion of the theology of marriage because the majority of the women coming into her seminary have already been divorced and, in many cases, remarried. Since addressing this issue with a degree of moral and theological seriousness would throw into question an action taken by a large part of the seminary student body, the issue simply isn't addressed. This is a particular instance of the limited role the seminary has, given the students who are attending it."

Not only today's seminary students but also today's churches are often roadblocks to joining theological education and moral formation. Pointing to his work with church boards that evaluate and judge candidates for ministry, Dennis Campbell noted, "The people on those boards haven't thought through their task. Consequently, they in fact often look to academic culture and psychology to provide the criteria for evaluating ministerial candidates. They want to look at the candidate's transcript and at his psychological testing. If you ask these boards to ask the theological question of candidates prior to, during, or after seminary, they're at sea. They don't know how to deal with it. The church has refused to make judgments about people's adequacy for ordination on the basis of spiritual and moral formation. Although the church should play a prominent role in establishing criteria and making judgments about adequacy for ordination, it has shied away from that role."

Another Candler professor, Dr. James Fowler, made an observation that drew the conferees into some self-examination. "We teach what we are. We really do teach what we are. That raises an important question: What are we, as ministers and teachers? It seems to me that rather than academic or church acculturation, most of us exhibit a pervasive pragmatism — not in the classic sense but in the popular sense. We live in a world shaped by the values of visible effectiveness. We live in accordance with various bottom lines that say there are no free lunches. Therefore, we have to justify our work by being productive in some visible and convincing way. Knowing there are scarce resources in this zero-sum game, we compete with each other for those scarce resources. In the face of massive evidence which says that individualism is a specious and false consciousness, we continue to believe that the really important actors are individuals.

"So, who are we? For the most part, we seminary professors are upper-middle-class folks. We are mobile, both vocationally and geographically — we're jet-setters. We move through time zones, cultural zones, and different communities.

We are people who are trying to deal with both the local level and the wider scenes. We try to be faithful, to some degree, to local communities where we do care about formation, and yet we're torn by a variety of other kinds of activities. We suffer under institutional constraints, yet we get immense support from institutional resources and have an unusual degree of freedom."

Neuhaus added to this observation: "Sitting around this table are people who have had significant influence in shaping the seminary culture, the church culture, and maybe even the wider culture of our day. So we're talking about a situation for which we are, to a significant extent, responsible. So if we're talking about major changes in the cultures of the seminary and the church, we may be talking about a major change in ourselves."

Unconvinced, Fowler commented, "We may be less responsible than we would like to think. The historical overview that Professor Holifield offers in his paper is a chilling recognition of how the deep structure of Protestant theological education has profound continuities that run from the eighteenth century up to the present."

"I read Dennis Campbell's paper at 35,000 feet. That seemed right!" joked Father James T. Burtchaell of Notre Dame. On a more serious note, Father Burtchaell argued that the seminary's biggest problem was its shrugging off of servanthood. "All Christians are servants of the Lord and therefore of the world. Ministers are also servants of the church. Accordingly, theological education affects not just those who will be ordained. How, then, can those ministers be readied for service in seminaries that are not servants of the church? Often the seminaries are not even *of* the church, though of course they are *for* the church.

"Through the centuries many good gifts have come to the church from the academy. But is it necessary for the academy, in rendering service, to be beyond arm's length of the church? That is, is it necessary for the seminary to be an offshore operation? Offshore corporations have proven serviceable in some ways. But in other ways they're not very edifying because they're nonchalant about the needs of their host societies. Only when the academy is *of the church* can it be a servant, though it need not be a slave."

"What do you mean by an academy 'of the church'?" Neuhaus asked.

"An academy accountable to the church," replied Burt-chaell. "And there are several ways to establish that account-ability."

Burtchaell went on to clarify his point. "Servants can be very troublesome and tenacious. I think of Thomas More, who acknowledged that he was the king's good servant, but More's loyalty to God made him more trouble than the king thought him to be worth." The seminary, Burtchaell was suggesting, should not be a lapdog of the church.

While the group was discussing the issue of accountability, Stanley Hauerwas interjected a personal note: "I'm a layperson who has the vocation of being a theologian. I take that seriously as a calling from the church. Therefore, my first task is not to train people for the ministry of the church. My first task is to undertake the calling that has been part of the Christian gospel from its beginning — namely, to think out, for the church, the intellectual love of God. That isn't just a 'head trip.' I understand it in Aquinas' sense — that is, fundamentally speaking, theology is joy in the truth. Some are set aside in the church to undertake that dangerous business. Therefore, I hold Dennis Campbell accountable to make sure that people pay me to do that."

"And pay him well, I might add," Campbell commented.

After the chuckles had died down, Hauerwas continued. "The church has found it useful to put seminarians in the context in which people are called out to do theology for the sake of the church. I take that to be the church's judgment based on usefulness. However, this context is not necessarily where the training of people for ministry must take place. It could take place in a cathedral school, where it once did. It could take place in an apprenticeship with a Puritan pastor, as it once did. That ministerial training today takes place among theologians I re-gard as an accident of history that we can continue but that isn't necessary.

"One of the things that happens, as a part of my vocation as a theologian, is that the church holds my feet to the fire by sending me all of these students to teach. I don't particularly like it, but I do it as part of the obligation of the call. But through it all I depend on Dennis Campbell to act as an institutional hold on me. He might want to fire me someday because I've become a heretic."

"Is there any other way you could fulfil your vocation as a theologian?" Neuhaus asked Hauerwas.

"Well," Hauerwas answered, "I'm really a traveling evangelist. I go all over the country giving pep talks for Jesus. I try to give people some idea of what it might mean to take seriously again the theological vocation of the church. That's part of my vocation.

"Here I want to throw in a note about the joy in the work of a theologian. This joy invites other people into the ongoing activity of the ministry of the church so that the ministry won't be so damned burdensome."

Dr. Philip Turner, formerly of General Theological Seminary and now the dean of Berkeley Divinity School at Yale, returned the group to an issue that Neuhaus had raised earlier — the who-is-attending-seminary issue and how that might be standing in the way of seminary re-formation. Said Turner: "Most of the individuals who come to our seminary have a certain character, a very clear character. There are, of course, exceptions. But most seminarians tend to be people who have a great desire to help others, and they derive a lot of personal satisfaction from this. Also, they have an enormous need for affirmation. Hence the character traits that are enhanced in seminary are sensitivity, kindliness, and so on. They get so nervous that they're paralyzed when you talk with them about power."

"Not to mention authority," Neuhaus added.

"Without exception, authority is considered a bad thing," Turner went on. "In the Episcopal Church the ordination vow has largely to do with promising to use power and authority rightly. 'Take thou authority . . . ,' the vow goes. But today that's the last thing in the world the church is really asking them to do.

"My wife is a priest. In her diocese recently there was another priest who got into New Age channeling. One day she announced that her particular spirit had informed her that

Jesus didn't really die; he married a druid princess, and they had little druids. This was the content of this priest's teaching to a group in her church. The senior warden of the parish thought that maybe something was wrong, so he called the bishop. The bishop, bless his heart, told the priest that she had three choices: she could recant, she could resign her orders, or she could undergo a heresy trial. Well, the bishop is the one who took the flak, because the dominant reaction was, 'We're Episcopalians, so we can believe what we want, and a bishop has no rights here.' " Realities such as these are quite sobering, Turner was suggesting.

Cultures and Countercultures

The seminary, a sociologist might say, is an institution embedded in three cultures — the academic culture, the church culture, and the general culture. Dr. Brooks Holifield of Candler had this to say about the seminary's host cultures: "In his paper Dean Campbell draws a sharp distinction between the culture of a seminary devoted to moral formation and an academic culture that militates against formation. The danger here is, on the one hand, making the academic culture a heavy, and on the other, idealizing the church. At its worst the academic culture is rife with relativism, secularism, and materialism. But at its best the academic culture embodies an ethic of honesty, an ideal of truth and truthfulness, an ideal of selflessness, and an ideal of self-denial. I don't want to identify the academic ethic at its best with the Christian ethic," Holifield qualified, "but I do want to question the sharpness of the distinction between an ideal academic culture and an ideal church culture."

Hauerwas judged that Holifield's account of the university came from "an eighteenth-century ideology used by upper-class students to dominate the lower class."

Hauerwas elaborated his critique: "Brooks' university is exactly the university that Nietzsche rightly condemned. He saw the university as embodying the ideology of a power relationship in the West that was coming unglued. One of the interesting things today is that the contemporary university is an unintelligible institution, intellectually speaking. Alasdair

MacIntyre is right in *Whose Justice? Which Rationality?* He says that the university became unintelligible when it ceased requiring loyalty oaths as part of joining a faculty. I'm for loyalty oaths.

"I just came back from Asbury Theological Seminary, where I gave a lecture. Larry Wood was being installed as a professor, and he took a loyalty oath before the entire community. I told them what a wonderful thing we had witnessed."

Glenn Miller pushed Hauerwas on this point. "Do you really mean that you'd take a loyalty oath?"

"Sure! Absolutely!" Hauerwas replied.

"But Stan, you'd want to write the oath," chided Neuhaus.

Undeterred, Hauerwas built on Neuhaus' comment: "It would be fascinating for the students and faculty of a seminary to have to write a loyalty oath to which they would be held accountable."

Then Glenn Miller spoke from experience: "I have publicly signed articles of faith, articles that are grounds for dismissal if they are violated. The problem is that since the time I signed, new articles of faith have been added, and new articles keep being added. Four years ago I took a great deal of comfort and security from teaching in a confessional seminary. I was proud of that. But since then I've watched the other side of that come down. It often means that you dare not question who wrote the book of Isaiah, and you had best not say anything good about women who want to be ordained as ministers, and you had better be very careful not to write about the problems of people who are homosexual. Still, I'm proud of our articles of faith. I don't think I've ever consciously departed from one of them — even the one on predestination. I'm greatly comforted to think that many of our trustees are predestined." That last comment generated considerable laughter around the table, as it was intended to.

"So," Miller continued, "while there has to be a responsible theological allegiance to the teachings of the church, there also has to be responsible recognition that the obedience of a Christian man is the freedom of a Christian man and that the two are always critically linked. You get into trouble when you talk about loyalty oaths rather than confessions of faith. I will confess my faith — one with the apostles, one with the fathers of Nicea, one with the fathers of my own denomination — anyplace. I will not take a loyalty oath, because that involves breaking the important theological link between obedience and freedom."

Neuhaus returned to Hauerwas. "Stan, are you suggesting that if Duke Divinity School was what it should be, it would be at war with the university?"

"We *are* at war with the university," replied Hauerwas. "But of course the university is so incoherent that it doesn't know it. The problem with the contemporary university is that within it you can't have meaningful disagreements because you have to agree on too much to have disagreements.

"So, in effect, what we in the university become are self-interested entrepreneurs whose business is ideas. For example, Paul Hardin, the new chancellor of the University of North Carolina at Chapel Hill, just yesterday defended the university as 'the marketplace of ideas.' That's exactly what capitalists want the university to be. Therefore, the university aims to turn out people who are refined consumers of ideas. Since the ideal of the gentleman, which the university once served, is gone — and let me add that I like that ideal, and I wish we could at least go back to that — we exist in a time that is culturally and academically at sea. That's causing part of our problem about what we're going to do about the seminaries. What we as a seminary can do is to remind the church why it sets aside some of us to do what we do. That is, interestingly enough, a very prophetic thing to do."

Taking the conversation in a different direction, Hauerwas asked, "What would happen if Dennis had to start going around to local churches in North Carolina to ask them to pay my salary?"

"Well, the churches do in fact pay your salary in large part," Neuhaus corrected.

"Only because the United Methodist Church acts like the federal government and taxes its constituency for things that otherwise the people would disapprove of," Hauerwas argued.

"If the church wouldn't contribute to your salary, Stan, what would you infer?" Neuhaus asked. "That there's something radically wrong with the churches, or that there's something radically wrong with your work?"

Half-jokingly, Hauerwas answered, "I would think that there's something radically wrong with the churches."

Next came a brief exchange between Hauerwas and James Fowler on why parish ministers seem to have dulled prophetic senses. Hauerwas commented, "As Reinhold Niebuhr said in *Leaves from the Notebook of a Tamed Cynic*, most pastors don't lose their prophetic edge because they're afraid of not being paid. Most lose their prophetic edge because it's very hard to be prophetic with those people whom you've learned to love. That's where the problem of sentimentality is absolutely destroying us. We haven't learned to love one another in the way that the Gospels teach — as a people destined to death. And we underwrite the sentimentality of bourgeois culture in the way that we avoid facing up to the fact that Christians are a people who are trained to die early."

The Reverend William H. Willimon, the dean of Duke University Chapel, was the next to engage the set of culture questions. Emphasizing the distinction between the moral formation of academic culture and the moral formation of church culture, Willimon recalled a seminary faculty retreat that he had attended. During the retreat, he said, "concern was expressed about seminarians engaging in substance abuse, sexual promiscuity, or other destructive practices. Then someone asked, 'What are we doing about it?' Another faculty member replied, 'We've got to respect our students' privacy and their rights.' This shows, I think, how far afield we are. We've adopted the moral formation of the academy — and it just happens not to be Christian."

Theologian George Lindbeck, a professor at Yale Divinity School, questioned Campbell about his handling of the culture issue. "It came as something of a shock to me," Lindbeck admitted, "when you mentioned in your paper how we should be educating students so that they're able to fit into the communities from which they came. That may in part be a difference between Duke and Yale. But since I began teaching at Yale in the 1950s, my way of approaching our problem has been to take a large portion of the students and train them *not* to fit into the communities from which they came. Why? Simply because the communities from which they came reflect what is here being called academic culture. That is to say, the incoming students represent a certain kind of middle-class, suburban culture — and that is the academic culture. So the challenge is to educate ministers against their churches, as they actually exist, for the sake of the true church."

Campbell answered, "I have increasingly felt that Yale's model, of which I am a product, is problematic. It has the seminary or theological school set over against the churches, as though we in theological education have got it right, and we're going to save the churches or the students from the churches. We've frequently congratulated ourselves for how we're saving the students and saving ourselves from the churches."

Then Neuhaus probed Lindbeck's point. "George, you're saying that, in some sense, theological education at Yale is seen as a factor for renewal in the churches. And you're saying that that renewal is achieved by theological schools standing over against the current state of the churches."

"If you were to look at the self-consciousness of divinity-school faculties," Lindbeck replied, "you would see that they think of themselves as trying to produce ministers who will try to help turn the church around. Now there are different models for doing that, and the kind of church envisioned varies considerably. The neo-orthodox model of the 1950s is very different from the Clinical Pastoral Education (CPE) model. Nevertheless, whatever their model, faculties share the same desire and the same hope, perhaps even the same conviction, that they are helping to produce ministers who will help to turn the church around. In turning the church around, they would turn it against the culture. Both the neo-orthodox types and the CPE types think they're opposing the culture."

David Schuller, questioning the seminary-against-church model, recalled an incident. "I was recently with a group of Baptists in the state of Ohio. The common denominator of the group was that each member had been in parish ministry between three and thirty-six months. One-third of them had already received notice that they were being asked to leave their pastorates. After spending only about seven hours getting to know them, I could easily have guessed which ones were leaving their present pastorates.

"The failure of theological education here was the failure to prepare these ministers to be both prophetic and pastoral. We failed to introduce them to the reality of where the world is, where the church is, and how the minister can be prophetic in those circumstances. Consequently, they didn't know these things, and as a result, they failed and were broken."

Minister as Exemplar, Church and Seminary as Tribe

The conference's fourth presenter, Father John W. O'Malley of the Weston School of Theology, noted that in Roman Catholicism "the person of the minister is fundamental and central. This emphasis can even shortchange the intellectual, which I'm not in favor of doing."

Geoffrey Wainwright provided the historical development in support of O'Malley's point: "In the Western church, both in the Roman Catholic Church and later in the Protestant churches, there has been a kind of assimilation between the monastic life and the ordained ministry. It takes various forms, and it is present in various degrees. Celibacy in the Catholic Church would be one example in the West. Celibacy also figures in the Eastern churches, though in a less thoroughgoing way. The East's distinctions between bishops, monks, and presbyters as marriageable is one sign of the difference between East and West.

"The question being raised concerns the need in any Christian community for some kind of exemplary presence. Monasticism, although at first it was simply anchoritism, arose in some sense as a protest against the world and perhaps against the church and the worldliness of the church. To be exemplary for the church, then, one had to go against some of the church's worldly manifestations. There is in the New Testament a peer expectation that those appointed, or ordained, to office should be exemplary. At least they should not be people who have done or who are doing things that would set bad examples for the flock. But that easily becomes a more positive role, with the expectation that ordained officers should serve as examples to the rest of the Christian community. Sociologically and psychologically, it's pretty common for the non-ordained to look to the ordained for some kind of exemplary role."

At this point Dr. George Marsden of Duke Divinity School built on Wainwright's historical sketch. Marsden added that in early Christian tradition there is "always a strong sense of the clergy being set apart. The clergy were often set apart early in their lives, even as teenagers. Protestantism has not had that. It compensated for that — particularly where Protestantism has been the establishment — with conversion. Pietism and Puritanism in America emphasized conversion as the means for setting people apart for ministry. The crucial question is this: What happens when conversion disappears? That's the situation of the mainline and the mainline theological schools that we're talking about. In a mainline Protestant seminary today there is no sense that to be clergy you have to be converted. Unfortunately, there are no other ways by which people are set apart, especially in university contexts. In addition, today we're often not dealing with young people at the formative stages of life; we're dealing instead with thirty-five-year-olds. Therefore, what we're talking about with regard to mainline seminaries is artificial respiration."

"As distinct from reformation," Neuhaus joked.

"Well, right," responded Marsden. "Maybe those are the two alternatives. But remember, artificial respiration is an important enterprise, though it isn't one through which you immediately expect the world to be changed. Still, it might keep the church breathing to some extent. Reformation isn't going to come from seminaries, even reformed seminaries. If there's going to be a reformation, which I think is needed, it will have to come from institutions other than seminaries."

Neuhaus then described what set-apartness once meant in the Lutheran Church–Missouri Synod: "We understood what it meant to go through 'the system.' When you went through the system, you started at age fourteen, the first year of high school. Next you went to the junior-college academy. Then you went to seminary. That was the system. And yet at no point was there a sense of set-apartness in terms of moral or spiritual formation. Indeed, the mere raising of the question of moral or spiritual formation would have been rejected as pietistic. Still, the system reflected a determination — though quite apart from any expressed concern for such formation — to begin forming people very early on for ministry. So the set-apart dynamic has taken strange turns in different parts of the Christian community."

"So you weren't taught that it was a good idea to read the Bible and pray on your own every day," guessed George Lindbeck.

"Right," answered Neuhaus.

"I didn't know that Missouri was that non-pietistic," confessed Lindbeck.

"Missouri was anti-pietistic," Neuhaus clarified, "not just non-pietistic."

Speaking next was Michael Graef, a recent graduate of Drew University's Theology School and a United Methodist minister in Spokane, Washington. He underlined the theological nature of ordination. He agreed with Campbell that ordination "begins with revelation. Ordination is the acknowledgment of the community of the word of revelation, the community of the gospel of liberation for the world. Ordination is a form of obedience of the church. It is for the building up of the laity, of the body of Christ, for the work of mission that is given by the gospel. We have ordination so that the church can accomplish what it is called to do — and that is to offer grace not only to the church but also to the world. The ordained are first and foremost laity. Nevertheless, they are set apart by their churches. As a preparation for ordination, theological education should make it possible to be theological in one's orientation to life, ministry, church, and academics."

"So you're saying that true theological formation will shape one's character to exemplify the theological truth one knows?" Neuhaus quizzed Graef.

"That's my perspective," responded Graef. "Learning theology did that for me." Graef remained insistent that the "moral formation of the clergy has to be theologically grounded. Moral formation in the Christian tradition has to be fundamentally theological in origin — otherwise it isn't moral formation in the Christian tradition. Moral formation of the Christian community has to do with God's claim upon his people. I also think that the issue of lordship is fundamental for ordination. So, as you can see, theological school helped me to be unashamedly theological about ministerial formation.

"Today formation is a hard issue to get at theologically because of the proliferation of theologies. Also, there's a tremendously volatile atmosphere in theological schools today. I'm not criticizing that — I'm just saying that that's the way it is. Feminist, black, liberation, and Hispanic theologies polemically place themselves over against the seminary as a symbol of oppression. So there's a kind of schizophrenia in theological schools."

Dr. Christa Klein of the Lilly Endowment was also interested in the sources and resources of the exemplary minister. "In the nineteenth century," she noted, "the American churches functioned as tribes. They were in intense competition. People then used theological language most often because they were in combat with each other. The seminaries were like fortresses. They were the closest thing to denominations at that time in that they were the organizations over and above the local congregations. People looked to seminaries for leadership. But the seminaries weren't solely responsible for nurture, because the churches' tribes were then very good at nurturing people. I'm not using the word 'tribe' negatively; as Martin Marty has taught us, tribalism has some good features. Tribes, after all, are on a scale that humans can easily cope with. Anthropologists tell us that people are provincial by nature. That's how we're formed; that's how we learn to be human beings — in our families, in our communities, in our congregations. The best thing that happens in a tribe is that tribe members learn they have a home base.

"There are tribes today, but they're much more complicated. We have the overlay of the denominational conglomerates on top of tribalism. The seminaries, which were once the focus or the apex of the tribe, no longer know what their place is. I heard one seminary president call the seminary a 'church agency.' That reference comes from an assumed conglomerate model, where we draw a flow chart to show where the seminary should be.

"Back in 1960," Klein continued, "I was Christian growth chairman of youth work in Lutheran Church–Missouri Synod. That was pivotal in my own formation as a laywoman, and that has kept me focused and concerned about the state of the church over time. Back then, church-related colleges were indeed church-related. Campus chaplaincies were indeed active — not like today, when college chaplaincies are highly privatized. Now what goes is what any particular college chaplain wants to do or doesn't want to do. There seems to be no accountability. Before, various youth movements created leadership in the church. But where are those youth movements now? I see them in evangelical churches, but I don't see them, alive and well, in the mainline churches. For example, 21,000 Lutheran kids of the Evangelical Lutheran Church in America gathered in San Antonio last summer. My daughter was among them. The best thing that happened there was that she got closer to a dear friend in her own congregation. But her accounts of the extravaganza, and the money and effort that went into it, were unbelievable.

"The point is that we can't look at the seminary as our salvation when something has eroded our pre-seminary formation. We did better when we were more self-conscious of our tribes."

Dennis Campbell agreed, noting that "youth work, church-related colleges, campus chaplaincies, Sunday school, and the Student Christian Movement, at least among Protestants, were once the feeder groups that sustained the seminaries. But a tremendous sea change has come about in the seminaries with the feeder groups so altered."

Suggesting that Christa had given the group license to be provincial, Neuhaus seized the opportunity and illustrated the point: "I have some tribal memories from my childhood. Growing up in the family of a Lutheran Church–Missouri Synod pastor, it was the most self-evident thing in the world, on any possible question that came down the pike, to ask what 'our position' was. So I would ask, 'What is our position on this and that?' It was clearly understood that I was asking, 'What is the position of the Lutheran Church–Missouri Synod?' And that was defined primarily by the seminary, Concordia-St. Louis, the definer of orthodoxy. Now it's ludicrous to ask, 'What is the position of the Evangelical Lutheran Church in America?' I can't imagine anybody in this 5.3 million-member body asking about 'our position' on anything — even though the new church has all of these divisions, units, agencies, departments, and so on."

Following Neuhaus' lead, Father Robert Leavitt of St. Mary's Seminary sketched the tribalism of the Roman Catholic seminary. "Before 1960," he said, "we were a mixture of monastery and novitiate school, and not one or the other. It was what some people have called a 'total institution.' Everything was managed from the inside. We used to have barbers in the seminary, so even your hair was cut by a Catholic priest. Then came the 1960s and the Vatican Council; the idea then was that the total environment provided by the seminary wasn't healthy, and that what was needed was diversity, pluralism, and interaction with all sorts of people. So the total institution fell apart. When that happened, the ethos at the center fell apart, and nobody could recapture or reconstruct it. They tried to put it back together piece by piece, and they found out it doesn't work that way.

"One of the pieces that did play an important role in Catholic seminaries in the 1960s and 1970s was what John Tracy Ellis has characterized as a deep-rooted anti-intellectualism among American Catholic clergy. So the priests — and, increasingly in the 1970s, women, religious women, and non-Catholic theological faculty — came into the seminary saying, 'The one thing we have to remedy for our Catholic community is the anti-intellectualism among our clergy. So we're going to turn out a generation of priests who can think and who can talk.' When that became the goal, the primary model of priesthood that was transmitted by the faculty to the students was in the form of a message: 'Be like us.'

"So today the seminary faculties at St. Mary's and elsewhere project an image of the priest as intellectual. But the students don't identify with that. What students are looking for today is witnesses — that is, a seminary faculty which stands, both corporately and individually, for something that the students admire."

"Again, what is it that students are looking for?" Neuhaus asked. "A radically Christian way of living?"

"They're looking for faculty members who embody some kind of priestly ideal," Leavitt responded. "That may include things like being prayerful, thoughtful, articulate, and skillful in certain things. But students certainly aren't looking for classroom performers, people who just have big ideas or blackboard ecclesiology that doesn't work in the streets. The seminary faculties first have to come to terms with the image they have of themselves. Because we still don't have what is essential in priestly formation: some kind of an image or model or exemplar toward which people can strive."

Picking up on Leavitt's remarks, Philip Turner examined how "the seminary as community might function as a tribe where certain kinds of socialization can occur. There are three things that we're bound to try that will fail. The first is curriculum revision, complete with courses on spiritual direction. The second is the provision of spiritual direction. That's not bad, but it gets very individualistic. All of my students have 'spiritual directors,' and I think it's a waste of time. They don't know what they're doing, and most of their directors don't know what they're doing. The third thing is the exemplar. I think we need exemplars, but they are models of something that is sufficiently and commonly held so that everyone in the tribe wants to follow them.

"So the question is this: Can the seminaries undertake to be a certain kind of community? Here I will cite Stan Hauerwas: Can the seminary be a community where we hold each other to the truth? I mean that in the sense of Ephesians; by that I mean we hold one another responsible for what we claim the gospel to be and for the life we live. Today we have such an enormous theological pluralism. A certain amount of pluralism is good, but it tends to get crazy today. To deal with that, to give people a sufficient common faith, you have to be able to say, 'I really think you're wrong.' My students find that very difficult. But that's one side of it.

"The other side is learning when not to speak, when to hold our tongue. The great enemy of the community in which I live is gossip, slander, malice, and other lovely little things that we usually don't talk about. I was once asked to preach a sermon on peacemaking. I made a lot of people angry because in my sermon I didn't talk about disarmament — I talked about not gossiping.

"Two little things, truth-telling and tongue-holding, are involved. But it would be horrendous to be a community that undertook simple truth-telling and tongue-holding. Being committed to truth-telling and tongue-holding in all their complexity raises the question of authority. What happens when, because of conflicting claims, a community can't sort things out? This also raises the question of obedience, because what happens when someone in the community says that things have to be sorted out a certain way?"

THE MINISTRY IN THE EARLY CENTURIES

After a brief luncheon break, Dr. Rowan Greer, a church historian at Yale and the second presenter of the conference, introduced his paper. He told of "a friend who defines history as old gossip. The nice thing about old gossip is that it's usually quite interesting."

Greer went on to give two reasons for talking about church history. "First, unless the church can come to terms with its past, it can't move forward. Coming to terms with the past means a realization that things are probably no worse — maybe no better, but certainly no worse — than they have ever been. We have a set of perennial issues that are always going to be issues and are always going to have to be addressed. This may be a prejudicial passion of mine, but I think we make a mistake when we turn everything into a problem that we think we can solve, and when we suppose the difficulties that we now face are difficulties never faced before." Second, he said, "to examine perennial problems in a completely different historical context provides a kind of foil and a purchase on the problems as they appear in our time."

Dr. Greer then selected a specific issue for closer examination. He defined the issue as "the tension between thinking of the minister as hierarchically placed over the flock and thinking of the minister as one in service to the flock and in solidarity with the flock. This is the peculiar thing about Chrysostom's treatise on the priesthood. He is clear that the priest is hierarchically placed over the rest of the people, but he is equally clear that there is solidarity between the priest and the people because the priest is really the people's servant. So from one point of view the priest as patron is superior to his 'clients.' But from another point of view the priest as patron is totally dependent on the 'clients' and must be their servant. There's a very complex kind of interaction here."

Greer went on to talk about ministerial character. "It's a mixed kind of character. There are various places where patristic writers speak of unworthy motives. What goes through my mind on this point is something that happened to me many years ago in Clinical Pastoral Education. We had somebody from Harvard at one of our sessions. He talked with us for an entire evening about the motives for going into the ordained ministry. He started by saying that he wasn't interested in talking about worthy motivations. What he wanted to talk about were the unworthy motivations — for example, getting to dress up and perform in public, having power over people's souls, disguising our inability to get along with people, and so on. The point of that long conversation was not to argue that these unworthy motivations should be eliminated but to say that they should be recognized for what they are — then they wouldn't have power over us. My point is that when we talk about character, we're not talking about perfected character. That, surely, will not be achieved until the age to come. Here we're talking about ministerial character in its imperfect state — its unfortunate aspects as well as its fortunate aspects.

"The ancient Christian writers thought about character not only in moral terms but also in spiritual terms. One of my hobby horses is this: Because in the West, philosophically, the will became divided from the intellect, we are left with a perfectly horrendous problem. Many people now suppose that the life of the will and the life of the mind are quite separate entities. The value of the ancients is that they were thinking of the human personality holistically, as a marriage of the will and the intellect. There is a unity in their understanding of what a person is that I daresay we have lost in contemporary society. We are incapable of solving this part of our problem: So long as we persist in thinking that 'the real self' is found in the emotions and that it has nothing to do with the mind or the will, we are lost."

Pointing out a prior question that deserved attention, Greer asked, "What exactly is the gospel? My own peculiar point of view is that Christianity in the West has developed in somewhat Islamic fashion in that it is commonly believed that there is one God and that Jesus is his prophet. But that isn't the gospel. That isn't the way I read the New Testament. I guess my trouble is that I've ended up believing all of these people in the early church. Unfortunately, the issue of what constitutes the gospel is now up for grabs in the churches. We can scarcely talk about ministers of the gospel without talking about what the gospel is."

Then Dr. Greer reflected on the morning discussion. "At Yale Divinity School we don't train people just for ordination," he said. "Another way to approach the issue of formation is to think not of ordination but of the priesthood of all believers, in the sense that the corporate body of Christ has a priesthood to exercise. Accordingly, what's going on in the divinity school or the seminary is presumably related to empowering the whole body of Christ for ministry.

"It has been pointed out that Yale Divinity School is actually a huge catechetical school. What we're doing in many instances is not really preparing people for ministry at all — we're catechizing them into the Christian faith. I don't see how at Yale we could possibly close our doors to those not seeking ordination."

Finally, Greer suggested that seminary re-formation will not be easily accomplished because, he said, "it's becoming increasingly difficult to find faculty people who are willing to make a double commitment — to the American academy and to the Christian church. We're going to have to recruit this kind of faculty member; I don't think such applicants are going to be there waiting in line. If we don't recruit them, we're going to get a faculty whose hearts aren't in their work."

What's at Stake?

The first to respond to Greer's remarks was Neuhaus, who referred to his years of ministry in a poor black and Hispanic parish in Brooklyn. "In reading your paper," he said, "I was struck for the first time by how critically important the patron model was to my parish ministry. I spent a lot of time as a patron in the courts, in the criminal justice system, in the welfare system, and in the school system. The parish I served functioned in a very powerful way as a community, like the old political clubhouse. You were considered a good pastor if you could get things done — that is, if you could pull strings to help people when they were in trouble or out of a job. It was a ward-political operation, but it was also a very communal-ecclesial operation.

"Your paper also made me newly aware of how dangerous what Chrysostom called vainglory, or exulting in a sense of power, is to a young pastor — one who's, say, twenty-five or twenty-six years old, as I was. All of a sudden that pastor is a wheel. And in New York City there are so many worlds within worlds that you can quickly become a very important person in specific little worlds. In this sense my pastoral experience was like the experience at most model black churches, at least the ones that are thriving. They put a huge emphasis on the patron role. They accent the advantage of belonging to and participating in a community because it does all kinds of good things for you.

"Looking at the negative side of my motivations in those years of pastoral ministry, I would say that it was very gratifying to be a very important person. I don't know what I would have done in an upper-middle-class, suburban parish that didn't need the kind of patron that St. John's in Brooklyn needed."

"In fact, there the patron role may have belonged to the laity," said Dennis Campbell.

"Exactly," Neuhaus responded. "So I was asking myself, as I was reading Rowan's paper, how day by day and year by year I sensed the consequences and the importance of what I was doing. I hope that, as an orthodox and sacramental Christian, I understood that the center of the ministry is the liturgy around which everything else turns. But seminarians studying for the ministry today — what do they think is at stake in their own ministries, aside from their personal failure or success in their ministerial careers? In his paper Rowan made it clear that Chrysostom and the others thought that the salvation of souls — meaning heaven or hell — was at stake; therefore, vainglory had to be avoided. Remember that the late catholic New Testament literature commands the laity to obey those who are over them in Christ; at the same time, the clergy must give an account for the laity's souls.

"Isn't a lot of what we might perceive to have gone awry in theological education and ministry in the life of the church attributable to the fact that a concern for the salvation of souls is no longer alive among us? Isn't it true that we have lost the sense that something monumental is at stake in Christian ministry? So how can someone take seriously a vocation and the shaping of himself or herself for a vocation if it is assumed that there really isn't something monumental at stake? Many of our ministries today — Lutheran, old-line, evangelical, fundamentalist, Anglican, and Roman Catholic — are debilitated and vacuous because nobody is quite clear about whether it matters all that much. Where did we get the idea that it doesn't matter all that much?"

"It isn't that it doesn't matter very much," replied Merle Strege of the Anderson School of Theology. "It's that in today's churches everyone is entitled to his or her own opinion. And who are ministers to intrude into the private world of religious belief? Religious belief is considered to be a matter between the individual and God. Any third party in that arrangement becomes intrusive."

Stan Hauerwas noted that in the not-too-distant past, Roman Catholics had assumed that salvation was at stake in the church's ministry. Today, things are different. Today, Hauerwas said, "we believe in illness, but we don't believe in God or in salvation. Consequently, we don't think anything is at stake in the ministry, so it's all right to be an incompetent minister. The real priests in our society are being trained in medical schools. I think our society's last schools of virtue are medical schools. There a belief in the significance of medicine is worked out in a rigorous formational system. If a student went to medical school and said, 'I'm really not into anatomy this year. I'd really like to get into counseling,' medical-school officials would say, 'Who do you think you are? We don't care what your interests are. Learn anatomy!' In medical schools a very definite formation occurs."

Perhaps when the church forgets about what is at stake in its ministry, as it often does, an unwillingness to exercise authority arises among the ordained, James Burtchaell suggested. Next he recalled a seminar he had conducted on Gregory of Nazianzus and his "Christian Meditation on Virtue." He noted that since Gregory's time, "Christians can only give you the servant church, talk about self-abasement, and accept suffering. But when it comes to being accountable for priestly presidency, that's quite a different matter. When reading Gregory, I was thinking that his unapologetic exhortation to exercise authority had no offspring." Agreeing, George Lindbeck quickly added that Gregory, unlike those who succeeded him, was not the least bit "embarrassed by power."

"You mean that others in the Christian tradition haven't addressed the issue of the exercise of authority?" Neuhaus asked Burtchaell.

"What I'm saying is that later exhortations for pastoral ministry downplayed high office, downplayed authority, and downplayed decisionmaking," Burtchaell replied.

"So we have to teach people not only how to accept suffering but also how to inflict suffering," Neuhaus joked.

Reporting on a recent conversation with a former student who now teaches philosophy, Burtchaell said, "The young professor told me that he wants to write about erotic love. But that's the most troublesome type of love because it fouls up agape and brotherly love. No Christian in our time writes about that, and that's embarrassing. It's like authority or power. It's something that's caused so much trouble that people haven't undertaken the task of discovering the ways in which it is an appropriate and integral part of life."

Ministerial Virtues

"We really do need to talk about the virtues for Christian ministry," declared Roberta Bondi. "Phil Turner discussed two of them this morning — truth-telling and tongue-holding. Both are also virtues for the academic community. It's important that theological school faculties teach what the virtues are. We need to be explicit about them. This reminds me of one of my favorite sayings of St. Anthony. He said that nobody picks up a piece of iron, like a blacksmith, and just starts beating on it and says, 'I think I'll beat on this to see if it turns into a plowshare or a weapon of some sort.' So it is with the virtues. We must decide in advance what it is we want to create and then move in that direction.

"Now I don't think that we can form the character of our students as if they were lumps of iron that we can beat into plowshares or swords. But we can take some responsibility for discussing with our students some of the Christian virtues for ministry. We can help them to dwell on the virtues — to think about them, talk about them, pray about them, and read Scripture about them. We have a terrible responsibility to do that. We must do that."

"And what if we don't do that?" Neuhaus challenged.

Then, Bondi speculated, we will continue with "the sort of mess that we now have among many of our seminary students who are bound for parish ministry. For example, take truth-telling. I find it very distressing that students don't seem to worry about cheating at Candler. This isn't just a matter of cheating on papers. It brings up questions about what the truth is and what the gospel has to say. Yet many students just sort of jostle along, unperturbed by the issue. The critical question is this: Are we as seminaries going to be just a small slice of American culture, or are we going to be something which stands over against that culture? We're not succeeding very well at Candler, and I don't believe that Candler is an unusual seminary."

Glenn Miller reinforced Bondi's concern about ministerial virtues with a historical example. "Nineteenth-century American seminaries were more concerned with the moral formation of character than anything else," he pointed out. "Therefore, the worst sin that a student could commit at early Andover was not to be stupid but to be immoral. The seminaries kept a very careful watch over the moral formation of their students and their character. Nineteenth-century Princeton was not as thoroughly infused with perfectionism as nineteenth-century Andover, but it also had a deep interest in formation. It devoted every Sunday afternoon to the question of ministerial character and piety. Union Seminary in New York devoted an evening every week to the question of character. This practice was picked up by some early Methodist seminaries. In fact, one of the original Methodist defenses of theological education was the way it got the process of character formation moving on the right path."

Today all of that has changed, Miller continued. "As seminary instructors we simply don't want to say to any of our students, 'Hey, you don't do that.' A friend of mine — who isn't a charismatic type, by the way — says one of the reasons he likes Pat Robertson is that Robertson is willing to say to his viewers, 'Hey, you don't do that. That's wrong.' Maybe the hardest challenge we now face is when to say, 'That's wrong.' A problem among Baptist ministers right now, something that causes a lot of ministerial relocation, is sexual immorality. Not just sexual immorality but *stupid* sexual immorality. Our failure to give some sort of moral direction or guidance in this area is indeed a crisis."

Merle Strege underscored Miller's concern with an example from his experience: "At our institution we have a nursing department, and last year there was a major incident involving a nursing student. While she was on nursing duty one time, it was discovered that she wasn't wearing a watch. Of course, if there's anything a nurse must have on her person, it's a watch. A watch enables her to perform her duties properly. Anyway, the Anderson nurse denied what was demonstrably true — that she was not wearing a watch. Her refusal to be honest is what caused the nursing faculty to raise the question about her character. On the basis of that question she was denied the opportunity to graduate. What made the case even more interesting was that her father was a trustee of the university."

Then Strege provided a counterexample, a case of institutional spinelessness. "When I first started teaching at our seminary, there was a student who found it as difficult as this nursing student to accept responsibility for his actions. But the faculty didn't know what to do with him. Finally we separated his character from his academic credentials, and ended up giving him a degree, although we really didn't want to recommend him to the ministry. Unfortunately, according to the standing policy of the Church of God, the recommendation of the seminary doesn't count much for or against a minister in preparation. So he went out and found a church and is now jumping from one pastorate to another, never accepting responsibility for his actions. This is the result of our seminary's being embarrassed to exert power" — especially with regard to ministerial virtues, Strege was suggesting.

The virtues required for ordination are similar to the virtues required for marriage, Hauerwas contended. He said that the church should challenge "the bourgeois notion that marriage has anything to do with romantic love. Christians are *required* to love one another — *even in marriage.* Furthermore, no one is ever prepared to be married. That's why the church holds itself up as an institution to which the married are called and through which they can discover that they have the beginnings of fidelity necessary for bearing with marriage for a lifetime. The same can be said of ordination. There's no way that anyone who is twenty-five or twenty-six or even forty can be prepared to know what it means to undertake a lifetime commitment of fidelity to the call to ministry. What is needed is a community. Character isn't some sort of individualistic thing. Rather, character has to be carried by an institution — for example, by marriage or by ordination — that draws from the determinative narrative of a community. So it's wrongheaded to say that people must have a certain character prior to ordination. Instead, the church must testify that its ordinands are beginning to develop the character for a commitment to fidelity, such that we can hold them accountable for their own failures."

"But how is that possible without a community that has a common understanding of holiness?" inquired Neuhaus.

"It isn't," Hauerwas answered. "But you Lutherans have never talked about holiness."

To some laughter, Neuhaus took up verbal arms: "We exemplify it, so we don't need to talk about it."

"Well I always say there are Christians and then there are Lutherans," Hauerwas shot back.

"I know, I know," Neuhaus acknowledged.

Burtchaell took the conversation back to Bondi's plea for a discussion of ministerial virtues. The basis of his remark was a conversation with yet another former student. During a session of spiritual direction with this particular student, Burtchaell recounted, "I had the occasion to ask him whom he trusts. He had grown up in a difficult family situation. He named several people, and then he said, 'I trust you.' And I thought to myself, 'He trusts me because I've been his mentor, or because my advice has been good, or because I've been his professor.' But these weren't the reasons, because he said, 'I trust that I won't wake up in the morning and read in the newspaper that you haven't been a good person.' That made me much more terrified than anything else he could have said. It was awesome that his trust was predicated on the kind of person I am and not on any describable skills I might have."

Morality Doesn't Just Happen

Philip Turner spotted a problem with the language of virtue and the pursuit of virtue today. "The people who wrote the texts that Rowan cites," he asserted, "were heir to a long tradition of moral education which they adapted for their own purposes. They did that rather successfully. One of the things that we lack in our time is a theory of moral education, both in political philosophy and in theology. The really great people in political philosophy and theology always had a theory of moral education. That is, as I said, notoriously lacking today."

"Philip, as you talk to your students, don't you know what the Christian tradition of moral practice and its underlying theory of moral education are?" Neuhaus asked.

"I'm beginning to have such an idea," said Turner, "but it wasn't taught to me; I've had to look for it. I found it in Thomas Aquinas, and behind him in Aristotle, as filtered through Hooker and a lot of other people. But when I went to seminary, that wasn't given to me or to my generation."

Neuhaus probed deeper: "Are we talking about a missing generation here? Do we assume that our generation's moral problem is something that the prior generation wouldn't recognize? If so, at what point was a moral ideal and theory more or less intact? With our grandparents? Or with our great-grandparents?"

"I'll tell you one thing I've found in my own tradition," Turner replied. "I've traced the worm back to Richard Butler and his view of conscience. He understands conscience to be a kind of sovereign arbitrator; conscience wasn't understood in that way by Hooker or others who went before."

Next Neuhaus posed a series of questions, requesting a show of hands in response: "How many of us assume that our grandparents, if they were Christian, had a more intact understanding of Christian character than our generation has? In other words, how many of you believe that two generations ago there was a firmer hold on a taken-for-granted but reflective understanding of what it meant to have Christian character or to live a Christian life?"

While most raised their hands, James Fowler did not. He explained why: "I resisted raising my hand because I'm not sure that my grandparents had a *reflective* understanding of who they were and what they were doing. Also, I couldn't say that their virtues and character were distinctively Christian. Their virtues and character might have been attributable to the ethos of small-town or rural America. Sorting that out would be an interesting task.

"Certainly theirs was a more coherent tribal existence, a more coherent 'village' existence. They lived in a face-to-face community where gossip was very important. We miss gossip today because it's one of the ways that people learn about life. In the sixteenth century, 'gossip' came from the word *godsibb*, which is French for one who takes a special responsibility for another at the point of sponsorship in baptism. So gossip helped to link the community together, and it shared wisdom. We really do miss good gossip today."

Connecting the rise of "progressive education" in America (with its assumption that it is better to teach the method of learning than content) and the recent rise of "values clarification," Fowler noted, "Part of the reason we don't teach the virtues is that we don't know which stories to tell. Also, there's a new complexity that has been introduced into our thinking about this problem. This has happened through our coming to terms with depth psychology, through our learning something about the elusive thing we call self-deception, and through the demise of heroic models. We're seeing the extraordinary, excessive working-out of this consciousness in the effort to scrape up anything that would make a political candidate vulnerable. Take, for example, Michael Dukakis being put on the defensive about the possibility of having consulted a psychologist at one point in his career.

"Virtue is a fact of communitarian life, not individual life," Fowler continued. "We need to concentrate now on *communities* of conscience and character. Somehow we still have the notion — partly because of American individualism — that the key to moral elevation of church and society is through the building of massively heroic characters. Yet at the same time we end up disillusioned with that."

Neuhaus wanted to make sure he had correctly heard Fowler, so he spoke up: "Jim, you're saying that the absence of heroes, or the loss of the recognition of heroes, may not be such a bad thing, because that kind of heroism was constructed on an American individualistic model; you're saying that now we have to find some new basis for heroic or exemplary life. But in the Roman Catholic community, among the traditionalists, there has been a powerful, lively cult of the saints that survives. And there has been a very clear understanding of what a saint is. In much of Roman Catholicism — and this is part of the Protestant problem — that has eroded. For centuries the saints

provided an alternative way of sustaining a communal sense
— not a rugged individualistic sense — of what the Roman
Catholic community was pledged to; this way pointed out
excellences historically achieved in extraordinary individuals."

Fowler was ready: "Augustine did his best theology after
having dinner with the community, when he talked about the
issues he was writing about. To see heroic, saintly characters in
their communal context was very instructive to him."

"The language of moral development will mislead us,"
Hauerwas cautioned. "After all, Aristotle thought that the way
to train someone morally was to teach him how to ride a horse.
And I think that's right. Aristotle's understanding of riding a
horse involved having the rider undergo a great deal of training
so that he didn't mishandle the horse. The same principle, of
course, applies to wrestling, mathematics, and so on. The best
moral training I had was learning how to be a bricklayer. The
point is that you never train virtue as an aim in itself. You
discover that the virtues are nurtured within activities. So the
very idea that you have to concentrate on something called
morality is probably a sign that you have a civilization in
trouble. That civilization probably doesn't understand the continuity between activities and genuine integrity."

At this juncture Neuhaus pointed out that moral confusion in the churches might have its origin in "the fact that
ordination has become what confirmation once was. Today, if
you're a serious Christian, you get ordained. As a consequence,
there is a dissolution of the notion of the seminary as a place
for the training of people who are set apart or called out. The
seminary becomes a place for the continued conversation of
people who happen to have an interest in things theological."

This led Dennis Campbell to clarify his position. Although
he didn't believe that everyone in theological school should be
en route to ordination, he posited that when "seminaries have
become places of study for people not seeking ordination, confusion regarding the unity and the purpose of the school usually sets in. Also affected is the question of moral formation for
ordained ministry. A theological school can't be all things to all
people."

At that point Rowan Greer admitted that he was uneasy

with the clerical focus of the discussion. "You should know," he said, "that I'm coming at this from the point of view of what I regard as a priest-ridden church. One of my objectives is to try to free my church, the Episcopal Church, from the domination of priests. Also, I'm unwilling to suppose that character should differ for the ordained person and the unordained person. Obviously, the conditions under which character is lived out will be different for clergy and laity. But it seems to me that the character of both needs to be *Christian* character."

"I agree with that," responded Campbell, "but the ordained person still has a representative role."

Greer provided a ready analogy: "The ambassador to the Court of St. James is the U.S. representative to Great Britain. But that is not to say that there might not be a private citizen who, under certain conditions and in certain circumstances, might succeed in representing this country far more effectively than the ambassador."

Then Neuhaus joined the conversation again: "You're talking about what has been called the 'double standard.' You're noting that priests have been badly trained, improperly schooled to equip the saints of God to fulfill their ministries. This hasn't happened because of an elitist approach to theological education. In my understanding of seminaries as places of moral formation for the leadership of the church, we're talking about self-consciously elitist institutions. They should be that, and we should be unembarrassed by that. Seminaries should accept both the power and the responsibility that comes with their service to the church. Even so, seminaries shouldn't use their power to lord it over people, as St. Peter says.

"Take, for example, the model of West Point. West Point is an unapologetically elitist institution for the training of leadership for the military. What would happen at West Point if, in order to increase its student body, the school let in people who were . . ."

"Pacifists," chuckled Hauerwas.

"Or just interested civilians," Neuhaus continued. "If West Point recruited people who were just interested in military questions, it would no longer fulfill its role."

Addressing Greer, Neuhaus argued that "if the training of the theological seminary is good, you won't end up with a 'priest-ridden church.' You'll end up with a clergy that is well-prepared, with the skills of excellence, to equip all the people of God to exercise their ministry in the world."

"I see the point," Greer acknowledged, "but I still disagree with it."

The lack of vital religion, suggested David Schuller, might be at the bottom of the churches' moral quandary. To make his point, Schuller described a meeting of minority main-liners — blacks, Native Americans, Hispanics, and Asians — that he had recently attended. "Mainline minority groups are growing, a trend that contrasts sharply with general mainline decline. Just prior to this meeting I was with an equivalent group made up of old-line denominational representatives. It was one of those typical shake-me-every-hour-to-make-sure-I'm-still-with-the-group meetings. By contrast, the minority group meeting was filled with vitality.

"The black perspective is particularly instructive here. At their meeting they kept describing the need of a suffering community. For years the black church has been addressing that in a very direct way. For them, Scripture isn't this detached, objective thing that needs to be examined histori-cally and critically; the Bible presents the reality of God here and now. So when they hear the story of Moses, it's real — that's why they have four-hour worship services. When the meeting I attended was over, I was asking myself, 'Is this the group that's going to reinvigorate us — those of us who suffer from bland, middle-class worship?' Sociologically, I have to answer 'No,' because we're going to make sure that, by the time they get to where we are, they'll be just like us. They'll be very objective about their religion. They'll have gone to our schools, and we'll have squeezed all this vitality out of them."

"I find that a sort of troubling set of observations," Greer replied. "You're quite right in discerning that I'm no crusader. I do have a very anti-apocalyptic point of view."

"And you're militant about it!" kidded Neuhaus.

"When we look at today's evangelical groups," Greer continued, "we see that they have numbers. Is that the criterion by which we should judge their truth? In addition, they obviously have deep commitment. On that point I always tell this story. There was an old Scotswoman who noticed one Sunday that there was a man rowing on the loch. She went to the minister and said, 'Minister, there's a man rowing on the loch on the Sabbath.' The minister replied, 'But after all, our Lord walked on the water on the Sabbath.' 'Aye,' she said with a heavy accent, 'but two wrongs do not make a right.'"

After a laughter-filled pause, Greer went on with his point. "Commitment isn't altogether a good thing without reference to what one is committed to. This holds with respect to enthusiasm as well. What troubles me is that enthusiasm can be an emotional thing divorced from the will and the mind. I see all of these things attracting my students. They like to be enthusiastic; they like to be committed; they like emotional expression. I find that deeply troubling because it strikes me that the real issue is this: Is the gospel true? Whether anybody believes it doesn't matter. How many believe it doesn't matter. The important thing is the truth of the gospel.

"Thinking of my own tradition and reading my tradition regarding character," Greer continued, "I put in first place the word *fallibility*. We Anglicans don't claim anything but fallibility. It strikes me that for a tradition to say 'What we preach to you is that we are fallible' isn't very persuasive in an age seeking certainties. But when I preach that my church is fallible and that I am fallible, what I'm actually preaching is that only God and his Christ are infallible. Today, that's a message worth hearing."

"You put that so winsomely, Rowan, that it's hard to resist," commented Neuhaus. "But I stand more with those who think that the message should be more radical. I can't imagine why it would be consequential to preach one's fallibility, unless there was a danger that people would suspect that you were infallible. I can't imagine — not just with respect to the Episcopal Church but with respect to any of our churches today — that anybody is fretted about their being infallible. Only when authority is asserted, only when one preaches a truth claim that implies obligation and commitment is it then necessary to relativize or temper the nature of the commitment that is being called for. This ensures that ministerial and biblical authority are not confused with the authority of God himself."

"I daresay we disagree," Greer replied. "Even in the long run we'd end up disagreeing. I'm taking a kind of F. D. Maurice line. He says at one point that if you start loving the church more than Christ, you'll worship the church and not Christ. And if you start loving the Bible more than Christ, you'll worship the Bible and not Christ."

"This is all probably a matter of different sensibilities and different readings of the signs of the times and the signs in the life of the churches," Neuhaus conjectured. "But it seems to me that the set of anxieties and the set of hopes for renewal that bring us together do not include the problem of people being so radically committed to the authority of the Word of God, the Bible, and the church that they're prepared to make idols of them. For the most part, what we're witnessing today is that the churches, the Scripture, the dogma, and the whole tradition of the community are placed at the service of the individual will for self-actualization, and people are not held accountable to the community in any disciplined way."

Purpose and Grace

Toward the end of the afternoon session, Professor Richey offered an observation. "The seminary that prepared the ministers who helped to produce the moral cohesion of our grandparents' generation was a seminary set in a context that was honeycombed with Protestant communities like the YMCA, the missionary societies, and the revival groups. The context and its communities had an ethos that was oriented toward a large ideal, a kingdom ideal. These communities and their activities were seen as part of the kingdom of God. They were attempting to bring the nation and the world to Christ. These folk did not create an ideal of moral character as an end in itself but made that ideal a by-product of the missionary enterprise. They had their exemplary models, particularly the missionary, who most concretely and faithfully exemplified what it meant to be a Christian in an authentic sense. What is important here is that many of the most evangelical of Protestant denominations — Methodists, Baptists, Presbyterians, and Disciples — have given up on the earlier ideal of Christianizing the nation and the world. As a consequence, the whole enterprise is in peril. And it isn't surprising that our seminaries no longer have within them those sorts of communal structures that produced an older ideal of character. Those sorts of societies and organizations no longer work. The YMCA is no longer a missionary organization; it's a leisure organization. And what we have in the denominations are caucuses and interest groups of one sort or another.

"Maybe we really do need to be talking about the gospel, the word that needs to be preached, and what the Christian witness is to the society. We shouldn't expect that character will take care of itself, but we should hope that the nature of Christian character will be brought along by our sense of what the appropriate witness is in this day and time."

As Richey highlighted the witness and mission of the church as essential components of the moral-formation project, Rowan Greer highlighted grace. "How can there be Christian character without grace?" he asked. "Augustine doesn't make the will a separate factor at all. What troubles him is that the will has been thought of primarily in terms of choosing. It has been thought that choosing is what willing is all about. Augustine rightly points out that the trouble with such a notion is that, first of all, when we make our choices, we're choosing not just between good and evil but also between goods. So even the choice of the good divides the will against itself. That's part of our problem. Moreover, Augustine says that freedom is no longer choosing. Freedom is cleaving to the good — 'In whose service is perfect freedom, in whose will is our peace.' At another level Augustine is concerned that to think of the will just in terms of choices is to isolate those choices from one another. Augustine believes that our choosing has a pattern which then becomes the condition of the mind and the soul and the disposition, almost what we think of as character. On that point, Augustine thinks that we're incapable of forming our own character because we're born with things that prevent the right development of character. For that reason, grace is absolutely necessary."

With Dr. Greer's word on grace, the second session of the conference drew to a close.

THE GENTLEMAN MINISTER

Opening the second day of the conference was Dr. Brooks Holifield of Candler. Holifield, the third presenter of the conference, informed the group that he had given Roberta Bondi a ride to the airport on the way to the conference. "The first words she said to me when she got into my car were, 'This is a depressing paper that you've written.' I thought then that her comment was susceptible to multiple interpretations.

"When I was given this assignment," Holifield went on, "I became immediately aware of the danger of nostalgia. The assumption is that they in the nineteenth century once had 'it' — that is, knew how to do moral formation — and we in the twentieth century have lost it and need to regain it. My paper does not, however, suffer from the problem of nostalgia."

Admitting that he doesn't dislike the ideal of the gentleman, Holifield continued, "I think we're struggling with precisely the same set of Christ-culture issues that nineteenth-century American Protestantism struggled with. Later generations of historians will be able to see that with far greater clarity than we do. Moral formation always entails working out some kind of combination of inherited values and affirmations of the Christian tradition with contemporary cultural forms."

Dr. Holifield drew his introductory remarks to a close by noting that those who live in the last decades of the twentieth century "have been given a critical sensibility. However, we suffer from an overweening confidence in our own self-critical capacity, and it may be that later generations of historians will look back and say, 'They thought they were so self-critical. But in fact they were merely buying into a set of cultural traditions of which they were only dimly aware.'"

The first conferee to respond to Holifield was Stanley Hauerwas. "I am obviously from the lower classes and have been pulled into a middle-class church which assumes that education leads to upward mobility," Hauerwas commented. "So I've always felt a certain oppressiveness on university ground because I've recognized that I don't have the requisite manners."

"But you've been working on them," Neuhaus nudged.

Undeterred, Hauerwas went on to make his point: "The ministry, obviously, doesn't occur in a timeless way. There are peculiar challenges that it faces at different times. At least the American Protestant clergy and seminaries in the nineteenth century were struggling with the peculiar challenges facing the people who were going to be sustaining the ministry in that cultural framework."

If American clergy faced up to demanding challenges in the nineteenth century, Professor Hauerwas continued, today "they're being nibbled away by ducks, so to speak. Today the assumption is that ministers are generally there to be helpful. So someone asks the minister to do this, and someone else asks the minister to do that, and before long the minister is missing an arm or a leg because the people have asked too much.

"What the nineteenth century was trying to do was to underwrite what it meant to be a gentleman. That included a sense of integrity regarding oneself, which meant that a minister knew how to say no. He also knew how to be insulted about the right things. Likewise, today we must train ministers to have a certain value in themselves that will issue in the kind of constancy and competency which was associated with what it meant to be a gentleman."

Here Glenn Miller put in a very strong word on behalf of the gentleman minister. "It took a great deal of courage to stand for gentlemanly values in the face of the militant, agrarian capitalism of America in the nineteenth century," he pointed out. "And it took a great deal of courage to stand for manners in a society that was unmannered. Back then, America wasn't the envy of the world. It was a land of yellow fever. It was a land of poverty, a poverty that drove people to move vast distances. Much of the nation was enslaved. People regularly lost their property and their land on the frontier. In that kind of rough, agrarian, early capitalist society — where getting-what-I-can-get-for-me was the real American virtue, and where liberty meant I-can-get-it-all — to stand for culture, for the best in literature, for the classics, for good music, for manners, and for a sense of decorum was a matter of courage. It was making a bet that the New World could be more than just an economic grab bag."

"To be a gentleman was to be heroic," inserted Neuhaus.

"Yes," Miller elaborated, "to dare to say that how you treat people counts more than the value you can get from people, to preserve the classics and the beauty of ancient literature by devoting your life to it — that was heroic! To stand at a seminary and convey to young men the importance of preserving the best of one's ancestors and of learning Latin, Greek, and good theology was to stand for nobility. It wasn't just a matter of social class. It was an attempt to make a statement which said that America could be more than laissez-faire economics."

Then Neuhaus, turning to Holifield, commented, "Brooks, your paper — whether you intended it to or not — does tend to debunk a certain style of moral formation in a certain sector of American Protestantism in the last couple of centuries. Glenn's point seems to be that that style of formation shouldn't be debunked, that it was marked by a seriousness of discipleship in its commitment to gentility in a very ungentle world."

"But was it a seriousness of *Christian* discipleship?" Richard Hays asked. "*That* is the question that Brooks is pressing. That involves a major distinction. In the same vein we need to address Roberta's earlier question about precisely which virtues we're seeking to inculcate in this formation that we're talking about. In order to give a substantive answer to that, I don't think we'd talk about how to ride a horse or how to lay bricks or how to use the military discipline of West Point. I think the place to look to find an answer to that question is in Scripture."

"But yours is just the bias of a New Testament scholar," Neuhaus joked, though with a purpose.

"But the New Testament hasn't played that much of a role in our discussion," Hays answered, "and I find that disturbing. We wring our hands and say, 'Oh, we don't know what stories form our life together.' Well, what the heck is the Bible supposed to be if not the source of the stories that form our life together? Now that doesn't solve all of our problems by any means. Because the more closely we read the New Testament, the more we see the same problem of cultural accommodation in the early Christian community that wrote those texts."

Refocusing the conversation on modern times was historian George Marsden. He reported what he'd discovered while working on the history of Fuller Theological Seminary. "I found that during the 1940s and 1950s, the gentlemanly ideal was something Fuller pushed. It tried to get its students to wear coats and ties. It had teas for the wives. It tried to teach the students manners, though basically that was a losing battle. But the ideal was still there." Still, teaching young men to be gentlemen wasn't central to Fuller's purpose. The inculcation of piety, said Marsden, which included prayer groups, daily worship, and theological-ethical conversation, always came first.

"In evangelical culture — both then and now — you're dealing with people who have a strong spiritual idealism," Marsden continued. "That can be taken for granted. I had a sense of that when I taught at Trinity Evangelical Divinity School for a year. People were converts there. They were dedicated. They were starting up prayer groups in which spiritual formation would be taken for granted. That's probably what was going on in the nineteenth-century seminaries too. So it might be something of a distraction to get off on the code of being a gentleman."

"It's difficult to get at the specific instances of nineteenth-century piety in the seminaries because it was taken so much for granted that they didn't even describe it for us," Holifield commented. "Generally we know what prayer meetings were like, but we don't know in any detail what the early prayer meetings at Andover, for example, were like."

Neuhaus thought it a good time to tell the story about the

British gentleman who was asked what his religious beliefs were. "He said, 'I believe what all gentlemen believe.' Then he was asked, 'And what is it that they believe, sir?' And he replied, 'Gentlemen do not say.' "

After the laughter had diminished, Russell Richey posed a question. "Were there any alternatives to the gentleman model that the seminaries of the nineteenth century could have pursued? In other words, was it thinkable for the seminaries to offer a viable model other than the gentleman for Christian formation? The answer is 'Probably not,' though in the nineteenth century there were lots of other models of Christian morality around.

"One of the historical ironies — and this is a depressing one — is to find Methodists and Baptists buying into the gentleman model. One of the important alternatives to genteel morality, particularly in the early nineteenth century — and this is well documented — was a morality that was explicitly defined over against gentility. The Baptists and Methodists in the Middle Colonies and in the South actually used gentility as the image of Satan. The reason that their coming to terms with gentility is ironic, tragic, and sad is that this development was related to their coming to terms with slavery. These denominations sacrificed their anti-slavery witness out of their sense of mission to the gentry and their sense of the gentry's importance as an access to slaves.

"So there are all kinds of complicated questions of priority. Does character have more value than witness? The Methodists and Baptists said, 'No. In the interest of saving the slaves' souls, we will live according to the canons of gentility.' That decision was, I think, a tragic one. The Quakers chose the other route. This raises a significant issue: whether a church wants to witness through character or through acceptance of the world's terms. So we have to ask what our priorities are. And to what extent do we, in focusing on character, make it a priority over other things — for example, the external missions of the church — that have legitimate claims?"

"Certainly there were models other than the gentility model in the nineteenth century," Holifield responded. "For example, as Professor Richey suggested, the Primitive Baptists represented very explicitly and often articulately another model that was directed precisely against the model of gentility. That, of course, didn't mean that the Primitive Baptists were free from their own cultural traditions. They were representing culture, frontier or rural. In the long run I'd have to say that I'm happy that the model of the gentleman won the seminaries. Otherwise, there wouldn't be many jobs for us."

"And we wouldn't be us," James Fowler kidded.

Before the conferees pursued another topic, James Burtchaell asserted that gentlemanly class status doesn't necessarily correlate with wealth. "Social class isn't always an economic matter," he explained. "For example, anyone who's an authority for a significant number of poor people is no longer in the lower class, no matter what his or her financial situation is. If someone can deliver for a lot of people, then he or she can deal with people of every class. Lech Walesa is still getting an electrician's wage, but he's still above the lower class as far as influence and social-economic-political clout are concerned. Other examples are Cesar Chavez and Mother Teresa. Each of Mother Teresa's sisters has in her possession two saris and one bucket to wash the saris in. When her sisters are transferred, the time required for departure is measured in minutes. That's done intentionally. And then there's Ralph Nader, who is said to lead a life of stoic frugality."

Employing Rowan Greer's description of a patron, Burtchaell said, "What I'm driving at is this: Isn't the patron of the poor obligated to remain at least symbolically poor? At the same time, the patron has to know how to sit across the table from very powerful and affluent people. In that circumstance a patron can't pick his nose because the welfare of many depends on his representation of them. The test of holiness for one who is a patron of the poor, the dispossessed, or the oppressed has to be that the patron is classless but doesn't use his classlessness to his advantage. So seminaries can't simply ask their students to adopt manners that will allow them to move freely across class lines; seminaries also have to attach warnings to the manners. These warnings would include the clear caution not to become a fop. A patron has to discipline himself not to ride the back of his patronage to self-aggrandizement. But the patron also has to be classless and have the manners that will carry him anywhere.

"This requires self-discipline. In the Roman Catholic tradition this discipline is implemented very easily. For example, every priest who is in a religious order has no salary. All of the diocesan clergy, regardless of congregation size, get a standard salary, which is basically less than anybody in the parish makes. The clergy wear those basic clothes, no matter where they go. And they go to a seminary that was always frugal. Priests learn to despise the pastors who found ways to get Cadillacs, though sometimes those pastors are pretty good patrons. But I'll say it again: the patron has to have solidarity with the people he loves, represents, and provides for, and at the same time he has to be accessible to everyone."

"Let's name that 'radical availability,'" commented Neuhaus. "Jim, you say you're not making a case for celibacy. But you're talking about a disciplined dispossession that makes one available to others. In theological education today, we must ask and answer this question: Are people being shaped to be radically available for the sake of the church?"

Holiness and Culture

As Brooks Holifield had noted in his introductory comments, the Christian tradition always finds visible expression in cultural forms. Christa Klein agreed, commenting, "Christian holiness finally has to take on the characteristics of its host culture in some way. Church historians could also tell us about how the forms of piety draw from the available culture. Earlier Glenn Miller was talking about the beginning of American-Victorian society, in which there really wasn't a well-established middle class. During that period, advising the minister not to spit while making a pastoral call was a very nice way of making the point that pastors should be gentlemanly. But then, as the Victorian era moved along, corruptions and self-serving middle-class behavior began to develop."

Klein then gave several examples. "At one time in American history, 'muscular Christianity' was an attempt to make Christian virtue attractive to men in a society that was defining virility in a certain way. It was an attempt to sell the faith. Here we're talking about Teddy Roosevelt. We're talking about 'the real man.' This was really an importation of the Anglophilia, the love of British culture, of that age.

"There were also Catholic versions of muscular Christianity. The Jesuits provide an example. One can see why baseball came to St. John's College (now Fordham). It gave the priests a way to relate to the boys. It made religious education far more attractive and created a special form of piety. During Holy Week the students basically alternated between the chapel and the baseball field. After all, during that week they couldn't read library books, and they couldn't receive outside mail, but baseball was allowed. Military drill was another attractive way of presenting Christianity. There were military masses at which everyone unsheathed his sword during the consecration. Again, there are always these cultural forms of holiness. They're always corruptible, but I don't see any easy way around them."

George Lindbeck, focusing on communal practice, was the next conferee to take on the Christ-culture problem. "Throughout history," Lindbeck claimed, "all serious Christian communities, from New Testament times on, have taken the Ten Commandments very seriously. They did in the China in which I grew up. They faced the old questions: What does it mean not to have any gods before God? What does it mean to not take the name of the Lord your God in vain? Also, what does it mean to honor the Sabbath day and to keep it holy? And so on for the second table. All of these things were endlessly talked about in sermons I heard, in catechetical instruction, in family discussions. If one was a Lutheran in China when I was growing up, one memorized Luther's *Small Catechism*, which covers the meaning of the Ten Commandments. So an entire set of practices that were common to the whole Christian tradition were being reproduced in a Chinese situation and being given a Chinese slant. Nevertheless, these communal practices, which developed in China over two generations, would have been recognizable to third- and fourth-century Christians. In fact, the early church fathers would have felt comfortable in this Chinese-Christian situation, and the Chinese Christians would have felt comfortable in the third- or fourth-century setting. I can't prove this; I wish I could. But there seems to be enough common practice to make mutual recognition possible."

Then Lindbeck brought in the clerical ideal, which, he said, "should be understood on the basis of a set of practices, communal practices. The clerical ideal can't possibly be understood unless one remembers that community is needed first of all. In the community, all Christians are expected, to put it bluntly, to obey the Ten Commandments."

Next Brooks Holifield led the group on a historical tour tracing certain developments in American culture. "Several years ago," he began, "I read a book on the images of the hero in American popular journalism — especially the popular magazines. What struck me was the extent to which the images of the hero have paralleled the images of the minister in mainline Protestantism. In the late eighteenth century and early nineteenth century, the prevailing image of both the hero and the minister was that of the gentleman. In the late nineteenth century the heroes in American popular journalism were Vanderbilt, Carnegie, and the people who built the great industries. This corresponded in remarkable ways to the image of the minister as the prince of pulpit: he had a commanding force and the power to persuade great crowds. Once the entrepreneur fell into disgrace and became a robber baron, the popular magazines picked up the progressive reformer as the hero. And that paralleled precisely, of course, the emergence of the Social Gospel minister as the paradigm of virtue in the church. World War I helped to destroy the image of the progressive; it faded into the background. During the war the popular hero in American journalism was the manager of mass bureaucracies. That was the person who, in mobilizing the nation for war, could take bureaucracies and make them work. And that's when we began to get the literature on the minister as church manager."

According to Holifield, the image of the local congregation went through similar changes. "In the seventeenth and eighteenth centuries," he pointed out, "there was an image in American Protestantism of the magisterial congregation. That church was perceived to have public responsibilities. It was the place where public proclamations were posted and public announcements were made. In some instances voting rights were certified there. That in many ways corresponds remarkably to a seventeenth- and eighteenth-century conception of the minister as a public person, a person with genuine civic and social responsibilities having to do with the maintenance of order in the wider society. Due in part to the market and to disestablishment, in the early nineteenth century the image of the church changed to that of the devotional sanctuary. The church became a place for withdrawing for the worship of God, a place apart from the public responsibilities which were then assumed by the large, voluntary, benevolent societies. That corresponds again to the image of the minister as a gentleman who shepherds a congregation aspiring to a certain kind of gentility and who has clear devotional purposes in mind. In the late nineteenth century there was a new image of the congregation in America. It was typified by Henry Ward Beecher in his series of lectures on preaching at Yale in 1872. In those lectures his advice to the clergy was to have more picnics. One of the pastoral theologians of that time talked about a revolution in understanding the church, and he said the symbol for it was the church parlor. The image was that of the convivial congregation. Fellowship, the fellowship hall, and the church parlor became important components of what it meant to be the church."

"Brooks, what do you take to be the image of the congregation now?" Neuhaus asked.

"You can see it in the architecture of new church buildings," Holifield answered. "It's an image of participation. You see this in various forms of worship, in the lessening of space between the altar and the place where the congregation sits. This is related to fellowship, but it's more than that."

Neuhaus pursued the implications of that image. "If participation is the dominant paradigm, then students who think the highest ministerial virtues are kindness, niceness, and sensitivity are really very smart. Maybe they perceive exactly what is required of them by their congregations."

"They are indeed responding to a dominant demand in congregations," Holifield replied. "Congregations are asking for ministers who have the personality — the friendliness and the warmth — to create a sense of belonging in a church."

Holifield had been edging up to a concern that Russell Richey made explicit: If the church isn't vigilant, culture can end up controlling important aspects of church life. "For example," Richey said, "the United Methodist Church could benefit from having a different model of spirituality and spiritual formation brought into the ministry. The present model is so inherently capitalistic that it is, from my point of view, seriously flawed. Most United Methodist conferences work with an estimation of the spiritual value of ministry that is rendered in precise dollar amounts. That is, appointments are ranked from top to bottom according to pastors' salaries, and the lists are published for ministers to see. Although the average ministers don't see the rank orderings, some of their bishops and district superintendents do. Pastors are rewarded by movement up this monetary ladder."

"The United Methodist reward-and-recognition system comes as a shock to some people," Neuhaus commented. "It did to me. We Lutherans weren't even supposed to mention salary. After all, one's call was a call of the Holy Spirit, so there was a piety that surrounded the minister's relationship to the local church. The very notion of a promotion, of a career, was considered odious, though this too is breaking down within Lutheranism. At least the United Methodist way is candid and straightforward. And it hasn't resulted in Methodist clergy having less spiritual integrity than Lutherans. So perhaps it hasn't done much damage."

Hauerwas disagreed on the amount of damage done: "In the United Methodist system the clergy end up having a constituency of one — namely, the district superintendent. Our fundamental doctrine is this: God is nice, and we ought to be nice too. As long as the minister reinforces the niceness of the congregation and doesn't cause any difficulty — doesn't adopt a new form of liturgy, say — the minister will probably be rewarded in the system. The minister will move up."

"That's too simplistic," James Fowler rebutted, and Dennis Campbell agreed.

"The corruption of the United Methodist minister isn't inevitable," Fowler explained. "It can be overcome by people who are trained to live with contradictions and tensions."

"That's true," Hauerwas conceded. "But a United Methodist minister with integrity almost has to fight the system. We Methodists used to produce some real characters. That was good. You couldn't anticipate what they were going to do."

Next, from a Roman Catholic point of view, James Burtchaell spoke on behalf of the United Methodist minister concerned about his salary. "To read the ranking of ministers by salary and to have an economic understanding of promotion might come from a minister's marriage and family," Burtchaell said. "A minister might be married to someone who hasn't embraced ministry, perhaps not even faith, and might also have children who haven't embraced ministry and who need to be raised well. If so, stress comes into play. A very important part of the married minister's life is the provision of goods and services that are required by the family. I've seen many of our most ardently socially conscious students put aside their social-justice concerns when they marry and have children. They put aside their dedication to the poor and their desire to be carefree about their own possessions, especially if the wives and children aren't in a ministry mode."

Get in There

At this point Neuhaus observed that it might be useful "to put some flesh on what we mean by moral formation. That is, why are we concerned with theological education and moral formation? As this gathering indicates, we don't think the two are happening the way we think they ought to happen, and that's cause for anxiety. Then we have to ask about the areas in theological education in which moral formation doesn't seem to be happening. We've already mentioned a number of afflicted areas and problems: vocation and careerism; marriage and divorce; questions of honesty; self-realization and obedience; a sense of community and what undermines it — gossip, conflictual caucuses, interest groups; spiritual discipline, prayer and worship, and sloth; and the issues surrounding authority." Neuhaus was asking how holiness might be culturally embodied today.

Easier said than done, noted David Schuller. "We've become so careful about the particular cultures that we may be incorporating or incarnating in the life of the church and the life of the Christian that we're almost paralyzed," he pointed out. "For example, we don't want a Christ who is simply a gentleman farmer out in Virginia. We're so conscious of making similar mistakes at the present time that we're left without alternatives. Still, one way or another, we have to incarnate the gospel and Christian formation in some sort of cultural forms. So, at this point, I'll call on Martin Luther, who said, 'Sin boldly.' "

"Wherever you are. Whatever the context is," Neuhaus added.

"Yes," Schuller agreed, "we have to plunge in and test the implications of what a possible effort would mean. Set this experimental mode against what we often see our students going through — and that's what Allan Bloom calls commitment to noncommitment. Our students oftentimes never get past it. They can't say, 'I realize the relativity of the entire world and of particular cultural commitments and embodiments, but finally I've got to come down somewhere. I must identify with one part of the world or another.' "

Revolution, Women, and Careerism

To get the discussion going again after a brief break, Neuhaus paraphrased David Schuller's first comment during the conference. "In responding to Dennis Campbell's paper, Dave said, in effect, 'That's all very nice, but look at the actual, institutional-structural situation in theological education today. Now tell me, how is your proposal going to be implemented without a major revolution?' I hope we can get to wrestling with that question. Otherwise, we may be just indulging our sentiments in drawing up a wish list of what we think ought to happen in theological education today. And that has limited utility."

Russell Richey indicated that revolution might come through seminary students, as it often has in Protestant history. "Seminary students have generated movements that were later adopted by the churches," he explained. "This pattern began with mission societies generations back. It may be that that's okay. Seminaries can offer courses that have spiritual dimensions, and the faculty can do all that can be done along these lines. But it is the students who create their own communities; they're not under control. We worry about our 'magisterium,' and how these groups are subversive of it. But maybe that's okay. These groups are generated out of the spirit of Protestantism, and the spiritual directions for the future may well come from them."

"Russell has to tell me that every morning so that I can make it through the day," Campbell joked. But Christa Klein worried that such renewal groups were too often disconnected from the teaching authority of the church and thus were just another form of religious privatization.

The revolution that Roberta Bondi had in mind had to do with women in ministry. "There are special problems in the ministerial training of women that we haven't discussed," she pointed out, "and I do wish we had more women around this table. It isn't irrelevant that one of the basic models of ministry in twentieth-century America is that of the *gentleman* theologian."

At this point Dennis Campbell asked Bondi, "Do you really think that in theological education there's a difference between moral formation for men and moral formation for women?"

Bondi answered, "My area of research is early monasticism. One of the things that makes me very sad is how little there is in scholarly literature on women's monasticism, despite the clear evidence that there were plenty of women monastics. One of the things that I've speculated on is whether the same virtues that were important to the male monastics were important to the female monastics and whether those virtues looked the same when they were lived out. For example, humility is a central virtue to fourth- and fifth-century monasticism, and my guess is that humility had a different character for men than it had for women. The way things are today may shed some light here. Men are constantly being told to cool it, to cut it down, not to dominate, whereas women need to assert themselves. So I suspect that the virtue of humility in the fourth century looked different from men's perspective and women's perspective."

Interjecting a more sociological note, Neuhaus commented, "It is self-evident that one of the most massive changes in theological education over the last twenty years has been the enormous increase in the number of women enrolled in seminary. Like every other historical change, this one is filled with ambiguity; it is uncertain what the consequences will be. This development will have to be reflected upon very carefully by everyone who is concerned about theological education, because the sharp rise in women's enrollments in seminaries isn't just a women's issue."

This prompted George Lindbeck to speak autobiographically. He recalled that the person who first exposed him to the ideal of the gentleman minister was a woman at Saint Adolphonsus College. "She earned her doctorate in mathematics at the University of Paris. Thirty years later this woman, who definitely had had a Christian conversion experience of some kind but who remained a very cultivated woman of the world, took it upon herself to turn into gentlemen those raw farmboys who were headed for the ministry. That meant, of course, that they had to have a knowledge of and appreciation for the classics of the Western world. She was a professor of mathematics, and a very good one, so she had enough leverage to gather groups together for literary discussion and for instruction in manners. This was an astonishing sort of thing, but she was utterly committed to it. She was a gentlewoman — of great force. The gender question," Lindbeck concluded, "strikes me as secondary."

Hauerwas followed up on Bondi's concern by noting, "There are different kinds of virtues that warrant concern in seminaries, according to the challenges of the day. For example, for women, justice is an important virtue today. That is, you're unjust if you fail to claim an honor that is due you — that's the worst injustice you can do. Democratic tolerance teaches the virtue of false humility in a way that destroys people."

Inserting a nineteenth-century perspective was Brooks Holifield, "In my paper I should have included a reference to Samuel Miller's *Letters on Clerical Manners and Habits*. It suggests some of the complications and ambiguities of the relationship between the sexes in the context of clerical formation. In his lectures at Princeton, Miller told ministers that they were to be especially careful with women in their churches because women held the balance of power. He also said that if ministers were going to be successful in the church, they had to be successful with the women. This is interesting commentary. If Miller was right, then the language of oppression that we often use today in discussing the sexes is probably a misleading language. After all, there were ways for women to exercise power in the church that we haven't discerned and begun to explore."

Hauerwas then expressed a more general concern about the direction of the conversation. "You've all been sucked into the language of character and virtue," he said. "But that isn't scriptural. Why aren't we talking more in the language of discipleship, in the language of witness? It may well be that the very fact that we're using the language of virtue is in itself an indication that something has gone wrong in the seminaries."

In a not-so-subtle reference to the prior speaker, Neuhaus responded, "There are notable teachers of ethics — not to mention any names — who have had a lot to do with getting the church to talk virtue and character in recent years. Are you recanting here, Stan? What are we witnessing here?"

Changing the set of issues under consideration, Roberta Bondi brought up a problem for United Methodist clergy. "Spirituality has become making it in the organization," she said bluntly. "Therefore, unfortunately, we in the seminaries don't talk much about internal resources or about the way ministry is related to growth in the love and knowledge of God."

So Neuhaus challenged the conferees. "What are the alternatives in theological schools today for students who want radically to throw their lives away for Jesus, quite apart from career pattern and upward mobility and so forth?"

The ordination track isn't the natural track for the pursuit of radical Christian discipleship, said Philip Turner. "In my church there's a system by which students are cleared for ministry," he explained. "Our students are terrified that they could be washed out of the system at any point for reasons that they don't know or understand. So they tend to be terribly cautious. And the one thing that Episcopalians — at least in my generation — fear more than anything in the world is any form of enthusiasm. My colleagues on the faculty are, on the whole, not concerned with immorality. But they are concerned with, and on the lookout for, enthusiasm — they really are. That stands in marked contrast with the traditional vision which says that seminary faculties are preparing their students to lead a community that has been entrusted with 'the life.' It's the job of faculty, seminarians, ministers, and the laity to live it and to be stewards of it."

"Philip," Neuhaus asked, "are you saying that it's unrealistic to expect that of seminaries and seminarians today?"

"I wouldn't use the word 'unrealistic,'" answered Turner. "But I would say that careerism is an enormous power that exerts pressure on seminaries and seminarians today."

Rowan Greer then pointed to a development that cuts against careerism and that might be reason for a modicum of hope. "One of the peculiar things that has happened at Yale since Berkeley, the old Episcopal school, joined up has to do with worship. When the merger first took place, there was absolutely no worship at all. Now, ten or fifteen years later, there is an old-fashioned, quasi-monastic routine: worship takes place every morning at 7:30 and every evening at 5:15. On any given morning there are never fewer than twenty-five people worshiping and often as many as forty, and on any Wednesday night there are often 150 people. It's the same thing over and over again: it's only the community telling the story. This worship has no purpose other than that. I don't think it's a way for the students to fulfill themselves. I don't think it's a way for them to have a support group." It is much more than that, Greer was suggesting.

The New Testament and the Churches

Now Philip Turner refocused the conversation on Brooks Holifield's theme, the gentleman minister. "The role of the gentleman had to do with more than etiquette," said Turner, "because the gentleman had a recognized social position to which bankers might aspire."

Holifield agreed and added, "Ministers, like others, were

explicitly aware of that. A gentleman's manners gave a minister access to people of influence and power."

"Which was part of the minister's mission," Neuhaus noted. "I mean, it wasn't something sleazy, a way for the minister to grasp for personal power. It was the minister's responsibility to influence the banker and the greater society."

"But do you influence that sector of society by mimicking it? That's the question," challenged Richard Hays.

Neuhaus came back with another question. "But how do you disentangle these various factors in a particular context where the minister is to be in mission? Undoubtedly the minister is influenced by his context and role. That is riddled with ambiguity from beginning to end, but the minister nonetheless is set to pursue a course of obedience."

Recalling that Turner had earlier mentioned the New Testament connections between marriage, household, and ministry, Neuhaus wondered, "Is that simply irretrievable today? Perhaps that particular New Testament transference can no longer happen. In most of the Protestant churches in America, the reality of disorderly households, of divorce and remarriage and remarriage, has in the last twenty years become pervasive. In Lutheran churches of, say, thirty years ago, a divorced minister, even if an innocent party in the divorce, was excluded from public ministry. Over the last twenty years, however, the proportion of divorced and remarried clergy in the Evangelical Lutheran Church in America is about equal to the proportion in the general society. Now nobody — no resolutionary body, no task force — has decided that the marital standard for clergy is no longer applicable. That just happened. Divorce and remarriage are now so entrenched among the ministers of the church that it would take a revolution just to raise the matter for discussion in the church — never mind trying to adopt some kind of disciplinary procedure for dealing with it. So it just may be that some clear New Testament indicators are no longer available to us — because of serendipitous, willy-nilly doctrinal developments, or because of an act of apostasy, or maybe a little bit of both."

Undeterred by Neuhaus' musings, Turner went to the New Testament again for instruction on the church and the ministry. "As I read the New Testament," he said, "I discover that the Christians for whom those books were written understood themselves as having been shown *the* way of life and as having been gifted with that life. So they understood themselves to be stewards of that mystery. They had to take care of it for themselves and for each other. Hence ministry was not so much a matter of doing good things in society as it was a matter of upbuilding the body in which the new life was known, lived, and made known. Ministry in the New Testament, in its many forms, was understood in terms of this new way of life. And many virtues went along with that. Ministers had to be zealous for the flock. They had to keep the wolves away, and the wolves weren't outside the congregation — they were inside the congregation. Ministers had to be judicious."

Then Turner looked at the Episcopal Church today: "Within my own church there are very few congregations that understand themselves in the New Testament way. As a result, most of my students have two models for ministry, which are related to the views that congregations have of themselves. (This is, admittedly, an oversimplification, and many ministers follow both models at the same time.) The first model is based on the premise that the congregation and the ministry exist to further particular causes within society which aim to achieve justice. The second model is based on the premise that the congregation and the ministry exist to be helpful to people in one way or another. Hence the models for ministry are those of manager and therapist, the main characters of our era, according to Alasdair MacIntyre."

"But Phil," objected Neuhaus, "you have a lot of students who graduate with a deeply internalized conviction that their business is to proclaim the gospel."

"But sooner or later," Turner responded, "they're swallowed up by these other models. The power of these social images is enormous. So whether you like it or not, sooner or later seminary graduates begin to pursue a 'career.' The career emphasizes one or another or both of the dominant models of ministry. On this path, clergy reach a certain point on the ladder of their careers and can't rise any higher; then they die. Their models set them up for this." They die spiritually, sometimes physically. The point, suggested Turner, is that "few ministers have a model of ministry that helps them to lead congregations deeper into the life of God in Christ. A minister can't exhaust that."

At this juncture Will Willimon commented from the perspective of church history. "It's dangerous to think about ministry before thinking about the church," he warned. "We make some of our biggest mistakes when we launch out talking about the special characteristics of ordained individuals without first discussing what needs to happen in the church. To me, ordination is comprehensible only as a function of the church. I guess I have a kind of low Lutheran theology of ordination. Luther talks about ministry in a functional, practical way. I like that. H. Richard Niebuhr, in *The Purpose of the Church and Its Ministry*, makes the point that without a clear notion of church we're never going to make any sense of why the church needs leaders.

"When you raise the issue of spirituality," Willimon continued, "who do clergy say that they read and like? They mention Henri Nouwen or Thomas Merton. This seems dangerous to me because these two authors are coming at parish clergy with a kind of monastic model of spirituality.

"In the earlier days of Methodism, there was a real attempt to form a peculiar people on the basis of what needed to happen to spread scriptural holiness across the land. Methodist leaders needed to know a few things relentlessly well, and they needed to be detached from other commitments. But today, in this society, what virtues are required to visit an eighty-year-old woman in a nursing home and have prayer with her? What virtues are required to prepare a sermon? What sort of virtues are required for one to invest one's life in doing something that often doesn't do any measurable good?"

Noting that it is especially important for the clergy to teach their flocks "a new language," Willimon illustrated his point: "Last summer an associate pastor on Long Island told me that he came into the ministry to help people adjust to their life situations. But his people on Long Island described their lives as if they were in constant combat. And I said, 'You mean like Ephesians 6?' And he said, 'Right. Until recently I didn't think of myself as someone equipping people for a struggle.

After all, I'm a Presbyterian, and Presbyterians don't struggle. We own the bank. But when I talk to the vice president of the bank and he describes his family life, it's as if he's in combat. So I've had to become a different kind of preacher because of the stuff that my people are going through.' It sounds to me like that congregation was on the way."

"Related to your learning-the-language school is the enormous popularity of expository preaching," Neuhaus added. "I think it's coming back. Despite all the years of trying to make the preached word relevant, people are saying, 'To hell with that. We want to hear what the Bible says.' People love a minister who can get up in the pulpit, take a text, and illuminate all aspects of it."

George Lindbeck then disagreed with Willimon's church-to-ministry line of argument. "There's no possibility of specifying the purpose of the family or any real community," Lindbeck reasoned. "Likewise, there are many different purposes of the household of God. The household of God is supposed to live as the body of Christ, but in different contexts the household has different purposes. The one thing you can always say about the household of God is that it worships together."

Geoffrey Wainwright had a different slant on the church-ministry issue. "As Paul — or whoever wrote to the Ephesians — says, 'Be imitators of me as I am of Christ.' That comes to be very important, because the baptismal character of the whole church is to be brought into conformity with Christ. The special character of the ordained ministry is not opposed to that in any way. It is seen as ministerial to the task of bringing the whole church into conformity with Christ.

"How do we do that? Principally by becoming familiar with Christ. And we become familiar with Christ primarily through the Scriptures, and the Scriptures as read and mediated in the public worship of the church. I try to hammer home to M.Div. students throughout their time at Duke that the most important thing that they can do while they're in divinity school is to become truly acquainted with the Scriptures. That is, they should hear, read, mark, learn, and inwardly digest the Scriptures as the primary locus for encountering Christ within the gathered community of the worshiping assembly."

"I thoroughly agree," said Richard Hays. "And by the way, Geoffrey, you can ascribe your quotation more confidently to Paul, because it also appears in 1 Corinthians 11. It does seem that the model of learning, understanding, and in turn teaching Scripture is really fundamental in the spiritual-moral formation of the minister. And here I'm not talking about going out and teaching the source theories of the Pentateuch."

Professor Donald Kortright Davis of Howard Divinity School concluded the session by asserting that "the discussion we've been engaging in up to now has been very homogeneous, to say the least. As a person who comes from a different cultural background, I can't help noticing the omission of some factors in the debate that surely cannot be omitted. First, there's a cultural captivity that seems to run throughout most of what we've been saying here. Roberta has spoken on behalf of women and their concerns, and that's instructive. But concerns about character formation and moral formation need to pay attention to the possibility that this enterprise needs to be liberated from a kind of cultural captivity. Second, there's not only a clash of ideologies going on here; there's also a clash of theologies. This isn't just pluralism; there's a real theological clash here. Third, there's a kind of ambivalence toward the foundation of Scripture. I'm not sure of the extent to which we've been taking the scriptural challenges seriously. We need to know exactly what the New Testament says about the church and the task of the church. Fourth, the mission of the church has been a very grave lacuna in this discussion. Mission isn't an option, an 'extra' in this conversation — it's something central to the Christian church. Formation for mission has to do with the mood of the age (that is, with what's happening outside the church) and with what's happening in the growth and development of Christian witness. The point about mission is that movement is involved, and wherever there's movement, there's a set of moral principles and attitudes that tends to shape and reshape how we view life and circumstances. And fifth, at this juncture — at the end of the twentieth century and the threshold of the twenty-first century — we're dealing with a situation in which some Christians aren't sure that Christianity is under siege. They're going to church, but they're not sure what's happening. They're living at the center of contradiction, whether they realize it or not."

THEOLOGICAL EDUCATION: THE CATHOLIC CASE

The fourth presenter of the conference was Father John O'Malley, who teaches at the Weston School of Theology. "My own field is what some of you would call a contradiction in terms," he began. "I call it the religious culture of the Italian Renaissance. Academically speaking, I really come to a dead end about 1527 with the sack of Rome. So I'm not really sure how I got dragged into this conference."

After the amusement had ceased, O'Malley continued, "There is in the Roman Catholic Church — because of a decision that has been made or because of the ratification of a situation — apparatus for spiritual formation. That is now unquestioned and, I think, unquestionable. I refer to that apparatus sometimes as 'the formation industries.' The formation industries assume, and even consume, the other seminary industries. It's quite impressive.

"The way the apparatus is in place today presupposes a degree of emotional maturity on the part of the student that isn't always present. This leads to problems in spiritual direction in seminary. The formation apparatus also presupposes a kind of confessional identity that isn't always present. Sometimes Catholic seminary students don't come out of solidly Catholic families like they did twenty or thirty years ago. So there's the problem of privatized spirituality, which is the inability to make a correlation between one's own life with God and public ministry."

Moving on, O'Malley reminded the conferees of his church's Thomistic understanding of nature and grace. "Although I like it myself," he said, "once it begins to work its way into formation issues, it creates a bias toward the church's adaptation to culture. There's a lot of rhetoric about the cost of discipleship in the church, yet there's a lot of continuity between the church and the world in which we live. In other words, the prophetic in Catholicism gets lost quite easily.

"In the Roman Catholic tradition, the theology of ministry and the theology of priesthood aren't well developed at all. The first official and elaborate teaching on the priesthood was as late as Vatican II. It produced three documents — the documents on priesthood formation, on the life and ministry of the priest, and on the bishops — in which a great deal is said about what priesthood is. This is the first time in Catholic tradition that the priesthood is defined in some detail. Despite all of the advantages that magisterial statement brings with it, it tends to be very general. The priesthood is almost always being defined magisterially in terms of parish ministry — that is, preaching the gospel and administering the sacraments. Yet 40 percent of the priests don't define their ministry in those terms. They have more specific missions and objectives. For example, the Jesuits can do almost anything *except* parish ministry. For another example, the religious orders not only targeted specific missions but also attempted an imitation of Christ. But the imitation of Christ is too full a reality for any one person or group to undertake alone."

Drawing his introductory remarks to a close, O'Malley noted, "You could say that Roman Catholicism has a managed model of formation."

Who's Going to Seminary?

Neuhaus was the first to engage O'Malley, and he did so by bringing up a rather delicate issue. "It is frequently said that the quality of students at Roman Catholic and other seminaries has declined dramatically in recent decades. I'm assuming that 'quality' is measured by academic transcript, by psychological evaluation, and by more religious tests. A friend of mine, who taught for twelve years at a Roman Catholic university that also has a seminary attached to it, said that the brightest seminarians in class were below the median of the university students. The seminary students were simply inferior students and not very impressive human beings. That's something we may have to be candid about. Because seminaries aren't getting quality material to begin with, moral formation and a lot of other things might be in deep trouble.

"The military metaphor was once important in training

for ministry," Neuhaus reminded the conferees. "That is, of course, very important in the Jesuit tradition, but not there alone. It also has strong New Testament roots. The military metaphor has a strong sense of mission. There is something to be done — that is the mission — and there are people deployed in order to carry out the mission. Obviously, the military metaphor engages, among other things, the question of authority. That's profoundly countercultural today. But in fact I kind of like the military metaphor."

"You love it," Stanley Hauerwas joked.

"That's true, but I don't want anybody to give me orders," Neuhaus replied in jest. Then he continued in a more serious vein: "Even in a non-hierarchical situation, there can be authority to which people can be called. So nobody is just a lone operator, conducting his or her own mission. In theory at least, the Scriptures and the confessions can be cited in the midst of a conversation as authoritative texts, and everybody has to sit up and take notice. But in my church today that isn't the case. If you're in a debate in American Lutheranism today — and I know this is true in United Methodism as well — you can cite an authoritative text, but it's taken as simply another interesting contribution. The response is 'Thank you. And now we'll move on to somebody else's opinion.'

"This ties into the question of mission. Is there now a deployment of well-equipped people from seminaries to fulfill the mission? The answer is no, even in Roman Catholicism, according to John O'Malley's paper. If anybody has any illusions that we're going to learn about formation from the Roman Catholic tradition, John's paper is a very disappointing paper indeed."

Part of this problem might be the anti-intellectualism that tends to plague Roman Catholicism, suggested O'Malley. "One of the extremely disheartening features of anti-intellectualism among Roman Catholics," O'Malley observed, "is that it seems to get quasi-official support. Take, for example, the canonization of the Curé d'Ars (Jean-Baptiste-Marie Vianney). What do you know about the Curé d'Ars? He was a good priest, but he didn't know any theology. That says a lot. And yet he's the patron of the diocesan clergy."

Another factor in the insufficient equipping of Catholic priests for parish ministry is the sea change that recently set in at Catholic seminaries. Robert Leavitt, who attended seminary in the late 1950s and early 1960s, argued, "During that time, Roman Catholic seminaries were transformed by the emphasis on biblical renewal. Biblical renewal supplanted Thomistic theology as the primary subject. People said you had to know the Bible to preach, so preaching and the Bible became the primary subjects. Teaching isn't so much emphasized in Catholic parish ministry. Catholic priests today don't think of themselves as teachers. Churches will simply hire a director of religious education to do the teaching.

"Pastoral theology became fashionable at the same time. All of a sudden it was decided that priests spent too long a time training in the seminary. They were there for twelve years. They were 'lifers,' since they started seminary training when they were about thirteen and finished when they were twenty-five or twenty-six. It was decided that the priests needed to get into the parish, that they needed to be introduced to the people they were going to be serving. They needed to get out of the seminary, out of this total institution.

"With that, of course, the total institution collapses. We don't have individuals coming in at thirteen any longer. Instead, we have older individuals who have had a great deal of life experience. They enroll in seminary and are sent out to get these little pastoral anecdotes that don't add up to a hill of beans. So we have lots of Catholic seminarians getting pastoral training, but there isn't much educational substance underneath that. I think that the pope and Cardinal Ratzinger are for eliminating this kind of pastoral effort. After all, a seminarian can't really accomplish that much in a semester in a little side sortie in the parish."

Next Leavitt half-jokingly described the traditional model of the Catholic seminarian coming out of the ethnic world as "a sort of Irish jock who wanted to say mass." That lasted, he said, until the 1960s. Since then, some rather dramatic changes have occurred. Leavitt used a personal recollection to illustrate. "A couple of students who resembled the old Irish-jock priest came to the seminary this fall. They looked around and said,

'The guys here seem very soft.' Likewise, people come out of the push-and-shove business world and into the seminary and say, 'Seminary people look soft.' It's as if the ecclesial world is softer, with rounder edges."

"In your informed opinion, is there more homosexuality in Catholic seminaries today, or is it simply being handled differently today?" Neuhaus asked.

"My feeling is that there is more," Leavitt said. "The number of heterosexual seminarians fell when fewer became willing to submit to the requirement of celibacy. Also, homosexual priests recruit homosexual seminarians. Everybody knows that church discipline is changed through power. If you can get more people on your team, you stand a chance of getting the discipline changed in your favor. If you're upset about church discipline regarding homosexuality, the best thing to do is to get more homosexuals into the ministry. I know that sounds like Joe McCarthy. But it's the fact of the matter."

On the issue of anti-intellectualism, Stanley Hauerwas spoke frankly. "I've never met a deeper anti-intellectualism than I meet in Roman Catholic seminarians who are concerned with spirituality. It's overwhelming. That's because many of the people in the Catholic ministry aren't very bright. They just don't have the basic intellectual stuff to do it. But I also think that Protestant seminaries today are beset by anti-intellectualism. There it primarily takes the form of various liberationisms. Feminists and people who get on the liberationist bandwagon are deeply anti-intellectual. But then we must ask, Where did we get the idea that intellectual life was so integral to the ministry?"

The next conferee to contribute to the discussion of the who's-going-to-seminary question was Philip Turner. Turner was more interested in students' religious backgrounds than in their intellectual caliber. "Many of my students are refugees from punishing religions," he explained. "Once you move from the aesthetic realm, they get very nervous. That makes them think of authoritarianism, dogmatism, and other punitive things from days past. It's hard for me, as a member of the faculty, even to raise the concerns of morality and authority with them."

"Are they really refugees from punishing religions? Or have they been taught by their churches and by their schools of theology the alleged dangers of these 'punishing religions'?" Neuhaus inquired.

"Most of my students are not former Episcopalians," Turner answered.

"Are they frequently former fundamentalists?" Neuhaus asked.

"Yes," Turner responded.

"That's extraordinary," said Geoffrey Wainwright. "My impression of the Episcopal Church in this country is that, frankly speaking, it's turning into a bunch of aesthetes."

"Yes, I call us the church aesthetic," agreed Turner.

Neuhaus pushed the group on this point: "What kind of punishing religion are we talking about? Unless it's in some kind of rigorous fundamentalism or very traditionalist Roman Catholicism, where in American religion today are people being socialized into a fearfully dogmatic, authoritarian, oppressive worldview?"

"It's possible to have an allergy to punishing religion," George Lindbeck asserted. "If one has this allergy, one forbids any talk of authority. Many of my students have it. So when I talk about authority, I never use the word. But this sensitivity doesn't mean that my students were exposed to punishing religion. This allergy is just part of the culture, which instructs one to be kind and permissive and to try to make everyone happy."

"This allergy is also part of the ecclesiastical culture," Neuhaus added. "It has a powerful myth of punishing religion. This myth has been internalized by the church culture and by the general culture as the great danger that must be avoided."

If many students at Yale have an allergy to punishing religion, they don't have an allergy to confessional teaching. Or so said Richard Hays: "When I simply stand up in class and make a confessional statement, I'm practically swamped after class by students coming up and shaking my hand and saying, 'Thank you for saying that.' Even if it makes students nervous to talk about authority, they have an enormous hunger for theological teachers who will give some definition to the faith."

Lindbeck said that the reason students affirm confessional teaching is that they don't perceive it as an act of authority.

"I've had the same experience as Richard," said Rowan Greer. "But I'm suspicious of that, because there's the risk that you end up talking only to like-minded people. What moves me more deeply is someone who will come in and say, 'You said that it's impossible to be a Christian without believing in the Resurrection. I'm troubled by that. What do you mean by that?' And then an hour of conversation follows. That, to me, is far more meaningful than the Hurray!-he-stood-up-for-the-Christian-faith experience."

Hays clarified his example: "Many of the students who say 'Thanks' are really saying, 'This has given me something to deal with.'"

Then Neuhaus cross-examined Hays: "Richard, will you say that you don't understand how any Christian can indeed be a Christian without recognizing that the Bible is the authoritative text? Also, can you use the word 'authority,' or are students repelled by it?"

"That's not a word that I use the first day of class," Hays admitted. "But when I teach a course in New Testament ethics, that ends up being the key issue. That is, in what sense is this text authoritative for the life of the community? I don't teach as if that question is up for grabs. I operate under the assumption that the text is authoritative. The question then becomes a hermeneutical one about how we construe the authority of the text. That, of course, introduces a whole series of complicated questions. But a huge majority of the students, at least the ones who take my courses, are willing to grant that premise. Once in a while a student will say to me, 'I didn't like that course. I couldn't buy that premise.' But that's an exception."

Lindbeck then noted that all the factions at Yale Divinity School — the lesbians, the gays, the straights, the liberationists, the neo-conservatives, the fundamentalists, the evangelicals, the old-line liberals, and so on — accept the premise of biblical authority. The trouble is, according to Lindbeck, "they all have different hermeneutics."

One who doesn't promote a pick-your-own-hermeneutics approach in his theology classroom is Stanley Hauerwas. "I politicize my classroom," he said candidly. "I start by telling my students that I want them to be different when they leave my classroom. I want to fundamentally change their lives. Part of the change is that I will make them very miserable; I will also make them very angry. That's all right. When they leave my class, I want them to believe what I believe. For example, I don't want any of them to leave my class and ever say again that they can enthusiastically support the military of the United States of America. If they do, they are decisively not people who are capable of ministry in the church of Jesus Christ."

"Do you mean that they just can't support the military enthusiastically, or . . . ?" asked Neuhaus.

Hauerwas interrupted: "If they're able to envision the possibility of being a servant in the U.S. military, they can do so only if their conscience is under very close scrutiny by the whole church. If they don't believe that they have that burden of proof, they're not worthy to be part of the ministry. If they say, 'Don't you believe in letting me make up my own mind?' I say, 'You don't have a mind worth making up. It's time for you to be trained.' If they say, 'That sounds awfully authoritarian,' I say, 'All you believe in is the tyranny of your own conscience. And that's exactly the reason why you're a liberal and corrupt. So it's time for you to face up to what you are.' And boy, have I got angry people in my classroom."

"That's your great eccentricity," Neuhaus congratulated Hauerwas, "and you do it very well."

On the general question of the moment — Who is going to seminary? — Dennis Campbell commented, "More and more theological institutions are opening more and more degree programs to fill in gaps left by declining enrollments of M.Div. students. That's happening across the board. There's a proliferation of M.A.s in this and in that. Some little seminaries are offering ten degrees of one sort or another. There's an M.A. in alcohol and drug rehabilitation, in music, in urban studies, and so on." Once again Campbell was suggesting how market pressures — which can endanger the very survival of seminaries themselves — can confuse the basic theological purposes of a theological education.

Hauerwas then asked, "Dennis, does the admissions committee of Duke Divinity School automatically turn down Unitarians who apply for the M.Div. program?"

"I don't know, but I don't think so," Campbell replied.

"Why wouldn't it?" Hauerwas wanted to know.

"Because you might have a chance to convert them," Neuhaus kidded, though with a note of seriousness.

Piety and Liturgy

James Fowler, who over the years has spent some time as a minister and teacher in Roman Catholic settings, noted, "Catholics often don't think to tell Protestants about the centrality of the Eucharist. For Catholics, all of the apparatus of formation is simply complementary preparation for full participation in the Eucharist. Also, when a Roman Catholic seminary celebrates the Eucharist in the middle of a hard day of academics, it declares that academics fit into what the institution is really about."

"That's true — there's a strong residue of the religious cult in Roman Catholicism," Donald Davis commented. "It still grips every level of the Roman Catholic community — from the pope to the member of the base community."

Robert Leavitt encouraged closer examination of this point because, he claimed, "even the cult has become politicized. The cult, which used to be the locus for common identification, has, because of the feminist issue, become a center of political controversy in the church. Young priests sometimes feel they're exercising an oppressive ministry by celebrating the Eucharist."

Such eucharistic dis-ease, said Stanley Hauerwas, "isn't all bad. In 1 Corinthians 11, St. Paul says that the reason so many of the Corinthians are dying is that they came to the Eucharist unworthily. It may be that one of the good things about the Eucharist is that we have to celebrate it in the midst of experienced pain. At Notre Dame we used to come together at the Lord's Table when we were divided, and it was painful. I always respected Ed O'Connor, who wouldn't serve me because I'm Protestant. It hurt, but there was something right about it. Maybe it's a good thing that God puts us through that."

Hauerwas went on to argue, however indirectly, for the normative character of eucharistic worship. "After I've been teaching at Duke Divinity School for twenty-five years," he projected, "I hope to have half the United Methodist clergy of North Carolina feeling guilty for not serving the Eucharist every Sunday. I know that they won't do it, but I just want them to feel guilty about it. I don't think that will bring any great, visible reforming movement. After all, look at the Anglicans: they serve the Eucharist frequently, and look what they're like. But at least the Eucharist has a foothold in the Episcopal Church."

George Lindbeck also spoke about the importance of worship, of liturgy, to a community of faith. "I've been a lay member of a parish for forty years," he began. "During that time I've seen seven pastors in the parish, and the parish has turned over in membership about three times. There are very few present members who were members when I first joined. We've never had a good preacher. Nor have we had someone who conformed to a 'Herr pastor' image. The pastors' assistants have usually been divinity school students who were usually better preachers than the pastors.

"It's not a great parish, but it has fumbled along rather successfully for forty years. The gospel has somehow been proclaimed. There has been great pluralism; there hasn't been theological or ethical uniformity. A wide range of views has been expressed publicly and vigorously, so the parish as a whole knows that there are different approaches to the faith and life. Still, many members have had their faith preserved. Some have learned the faith in new ways through being a part of that parish.

"Yet all the pastors of my church have been the type of pastor that we've criticized during this conference. They have been kind people who have helped others to get along. Here my Lutheran bias is about to surface, because I can't imagine that my church would have worked without the liturgy. But it has worked."

To which Neuhaus replied, "We would all want to say, *Deo gratia,* that God keeps his promise with his church, despite the absence of the excellences that we would like to see exhibited by the church. But I hope that you're not inviting anyone to draw the conclusion that we can thus resign ourselves to the absence of the excellences."

"No," Lindbeck answered. "What I'm suggesting is that these ministers had structures. Not one has tried to monkey with, or 'revitalize,' or change the liturgy. The congregation wouldn't allow it. The pastors have simply done the liturgy. In addition, none of them has wanted to change the confirmation structure, and all have followed the lectionary in preaching."

At this juncture Geoffrey Wainwright pointed out a feature of Catholic seminary life that is surely related to its eucharistic piety. "As a theological student," he recalled, "I visited Roman Catholic seminaries. What I remember most strongly of all is that I've never been treated so hospitably by any institution that I've entered as I was by these half dozen or more Roman Catholic theological seminaries. Hospitality, you will remember, is a New Testament virtue and skill. And it's not without its Christological meanings."

"Catholic seminary hospitality comes from the people there being at home there," James Burtchaell explained. "It has attenuated since your visits, Geoffrey, because the students today are often away from the seminary — out and about in the ghetto, in Appalachia, and in Chile. But it hasn't vanished. By the way, you would have found it in a monastery too. These are people who know they are at home. When my students say, 'I'm going to visit my family, but I'm coming home soon,' then I think they have truly found community there."

Robert Leavitt underscored Burtchaell's point: "Catholics used to refer to the seminary itself as 'the house.' This is, of course, a familial metaphor. The duties of the house — cleaning the floors and tending the grounds — were done by the members and students, and that furthered the sense of ownership of the place. Now we strive for community without that kind of investment in the more menial aspects of life together. That poses a danger for celibate clergy, because they end up living in an idealized world where they don't have to attend to the basics of living."

Citing *The Seminary — Protestant and Catholic* by Walter D. Wagoner, Burtchaell observed that contemporary Protestant seminaries seem to be populated with refugees from rigid pietisms. As Philip Turner had suggested earlier, these refugees have often lost much of their spirituality in flight. Also, Burtchaell noted, the schools they have ended up attending are often on the verge of becoming graduate schools of religion rather than remaining theological seminaries. In other words, the Protestant seminaries emphasize academics almost to the exclusion of spirituality.

Neuhaus added, "What I call the 'narrow escape syndrome' dominates a lot of church leadership and religious academe. Many there feel like they've narrowly escaped. In the case of Protestantism, they feel that they've escaped the fundamentalism of their earlier life. They're frightened by any mention of authority, because they're concerned that they'll get sucked back into what they narrowly escaped. Today you see a lot of that in Roman Catholicism too. There you have traditionalism and *The Wanderer.* There the suggestion of authority sets off red lights that are set off by any hint of pre–Vatican II."

Next Hauerwas offered an observation to those around the conference table who seemed to be neglecting the problems of the Catholic seminaries today. "When I go to Roman Catholic seminaries today, I find a deep sadness there. At St. Mary's of the Lake, or St. Charles in Philadelphia, or Notre Dame in New Orleans, there is a deep, deep pathos and sadness. I was just at Notre Dame, New Orleans. There they've turned what was at one time a chapel in the residence for the future priests into a weight room. That's got to break your heart. St. Mary's, Mundelein, was built for 3,000 seminarians; today there are eighty-six. There's a sadness there that I don't know how to get at. I think it has a lot to do with the damned buildings the seminaries are stuck with."

What Then Is to Be Done?

As the conference neared its conclusion, moderator Neuhaus suggested that the conferees remember Lenin's famous pamphlet entitled "What Then Is to Be Done?" Neuhaus asked for an emphasis on specifics, hoping that they would guide the remainder of the conversation. "If theological education is to be more effectively and self-consciously concerned with moral formation, what kinds of things should be done? And can they be done? Include little changes — like saying prayers in the classroom — and larger changes."

Urging seminary faculties to reform their own households so that they might better form and re-form their students, William Willimon observed, "Why can't we faculty members simply decide just what *we* need to do to form clergy? For example, on this campus — and I've also seen this at Harvard — the business school has, for good or ill, radically influenced other schools through its case-study method. Now there's a school that decided that it needed to work on its stuff in a creative way. The divinity school needs to say to the rest of the university, 'We don't buy into your notions of scholarly objectivity and your mushy notions of smorgasbord curriculum.' We need to go head-to-head with the department of religion and say, 'We want to frame the intellectual questions in a way that is much more intellectually dynamic.' We can do that now. Granted, it will be very difficult, because when you talk the way we've been talking, you go against an academic tradition that is at least a century old."

Ethicist Philip Turner then spoke briefly about what he's attempting in his own household. "I've been rather hardheaded about picking out certain students who I think are promising," he explained. "I try to get them into my classes. To do that I've moved almost all of my teaching out of the classroom. I teach out of my living room. I've also had to go outside the confines of my own discipline. I couldn't simply offer courses in ethics and do what I want to do. So on my own I'm teaching a course on Calvin this year, and I taught a course on the creeds last year. I follow an interpersonal model of teaching, because I came to the conclusion, rightly or wrongly, that nothing could be done at the curricular level. There wasn't enough agreement among faculty and administration for that."

Also concerned about the seminary household was George Marsden. "What we need to do," he said, "is to go back to Christianity. We should start talking about God and the authority of the Bible. We should pray and teach the liturgy. But in most Protestant seminaries, if we went back to that kind of Christianity and came out with it as authoritative, we'd get kicked out. You might be able to get away with it at Duke because of its traditionalist ethos."

"Is Duke really that different than, say, Union in New York?" Neuhaus asked the group.

Geoffrey Wainwright took up the question: "While teaching at Union in New York, I always felt that the assumption was that Christianity was wrong unless it could be shown to be right. At Duke the assumption is that, on the whole, Christianity is the agreed-upon basic, though there are problems here and there that can be debated."

"At what point would you get kicked out of the University of Chicago Divinity School for authoritatively teaching orthodox Christianity?" Neuhaus asked.

"When you offended the feminists or the relativists or the gay caucus," Marsden answered.

"How might you offend the relativists at Chicago?" Neuhaus probed.

Marsden replied, "By implying that Christianity is a religion that has some exclusivism. By implying that relativists weren't Christians. After all, if you're talking about traditional Christianity, you're going to have to isolate and argue against ways of believing that are different from traditional Christianity."

"George, you're saying that there is a normative Christianity," Neuhaus observed. "For example, if someone doesn't believe in the resurrection of Christ, then he or she isn't a classical Christian."

"Yes, and if you say certain people aren't Christians, you'll get booted out," Marsden responded.

"Do you really mean you'd get fired from the faculty?" Richard Hays asked with a note of disbelief.

"Well, you'd get hooted down and eventually called a crank," guessed Marsden.

"I question that," said Hays. "I think we've allowed ourselves to get buffaloed, to be intimidated into thinking that we could never say anything like that."

Then Neuhaus continued his line of questioning. "How

much could be changed if seminary professors taught more confessionally?"

Marsden attempted an answer: "In today's seminaries you have pluralistic institutions, and you have to be careful about whom you offend. If you go into a seminary classroom and say, 'Your problem is that you need to be converted,' what you're saying is that some people there aren't Christians. That might not be an appropriate thing to say in a school that isn't restricted to one denomination."

Neuhaus wasn't so sure. "In a theological faculty," he said, "it should be inescapable that at some point you're going to be teaching about the idea of conversion. If you make it clear that your understanding of conversion is that it is constitutive of being a Christian, you're not browbeating the class. You're simply making clear what your understanding of the Christian life is. And that includes conversion, in the born-again sense and/or in the baptismal-renewal sense. You wouldn't be a good teacher of the church if you didn't teach that."

James Burtchaell was also interested in how theological schools might reinsert moral formation into theological education today. His first suggestion was that seminaries adopt a model for theological education based on the biblical image of the rabbi with his students. "Remember the Passover?" asked Burtchaell. "It had to be celebrated in a family home. The lone exception was the rabbi and his group of disciples, who together formed a family. This is an instructive model. If a seminary isn't a church, if a seminary doesn't have a regime of community, if a seminary cannot and does not celebrate the Eucharist, then something is missing. The seminary must have a regime of appropriate asceticism and prayer. This reminds me that I am a father to those who enter my seminary community. I must work with them."

To this Neuhaus responded, "Jim, aren't you just whistling Dixie on this? What Protestant theological school do you know of that has in its admissions criteria a commitment to the community?"

Burtchaell didn't answer, but Philip Turner did. "That's an irony," he said to Neuhaus, "because the students now coming to seminary are looking for community. What they want is what Victor Turner called 'communitas,' an immediate translation to the heavenly state."

"And that includes a discipline of worship and mutual accountability?" Neuhaus asked.

"Mutual accountability is where the problem comes in," Turner admitted.

"But a sense of accountability is growing," noted Jay Rochelle of the Lutheran School of Theology at Chicago. "At our place we have an entire chapel program. Out of that are spinning small groups of people who talk to each other about what it might mean to live the whole Christian life and be accountable to one another. I'm hopeful about that."

Less hopeful about what is happening in Protestant seminaries these days was Michael Graef, a recent seminary graduate. "Discussion regarding community, at least during my years at Drew, was a rhetorical device which abounded," he contended. "It was used to try to hold together some semblance of consensus in an extremely diverse place. The only actual community that existed there was our gathering silently around the Lord's Table to receive grace. Otherwise, community in any meaningful sense was problematic."

At this point James Burtchaell offered a second suggestion regarding the most important time in training for ministry. "Unfortunately," he said, "that happens in the first two, possibly three years after ordination. Then we in the seminaries do zilch. But that's when all of the lifelong ministerial habits are formed. That's when sexual strain shows. That's when prayer is under attack from work. That's when the exhilaration of sharing people's private concerns is overwhelming. That's when money becomes an issue. And we do nothing. We figure that clergy are journeymen from the moment of ordination. And those who are ordained are insulted at the thought that any future formation is needed."

Rochelle agreed with Burtchaell. "I'm very worried about that three-year period after seminary graduation," he admitted. "I get a lot of people who come back to the seminary bleeding after a year and a half. Many were assigned to be associate or assistant pastors. What makes the hair on the back of your neck stand up is that they put up with crap from senior pastors that couldn't be gotten away with in the world of business. It's covered over with smarmy religious talk that doesn't mean a damned thing. Underneath it all are issues of power and sex that, in most cases, the senior pastors are unwilling, inadequate, or unable to address. What happens is that the senior pastors engineer it so that the assistant pastors get booted out after a couple of years. This just makes you mad as hell. So if we're going to talk about moral formation, maybe we should talk to people who take on assistant ministers during their first three years out of seminary."

"It has always been astonishing how few instances there are of happy team parish ministries," Neuhaus acknowledged. "They are rare exceptions. Moral formation needs to address the problems of ego, competition, unwillingness to share credit, and so on. These problems run very, very deep. They're busting out in the Roman Catholic situation, the Lutheran situation, and in every ecclesial situation that I'm aware of. We haven't trained people to be in ministry with others. We use the language of collegiality, but we don't live it. I would guess that more difficulties with women ministers in the parish have to do with this problem than with the male-female problem. There's an inability to subordinate the ego to the task at hand."

Dennis Campbell followed Neuhaus' point with a question: "The worst examples of collegiality are often found in seminary faculties. So how can we expect theological students to develop a sense of collegiality if the ones they watch are lone rangers on the faculty who engage in backbiting and gossip?"

To reanimate the goal of moral formation, seminaries should develop and transmit to their students "a wisdom tradition," according to Michael Graef. "I'll use a biblical image," he said. "Jesus, being tempted in the wilderness, hears, 'If you are the Son of God, command these stones to become loaves of bread.' Jesus responds, 'It is written . . .' Jesus' response refers to a scriptural, authoritative wisdom tradition. Seminarians badly need such wisdom."

But Stanley Hauerwas warned that transmitting a wisdom tradition is something which, like most tasks, is easier said than done. "After all," he said, "you can't properly attain wisdom without going through the sufferings that are necessary to embody it and that have achieved it from the beginning."

Such a wisdom tradition now exists, suggested Neuhaus. He elaborated: "There is in Christian tradition a tradition of experience that has been discovered which indicates that some things in ministry don't work. If you live or minister this way, the tradition instructs, this will happen. Unfortunately, this tradition is powerfully resisted by those who refuse moral instruction."

Geoffrey Wainwright agreed with Neuhaus by hinting that a ministerial wisdom tradition need not be composed ex nihilo. It simply needs to be recovered from the riches of church tradition. To make his point, Wainwright referred to Duke's church-and-ministry course: "Two of the texts that we have had students read are *The Book of Pastoral Rule* by Gregory the Great and *The Reformed Pastor* by Richard Baxter. Despite all of the social and cultural changes that have taken place between those authors and us, there are some quite startling continuities. There is this timelessness about the Christian church and the nature of its ministry. Gregory the Great knew very well how to deal with issues like self-deception, motivation, reluctance, and so on. And so with Richard Baxter. When he lists the things that a Reformed pastor is to do, students who read him say, 'Yes, he's right. These are very basic functions within the life of the congregation.' We should be aiming to help students to become people who can do that sort of ministry. This involves a small number of classical models of things that Christian ministers have always done in the life of the church."

The next item that was placed on the wish list for theological education was an increase in religious practice. Stanley Hauerwas put this on the agenda with this comment: "My most important formation took place with Roman Catholics. I was formed at the University of Notre Dame. Until I was at Notre Dame, it never occurred to me that there was any connection at all between being religious and being a theologian. I remember when I went to Notre Dame, I was asked, 'What difference will your being a Protestant make in your teaching of theological ethics?' I answered, 'I haven't got the slightest idea. I'm not a Protestant. I went to Yale.' My point is that, for many of us, more important than our denominational identification is the graduate school we went to. That's where our fundamental formation took place. At Notre Dame I saw for the first time how ecclesial presuppositions determine theological agenda."

Roberta Bondi followed by suggesting that the spiritual formation of most seminary professors was really nothing but their graduate work. "Part of that training," she said, "systematically trained out of us habits of prayer and Scripture reading, which were considered suitable only to pious fundamentalist types."

"So a spiritual deformation, or a dropping of the baggage of real spiritual formation, was taking place in graduate school," Neuhaus ventured.

"Yes," Bondi replied. "For example, during my graduate days I was informed that if I was inclined to pray, I was to repent of the inclination immediately, because it was implausible that I should even think of it. From such experience we have brought into our own seminary teaching an inability to figure out what to do with prayer and Scripture reading with respect to students. So in seminaries today there's a lot of automatic suspicion of prayer and Scripture reading.

"My continuing study of monasticism has led me to understand the importance of Scripture and the necessity of every Christian establishing a daily discipline of reading Scripture and praying. What I'm saying is that Protestants — and here I'll note that the Catholics aren't as bad off as they think they are — really do need to rethink the place of prayer and Scripture reading in the training for ordained ministry. We need to put aside our fear that if we pray or read the Bible we will become, or be perceived as, frothing-at-the-mouth fundamentalists. We still have this knee-jerk reaction against piety. At Candler it's easier to talk about your sex life than to talk about the necessity of prayer and Scripture reading."

"I don't see this the same way," James Fowler commented. "I see the problem in terms of our seminary regime building no leisure into life. I don't see it in terms of an external or internal denial of the importance of prayer and Bible reading. It's just that our manner of ordering life is, on the one hand, individualistic and, on the other hand, exceedingly full."

Then Hauerwas spoke: "I'm not naturally religious, so I don't want to blame graduate school for my lack of piety. Prayer doesn't come easily to me. Praying isn't something I do privately. I pray when people help me to pray. That's the reason I attend church. I'm not saying that's good. I'm just saying that that's the case."

Addressing Fowler in particular, Hauerwas continued, "Jim, what Roberta is suggesting is that our seminaries presume that methodologically one can understand the biblical text without moral formation. Athanasius wrote that you can't tell someone how to get to a city just by pointing it out on a map. You have to show him the way. Athanasius also said that trying to find the city without being shown the way is the equivalent of trying to read the Scriptures without attending to the lives of the saints. Of course, that's the way we were taught. We were taught to deal with this literature without having our lives changed. Roberta is suggesting that praying and reading the Bible can sometimes change a person's life. Basically what changes one's life is other people, but sometimes that happens through the mediation of that literature."

"But more basically, isn't it true," Neuhaus inquired, "that seminary students are taught to read the biblical text in a way that makes it exceedingly difficult to read it devotionally, to read it in the way the Scriptures were given to be read, to read it in terms of the revelation that can change one's life? Ron Thiemann at Harvard and George Lindbeck speak about the biblical text as a 'habitable text.' They say that the historical-critical method, as it is taught, has tended to make the Bible an uninhabitable text. That is, you can't live it; you're always apart from it because of the exercise of a critical consciousness. What is needed is a second naiveté in which you can, in a childlike way, read the Scriptures. This is something that most of our theological schools aren't equipping people to do."

After Roberta Bondi raised a question about Neuhaus' use of the word "childlike," he replied, "As Alfred North Whitehead said, the only simplicity to be trusted is the simplicity on the far side of complexity. That's what I take to be the second naiveté. In it we don't put the critical aside; we work through it. As our Lord said in Mark 10, 'Whoever does not receive the kingdom of God like a child shall not enter it.' That's the second naiveté. It isn't pretending that we don't know all of the complexifications which stand in the way of an obedient reading of the Scriptures."

After disagreeing with Neuhaus' interpretation of Mark 10, Bondi yielded the floor to James Fowler. He explained that he had learned a new method of biblical interpretation from the *Spiritual Exercises* of St. Ignatius. "The biggest obstacle for me in this new method was to submit myself to the text and to let the text read me," he said. "It had to read me at points other than my cognitive intellectual capacities. Sometimes I ended up spending a week on a pericope. As that text got me into it and began to work with me, a kind of hermeneutical reversal took place. If that's what we mean by the second naiveté, it is something very powerful."

James Burtchaell joined several others in expressing concern about the paucity of piety, not to mention belief, in seminaries. He related an anecdote to illustrate his concern. "I have four former students, all quite bright, who went to Yale Divinity School and left before receiving the doctorate. The reason that they gave was that they couldn't find any faculty member who would say in public that he believed in God."

"Because he privately told me, I happen to know that George Lindbeck believes in God," Neuhaus joked.

Then Burtchaell told a second story: "In a course last year I was trying to teach the difference between professed and functioning theology. The students in the class had to investigate how theology is implicit in various programmatic Christian undertakings. One of the students did a project for me titled 'An Inquiry into Beginning Classes with a Prayer.' He chose as his test population my colleagues in the department of theology. He interviewed more than half of the theology faculty. First he asked, 'Do you believe that at a Catholic university — say, here at Notre Dame — piety is an appropriate part of the academic experience?' Everyone said yes. Next he asked, 'Do you believe that faculty should have some opportunity to share in this?' They answered, 'Well . . .' Then he asked, 'Do you begin your classes with a prayer?' Out of the twenty-four professors interviewed, only two or three said yes.

"Mind you, when I came to Notre Dame, *all* classes, no matter who the instructor was, began with a prayer. If the instructor wasn't a Catholic and felt awkward praying, then that instructor would ask a student to pray. To my knowledge I have never begun a class without a prayer. Usually I pray the first day of class and then I ask the students to pray after that. I say, 'Will you pray? Those of you who have a cardiac arrest when you hear this question I'll put on my cardiac list. As for the rest of you, I'll simply ask one of you to pray before class begins.' It's a wonderful experience in prayer.

"But to get back to my student's survey: In trying to justify their responses to the survey questions, my colleagues fell prey to all sorts of explanations. 'The students would think that I'm into some sort of catechetical fling and not interested in teaching Scripture.' Or 'They would be confused about scholarship.' Or 'They would be irreverent during the prayer.' This is absolute crap! The student was scandalized by these findings."

Burtchaell moved from this specific incident to a generalization: "Everybody today who comes out of the academy and stays in the guild is familiar with this toxic reaction to the notion of public profession of the faith, because scholarship and faith are thought to compromise one another."

Burtchaell then urged seminaries to change their hiring procedures. The impious seminary classroom will become pious, he said, only when the seminary begins asking a significant question of its faculty candidates: "What will you do to make your students more holy and more devout ministers of the gospel?" Burtchaell concluded, "Even if the faculty candidates *want* to assist in forming their students in holiness for ministry, they may not know how. For some years Notre Dame has gotten most of its Scripture people from Harvard. It takes years to bring Harvard grads back to life again. If formation for the student is most important when he or she is actually in our harness, then it's important for us to realize that formation will probably take place only when the right people come into our company.

"I will end with a statement of the Burtchaell Principle: Any adjective by which an institution wants to be known has to represent a quality explicitly and unashamedly sought after in all personnel decisions. If you want to be a place that turns out holy, integrated ministers, then you have to make holiness a spoken-out-loud issue in the recruitment and development process."

Neuhaus then applied the Burtchaell Principle to the local church. "A Lutheran congregation was calling a pastor," he recalled. "The call committee consulted with me about how it ought to go about its work. I suggested that the committee ask each ministerial candidate about his prayer life. If the candidate was embarrassed or incapable of talking about that, he probably wasn't the pastor they needed. The committee took my suggestion, interviewing three candidates recommended by the bishop. It rejected all of them. Then the bishop's assistant came to the call committee and asked, 'What in the world are you doing? What kind of questions are you asking?' The committee members said, 'Well, among the questions we're asking is a question about the candidate's prayer life. And these candidates seemed taken aback by it. They couldn't talk about it.' The bishop's assistant promptly instructed them that that wasn't an appropriate question to ask."

Heroic Ministers or Heroic Communities?

The holding up of exemplary ministers and exemplary ministries to the seminaries and the churches was the next item placed on the what-then-should-we-do list. Jay Rochelle initiated this discussion: "Seminarians are trying to be true to their commitment to Jesus, to use words that fall pretty easily from my lips, and on the other hand they want to figure out how best to use their creativity. In the churches that exist now, they perceive that that will not be easy."

"In other words, " Neuhaus responded, "students fear that what they hope is the radicality of their devotion to Jesus is somehow going to be diluted. When I was in seminary, I looked at parish ministers who were ten years out of seminary. And with a few exceptions, it seemed to me that they were all washed out. Of course, I was certain that that wouldn't happen to me. But I'm keenly aware that there are a lot of students who would look at me now and say, 'Boy, there's a washed-out case.'

But what ministries are lifted up in theological education today as exemplary ministries to be emulated? On the American scene do we have any exemplary people in ministry?"

"Yes, those in the Bronx, those in Appalachia, and those working with Hispanics," Burtchaell answered.

"But there isn't much interest in inner-city ministry in seminaries today," Neuhaus replied. "At least from my experience today, you can't get clergy to go into inner-city work, into socially and economically marginal situations. If that's the case, who do the seminaries lift up? And what about middle-class and upper-middle-class parishes?"

James Fowler then questioned the question itself: "I think it would be specious to offer up exemplary ministers apart from the context of the ecologies in which they found it possible to be the kinds of ministers we admire."

"Jim, I'd like to pin this down," Neuhaus responded. "Is it really agreed around this table that there are no exemplary ministers who we can hold up as models in our seminary classrooms? If that's true, that's a very sobering reality. After all, every profession, understanding that word in its classic sense, has to have some excellent *professors* who aren't academic professors. Can you imagine a medical school that wouldn't hold up to its students models of the kinds of doctors they ought to be? Maybe that is the case in medical schools today. I'd be very surprised, however, if it were."

"That's precisely the case in medical schools," Fowler asserted, "because the medical specialist is so highly supported by a whole ecology of assistants.

"This doesn't mean that I wouldn't bring a minister in to talk to a class," Fowler continued. "But if I did, I wouldn't say to my class, 'That minister is a heroic model whose example you should use to shape your ministry.' I would say, 'You should learn from some of the virtues that he has. But you should also look at the history of the church that empowers him to do what he does in that particular place.' What I'm trying to do is to break down the notion of the heroic exemplar. The minister can be competent, committed, passionate, and spiritual. Yes! But he isn't the sole maker or breaker of a particular congregation."

"Why do you want to break down the notion of the heroic

exemplar?" asked Neuhaus. "In a world without heroes, that's unnecessary. That notion has already collapsed; you don't have to break it down. It seems to me that today we need some heroes."

"But we've seen the backside of too many of those heroes," Fowler argued.

"All of them have clay feet up to their armpits," Neuhaus agreed. "But the masters of suspicion and skepticism now get to gut . . ."

"But by singling out the hero you're denying that group of people who worked with the hero to make heroism possible," Fowler interrupted Neuhaus.

"But why is this an either-or proposition?" Neuhaus challenged. "The exemplary pastor isn't simply a great persona and presence. He is someone who, in an exemplary way, is equipping the saints for their growth in grace and ministry."

"But I want to talk about the way the saints equip and empower the minister," said Fowler, "and I want to argue that the model of heroes may not be a helpful way to look for exemplary ministers. I'm trying to get the clergy out of the center here."

Sensing that an important conflict had surfaced again, Neuhaus commented, "Yesterday a good many of us were saying, 'What the clergy are scared of and what the students are scared of is that there is, at the center of the ministry, an authoritative word, borne by someone who has been given authority to speak that word. We're afraid of that because with authority comes responsibility, and responsibility suggests that we might be irresponsible and fail.' Reading the signs of the times, so to speak, it seems that that is our historical moment.

"On the other hand, Jim and Rowan are reading the signs of the times in a very different way. But I don't know where in our world there is a danger of the minister standing at the center and bearing the responsibility for leading that community. Where exactly is that so strong? Where is it so dominating that we need to be fighting against it? I think we need to be fighting against people who aren't prepared to stand at the center and say, 'I am the shepherd of this flock. I accept full responsibility, temporal and eternal, for that.' "

At that point Rowan Greer clarified his position: "I'm not arguing for an abdication of the authority of the minister," he said. "I'm arguing for a redefinition of authority in the community context. If I understand what our new prayer book is up to, it has moved away from the shepherd-sheep model. No longer is the rector up front reading the service at the people. Instead, the service is an act of the people of God, and everyone is involved in it. That doesn't get the ordained minister off the hook. It simply means that authority has to be embraced in a new way."

Stanley Hauerwas tried a different approach to the minister-congregation impasse that had developed by comparing the pastor with the jazz musician. "You can't have someone like Joe Hooker until you have audiences trained in Dixieland jazz. In other words, to get great jazz musicians, you've got to have trained hearers. You can't separate the musician from the hearers. Likewise, the Christian preacher has to have hearers. Even when Israel was unfaithful and a prophet rose up to say so, at least someone was around to say, 'That's a prophet!' I'm trying to break down the model of the lonely, isolated hero out there. I'm saying that ministry occurs in heroic communities because the story is heroic. What the community has to do is have confidence that when the Word is rightly preached, it will bear fruit. And a pastor has to trust the people not to be audience but to be congregation."

"Do you know any heroic congregations, Stan?" Neuhaus inquired.

"Yes, I do," Hauerwas replied, "and you do too."

"No, not heroic congregations," Neuhaus corrected. "But I do know heroic people in congregations. And I know congregations which have been shaped by leaderships that were radically devoted not to prima-donna-ish heroism but to their people. The people then became obedient listeners. That is, in the proper sense of the word, they listened responsibly. But I would say that it never happens that there are congregations which are alive, vibrant, and growing in grace where there is not a great pastor.

"Let me say again that by great and heroic pastors I don't mean prima-donna-ish pastors. I don't mean Lone Rangers.

The heroic pastor may not even be great in any obvious way. But if you look carefully, you find someone who is unabashedly the shepherd of his sheep and who readily accepts responsibility for that. So I think it's a great shame, Rowan, that the prayer book has dropped this metaphor. It's exactly right, and it isn't demeaning to the sheep in any way, if properly understood."

As this segment of the conversation wound down, Philip Turner briefly attempted mediation: "These notions of minister and church, authority and community, logically presuppose each other. You can't have an authority or hero apart from the community which embodies, in some way or another, what the authority furthers and the hero exemplifies."

Beyond Anti-Authority

Leaving aside the minister-church dialectic, James Fowler offered a possible means toward the end of reconstructing authority in the churches, which might then lead to moral re-formation in the seminaries. In the churches and the seminaries, he said, "we need to create public space where we can appeal to classic texts, offer an interpretation which doesn't say that one person's interpretation is as valid as anyone else's, and locate the authority of the text. Also, we need to practice a kind of hermeneutics, exegesis, rhetoric, and persuasion that constitutes a sort of authority that isn't authoritarian. This is a forceful and authoritative authority, yet it's one that can entertain conversation."

According to Fowler, the creation of this kind of public space would be a great improvement in today's seminary, over which Clinical Pastoral Education (CPE) continues to exercise authoritarian, if not totalitarian, rule. "Unfortunately," said Fowler, "the CPE model has great residual power. It has become almost universal for Protestants. It's used for evaluating whether or not a student is ready to go into the ministry. Then there's a kind of Carl Rogersism running through ministerial training. It was a powerful corrective at one point in American culture, but as a positive principle it simply doesn't work. The symbols of that are the assertion 'I must get my needs met' and the question 'Are you getting your needs met?' That kind of attitude creates an ethos that undermines a lot of the positive dimensions of calling and vocation and the readiness to counter our culture's images of success and reward."

Philip Turner, who had been addressing the issue of authority during much of the conference, followed with this comment: "In seminaries' practical training, where students actually start doing things and where real formation begins to occur, we have virtually nothing that would, in an experiential way, acquaint students with the exercise of authority. I have often thought that what I would like to do is send some of my students to work in a black parish in Harlem where the patronage model of ministry is much stronger. There authority is up-front, and it is openly handled. And that setting provides the same kind of scrutiny that a student gets in the one-on-one-CPE-how-did-you-react-when-someone-was-dying training that almost all seminarians go through today. We really underestimate the current power of the CPE model."

William Willimon was quick to remind the conferees — even if they didn't need to be reminded — of the contemporary churches' unwillingness to accept and exercise authority. "Some seminary professors are struck by the complete irresponsibility on the part of the church," he pointed out. "The church is saying to us, a bunch of professors, 'Come on, *you* decide who ought to be serving as a United Methodist minister at Bunnlevel, North Carolina.' Behind this problem, of course, is a demoralized clergy. The other day a Roman Catholic priest told me that he wouldn't encourage anybody to go into the priesthood today. 'All I do is bury people, marry people, and shuffle out the Eucharist,' he said. 'Twenty years ago I would have encouraged young men to enter the priesthood. But now I wouldn't.'

"Right now the clergy suffer from a crippling inability to discipline one another, even in some of the grossest breaches of moral conduct. I'm thinking particularly of United Methodist examples, but I could think of others. In my own annual conference there are cases of wife abuse, income tax evasion, and worse. This happens yearly. The United Methodist system is predicated on the assumption that clergy will discipline their own, and the laity wait for us to do that. For example, there was a district superintendent, a Duke graduate, who didn't pay income tax for twelve years. He was indicted and convicted. When this came before the annual conference, people took the floor and talked about the one who was without sin throwing the first stone. I asked, 'Does anybody have a rock?' When I left the meeting, my dominant impression was this: Here's your typical United Methodist ethical mush at work. Later I came to a much more devastating conclusion: We don't even respect ourselves enough to say to this guy, 'We don't want you to be a part of us.' We United Methodist ministers should think so much of our God-given vocation that there will be some colleagues to whom we must say, 'You can be a wonderful Christian. But you can't be a United Methodist pastor anymore. You forfeited that possibility. We can't use you.' It's sad that six hundred people sat in that room at the annual conference and none of us said, 'We treasure so much the yoke under which we serve that we cannot use you.'"

Willimon continued his point by noting that demoralized clergy lead to paralyzed churches: "As a United Methodist, I'm part of a denomination that over the last decade has lost six hundred members a week. All of the mainliners, or old-liners, are in the same situation. How much more dissatisfaction do we need? This summer I went to the jurisdictional conference. A bishop got up and said, 'The good news is that our rate of decline is one of the lowest in the United Methodist Church today. The good news is that we have lost only 120 members a week since we last met.' Despite this 'good news,' he expressed regret and said we needed to work on evangelism. Then, when we had finished with that, we proceeded to elect a group of people as bishops, not one of whom, in my humble estimation, knows what to do about the losses.

"I have this myth — and the historians could probably tell me that it's a kind of romanticism — that a hundred years ago, when Methodist clergy got together, we impressed people. We were tough on each other. We were God's storm troopers. We were the Jesuits of Protestantism. We could do it. Now when we get together we look like a closed union shop that doesn't give a damn that we lose 600 members a week." It seemed that

Willimon was calling for clergy formed by a church not afraid of authoritative teaching and discipline.

Thinking that she had spotted a way out of the churches' present deformations, Roberta Bondi said, "There are a lot of parish-willing women in seminaries right now. They're eager to go through seminary and then take up parishes. Many of these women don't feel the same way as our men students. A lot of the male students say, 'Well, I'm not smart enough to be a doctor, and it looks like a lot of work to sell insurance. So I think I'll go into the ministry.' Women don't go to seminary with that sort of attitude. They go thinking, 'This is going to cost me a lot: I'm going to face a lot of opposition all along the way. But this is my calling.' In our seminaries, I'm sad to say, we don't support the women who are most enthusiastic about going into the ministry."

Willimon recalled a field-education seminar for first-year students at Duke: "The male students in the seminar started griping about 'the dumb bishops and district superintendents.' One of the women, who was about forty-five years old, said, 'I find this an utterly boring discussion. I'm dying to get out there and serve a church; I feel that God wants me to be there. It's taken me twenty-five years to get here. I want to discuss something more interesting — like how I can give my all to the service of God and the church.'

"When I met this woman again three years later, I worried that we divinity school professors had done something to her, because she was using a different language which we had taught her. She was talking about her rights and prerogatives."

"Let's put something forward that's positive," urged Bondi, "rather than saying, 'What's the trouble with all of these damned angry women?' Let's talk about some virtues for the Christian ministry, like tenacity."

Donald Davis addressed Bondi's concern by describing the situation of the women at Howard Divinity School, a school of 260 students. "About 34 percent are women," he said, "and they are among the best students in terms of academic work and in terms of dedication to the ministry." According to Davis, although the women graduates face placement uncertainties that are discouraging, they persist as students and often pioneer new churches after completing seminary training.

Today's churches, which often repress the issue of sexuality and which are easily threatened by societal changes in sexual dynamics, aren't sure what to do with women in ministry, Stanley Hauerwas noted.

Then Brooks Holifield spoke up: "The possibilities for ministry in the Protestant churches have been immeasurably enriched by women entering the ministry. This has happened simply because the influx of women has provided a wider pool of talent than was previously available. Still, I feel uncomfortable with Roberta's statement. Eight years ago the women in the seminary where I teach were among the very best students. But as their numbers have increased and as it has become more acceptable for women to go into the ministry, we have ended up with women who are mediocre and moderate, as we have men who are mediocre and moderate. I'm reluctant to say that there is one gender that's not eager and enthusiastic about ministry. I think that romanticizes the gender issue, and romanticizing the gender issue is one of the worst things we can do."

Addressing women's virtues in ministry, James Fowler recalled a meeting of ministers in which a woman pastor described her experience. "She was a couple of years out of seminary and was serving a church; she was about six months pregnant. She talked about the difference between the way she led meetings and the way her male colleague led meetings. Her male colleague would come into a meeting with his agenda set, explain the agenda, move through it efficiently, and finish. 'When I go into a meeting,' she said, 'we begin by renewing our relationships with each other. And then we talk about what needs to be on the agenda. And then in the fullness of time . . .' She was unselfconscious about this, and her colleagues began to smile knowingly. She was demonstrating that a woman can introduce a fundamentally different understanding of process and time."

Women in ministry can be a source of other salutary effects, according to Fowler. "We now have students in seminary who have lived through various sexual revolutions," he explained. "From them we are seeing emerge some genuinely new and potentially helpful models of relationships between men and women. These models don't deny sexuality, but they don't fall so readily into the trap of seductiveness that besets my generation. In this instance we can learn a fair amount from our students. And," he added, "it isn't just men and women who need to learn to be colleagues. Men need to learn to be colleagues too."

At this point Dennis Campbell addressed the feminization of the clergy. "I'll be up-front in telling you that I would be very worried if the student population of Duke Divinity School was almost 50 percent women. Maybe that's a shockingly sexist statement. But the observation I would make is that an institution's strength in institutional indices is affected by that. As seminaries have admitted more and more women to fill up their student bodies — and there's no question that this has happened — there's a flip side that isn't very pleasant to consider. Deans of other professional schools worry about the same thing. The law school, for example, is concerned about becoming 60 percent women and 40 percent male.

"Regarding the clergy, think for a minute about the market model. There's a fear that the clergy might go the route of elementary education. That is, because of low salaries, the ministry could become feminized, and then the male component would diminish even more rapidly and might reach a point of no return."

"So Dennis is worried about the ministry being perceived as an essentially feminist profession," Neuhaus summarized.

"Would that be worse than its being perceived as a masculine profession?" asked James Burtchaell.

"Yes, because that's so low status," Bondi answered.

Stanley Hauerwas also answered: "Women are considered low-status people. When they take over a profession, the profession drops in status. Consequently, it loses the patronage power that Rowan was talking about. Good examples of this are elementary education and nursing. But I think this is good. It will ruin the Constantinians among us."

Neuhaus remarked, "Your point, Stan, is that the worse things get, the better they get."

Getting away from the gender issue and concluding the conference conversation, Burtchaell set forth two additional approaches to re-establishing moral formation in theological schools. First, he suggested that in its visits to seminary campuses, the Association of Theological Schools should begin routinely investigating "what is being done for the seminarians' moral formation and godliness." Second, Burtchaell said that the visiting committees of the theological schools should begin assessing their schools on the basis of criteria pertaining to moral and spiritual formation. These committees, Burtchaell said, could see "whether or not seminarians were being schooled in the Holy Spirit."

After Burtchaell's comments, moderator Neuhaus thanked Dennis Campbell for the hospitality extended to the conference by Duke Divinity School. Neuhaus also thanked the four presenters of the conference as well as all the assembled participants.

A CONCLUDING WORD

It can safely be said that every church has, in its living tradition, vows into which its ordained ministers enter at their ordination. When, for example, individuals are ordained as elders in the United Methodist Church, they must take the vows contained in the church's Historic Examination. All Methodist elders, from the time of the brothers Wesley to the present, have been required to respond appropriately to Methodism's historic ordination vows, which were originally composed by John Wesley himself. The common practice has been for the bishop, standing in front of the members of the annual conference he serves, to pose the questions of the Historic Examination to those about to be ordained. Again, United Methodism is not extraordinary here. All churches today employ ordination vows in one form or another.

Continuing with the Methodist example, it might be useful to recall the precise nature and content of Methodism's ordination vows. They are made up of nineteen questions, asked in the following order: "(1) Have you faith in Christ?

(2) Are you going on to perfection? (3) Do you expect to be made perfect in love in this life? (4) Are you earnestly striving after it? (5) Are you resolved to devote yourself wholly to God and his work? (6) Do you know the General Rules of our Church? (7) Will you keep them? (8) Have you studied the doctrines of The United Methodist Church? (9) After full examination do you believe that our doctrines are in harmony with the Holy Scriptures? (10) Will you preach and maintain them? (11) Have you studied our form of Church discipline and polity? (12) Do you approve our Church government and polity? (13) Will you support and maintain them? (14) Will you diligently instruct the children in every place? (15) Will you visit from house to house? (16) Will you recommend fasting or abstinence, both by precept and example? (17) Are you determined to employ all your time in the work of God? (18) Are you in debt so as to embarrass you in your work? (19) Will you observe the following directions? (a) Be diligent. Never be unemployed. Never be triflingly employed. Never trifle away time; neither spend any more time at any one place than is strictly necessary. (b) Be punctual. Do everything exactly at the time. And do not mend our rules, but keep them; not for wrath, but for conscience' sake" (*The Book of Discipline*).

It must be reported that a few of the ordinands who are being examined with these questions by their bishop in front of the ministers of their annual conference will snicker at a question that they perceive to be otherworldly in demand. And sometimes during the examination ritual, the ministers of the annual conference, who have taken the vows in prior years, will knowingly wink at each other during the reading of a question, thereby acknowledging to each other the impossibility of meeting its requirements. And sometimes, by providing humorous commentary on a question or two, the examining bishop will even enter into the fun and games of taking the ordination vows with a grain of salt. Given the demanding nature of Methodism's ordination vows, such attempts at comic relief are understandable. But these comic gestures — which, once again, are surely not confined to the United Methodist household — might indicate that ordination vows are not perceived to be all that serious a matter, and therefore that the moral and spiritual formation of the ministers being ordained is not considered to be that serious a matter.

The two-day discussion that is reported on here is built on at least two strong assumptions. The first assumption is that ordination is always a very serious matter — for the churches that ordain, and for the men and the women who are ordained. The second assumption is that theological education should morally and spiritually (as well as academically) prepare those seeking ordination to enter joyfully into their ordination vows with integrity, with fidelity, and even with zeal. When the second assumption is accomplished in practice, the connections between theological education and moral formation will have been made. Exactly how that is to be accomplished in the various churches and seminaries remains one of the great tasks confronting the church — as, I suppose, it has, albeit in different forms, confronted the church of all times and places.

Participants

Roberta C. Bondi
Candler School of Theology
Emory University

James T. Burtchaell
Department of Theology
University of Notre Dame

Dennis M. Campbell
The Divinity School
Duke University

Donald Kortright Davis
The Divinity School
Howard University

James W. Fowler
Candler School of Theology
Emory University

J. Michael Graef
Covenant United Methodist
  Church
Spokane, Washington

Rowan A. Greer
The Divinity School
Yale University

Stanley Hauerwas
The Divinity School
Duke University

Richard B. Hays
The Divinity School
Duke University

E. Brooks Holifield
Candler School of Theology
Emory University

Christa Klein
Lilly Endowment, Inc.
York, Pennsylvania

Robert Leavitt
St. Mary's Seminary

George A. Lindbeck
The Divinity School
Yale University

George Marsden
The Divinity School
Duke University

Glenn T. Miller
Southeastern Baptist
  Theological Seminary

234

Richard John Neuhaus
New York City

John W. O'Malley, S.J.
Weston School of Theology

Russell E. Richey
The Divinity School
Duke University

Jay C. Rochelle
Lutheran School of
   Theology at Chicago

David S. Schuller
Association of Theological
   Schools in the United
   States and Canada
Vandalia, Ohio

Paul T. Stallsworth
Creswell, North Carolina

Merle D. Strege
School of Theology
Anderson University

Philip Turner
Berkeley Divinity School
Yale University

Geoffrey Wainwright
The Divinity School
Duke University

William H. Willimon
Duke University Chapel